THE EFFECTIVE TEACHER

Also available from Cassell:

M. Buchmann and R. Floden: *Detachment and Concern*
G. Claxton: *Being a Teacher*
C. Cullingford: *The Primary Teacher*
C. Cullingford: *The Nature of Learning*
C. Cullingford: *Children and Society*
C. Cullingford: *The Inner World of the School*
A. Hargreaves: *Changing Teachers, Changing Times*
A. Hargreaves and M. Fullan: *Understanding Teacher Development*
W. Louden: *Understanding Teaching*
A. Pollard: *Learning in Primary Schools*
A. Pollard and S. Tann: *Reflective Teaching in the Primary School – 2nd Edition*
J. Scheerens: *Effective Schooling*
E. Sotto: *When Teaching Becomes Learning*

The Effective Teacher

Cedric Cullingford

CASSELL

Cassell
Villiers House   387 Park Avenue South
41/47 Strand   New York
London WC2N 5JE   NY 10016-8810

First published 1995

British Library Cataloguing-in-Publication Data

A catalogue record for this book is available from the British Library.

ISBN 0-304-33177-5 (hardback)
      0-304-33180-5 (paperback)

Typeset by Colset Pte Ltd, Singapore
Printed and bound in Great Britain by Redwood Books, Trowbridge, Wiltshire

For Nichola

Contents

Preface and Acknowledgements

This book celebrates the art of teaching as well as giving insights and practical support to teachers. Teaching is a complex matter to anyone who wants to do a good job. It is also very demanding.

The complexity of teaching is not always understood. A doctor can rely on a mixture of knowledge and experience in dealing with one patient at a time; dealing mostly with the physical symptoms of people who explain what they feel is wrong. A teacher deals with about thirty individuals all at the same time, having to analyse what is going on inside their minds and working out, even for those who do not want to cooperate, how best to help them. A teacher's knowledge and experience need constant updating.

This book is not just for new teachers, but for teachers with years of experience. It draws on many research studies of teaching as well as the experience of many teachers. It provides an analysis of the effects of teaching and draws attention to the dilemmas and interests that affect all teachers. It is a book designed to help as well as celebrate, not by giving 'tips' but by helping to define what teaching is.

I called teaching an art, but it is also a science. There are certain characteristics of teaching that apply whatever the age of those taught. Whilst the book is called *The Effective Teacher*, it is targeted particularly at the primary level – since it is in the younger age range that the greatest complexities lie. I have personally taught all age ranges from pre-school to undergraduates at an ancient university. The greatest intellectual challenge lies in the infant school. The fundamental problem of any education system is that people do not wish to acknowledge that fact.

The book is designed to be of relevance to all teachers. It owes much to the experience of children in more than one country. The unwitting help of many children and many teachers needs to be acknowledged, for the book is based on observation and conversations as well as teaching. Teachers do not like being observed, but once they are accustomed to it they share their insights with their colleague in ways that show great thoughtfulness and ability to analyse.

Many teachers, especially in primary schools, are women. This raises the question of how to refer to individual teachers without using the visual disfigurement of 's/he'.

Sometimes I have, in other books, used 'she' for teacher and 'he' for the pupil. Here, however, I would like to use generally the ultimately more neutral 'he'. Given the disproportions of gender, and of power, and drawing attention to individuality rather than status, however, this will not be consistent. It is the teacher (him *or* herself) that counts.

There are many reports on research and illustrations of ideas which interpose and further enliven the main text. They do not have to be read at the same time when the reader follows the main argument.

I have received a great deal of help, both willing and more grudging, from hundreds of teachers in many schools. This book owes its existence to their interest and experience as well as to the encouragement of Nichola Tooke and Naomi Roth.

Introduction

There is a well-known quotation from Erasmus: 'The important thing is not how *much* you know but the *quality* of what you know.' This is difficult to disagree with. But what is meant by 'quality'? How can it be learned or taught? It is easy enough to acquire facts but more difficult to know what to do with them. It is always possible to accumulate information, but how do we acquire wisdom?

One underlying theme that runs through this book is the way in which we learn to become more effective teachers than we already are. That means addressing the essential facts about learning and teaching. Can effectiveness be 'taught'? What is the balance between the individual striving to learn and the techniques, formal and informal, that are offered by others? Many people like to learn but resent being taught. Or, rather, they do not like to notice that they depend on others than themselves. There is a natural instinct that leads individuals to believe that they are 'self-made': their own natural creators.

This book rests on the premise that we are learning all the time, either positively or negatively; learning to change and develop, or decaying into unthinking habits and attitudes. It is also written in the knowledge that, given the will and availability of help, it is always possible to learn not just facts but a new quality of effectiveness.

Some have doubted whether this can be so. It has been fashionable, and to some extent still is, to question whether teachers can learn the art of teaching, rather than the subjects they teach, as if teachers were born rather than made, and naturally gifted rather than constantly learning. Those who think so are retreating from the demands of the profession which reveal the range of effectiveness among teachers and the responsibility of all teachers to reflect on their own performance.

There will always be some teachers who are more effective than others, some who seem to have an innate flair. There will always be some trainee teachers who will never learn the essential role of the teacher. This is not to criticize them as individuals; the fact that they are not suited to the particular demands of the profession takes nothing away from their virtues. It means only that their personal characteristics are inappropriate to teaching.

Years of experience in universities and colleges have revealed how students and practising teachers have changed and improved their skills. The claim that teaching cannot be taught is not only a curious denial of the role of the teacher but is countered by a mass of evidence. Clearly the development of the individual teacher is not a steady one, with constant additions of knowledge; it is a more varied, more personal matter. Clearly, too, the personality of the teacher plays a central part in forming the teaching style.

The important argument is that there are different kinds of effectiveness. There is no one style or personality that by dramatic gestures or flamboyance lends itself to effective teaching. We have all witnessed the teacher who might appear to be unprepossessing, or lacking in social graces, or shy, but who runs a magnificent classroom, with a minimum of fuss and a quiet attention to detail. The teacher is judged not on personality but on effectiveness. Being effective does not mean being perfect, or giving a wonderful performance, but bringing out the best in pupils.

Those who deny that teaching can be taught on the grounds that research has not detected *how* it happens give themselves away in their own arguments.[1] They point out that effective teachers are those who provide pupils with many opportunities to learn. But isn't this a satisfactory definition of teaching? The art of teaching lies in understanding how people learn and what to do about it.

To question whether it is possible to educate teachers is to undermine the professionalism of teachers and provide an excuse for not improving the opportunities that children have. When there is a desire to remove control of the curriculum from the teachers and to impose a set of standard tasks so that one school can be tested against another, the possibility of improving education begins to recede. When there is an assumption that anyone with a modicum of common sense can 'teach', especially younger children, standards rapidly fall.

It is an unfortunate truth that education has not yet been taken seriously, and the doubts about teachers are just one manifestation of this. Glib dismissals such as the claim that 'those who can, do, and those who can't, teach' indicate a cultural malaise which it is difficult to define. But it is one example of a general suspicion that education does not change things and at best maintains the status quo.

Despite all evidence to the contrary it is still fashionable to assume that there is already nothing a teacher can do by the time a child starts school, and that all depends on socio-economic background. Whilst the importance of the first five years must not be underrated,[2] the weight of evidence clearly demonstrates how different formal programmes actually help children. The fashion to deny evidence is shown in reactions to the Head Start programme in the United States. It was held that there were few cognitive gains which could clearly be attributed to all the additional educational help that young children received. But then the evidence emerged. The children were not providing measurable 'cognitive' gains, but they were learning social skills, through relationships, self-belief and motivation. This proved beneficial for their subsequent academic achievements.

Another example of the fashion to deny the effectiveness of teaching can be found in the teaching and learning of reading. A number of popular texts suggested that teaching did more harm than good and that children would learn to read despite the teacher. Apart from the fact that countless studies[3] show that children gain insight into reading by being formally taught, such texts again reveal a misunderstanding of the role of the teacher as enabler. Can children learn to read without access to books?

Do they understand phonemes and graphemes and reading from left to right without having them demonstrated?

The mythology that schools, and the teachers in them, make little difference has been analysed in two large research studies.[4] The first looked at secondary schools with very similar intakes of pupils of similar abilities and home backgrounds, and discovered that some schools were much more successful, both academically and otherwise, than others. The second looked at primary schools and again showed how schools varied greatly according to the attitudes and performance of the staff as a whole.

But we have all known, from experience and observation, that some teachers are more effective than others. We might not like it, but it is a fact. We have known, too, that 'culture' in the broad sense is a product not of genes but of circumstances. The use of language might be an innate ability but every language is learned in a context.

The teacher is one of the main providers of the 'culture' that enables the child to learn. The teacher cannot *make* a pupil learn or guarantee that he or she will remember and act on all that is heard, but the teacher can create conditions for motivation and have a very subtle and profound effect on the pupil. There is a constant relationship between the need for the learner to *want* to learn and the provision of material from which the learner *can* learn, and that is equally true in relation to the reader and this book. Any book can be ignored, but if the reader wants to learn there should be enough in the book to make it possible.

The nature of the book, like the nature of teaching, needs a little explanation. The book is designed to be clear and easy to read, although it is based on extensive research. The research is not intended to be intrusive nor is the author trying to parade his erudition by means of a series of footnotes. A little earlier, for instance, a reference was made to 'countless studies'. Actually the published studies probably could be counted. Instead of two or three examples, we would then have several pages of footnotes. That is not appropriate here, but it is important for the reader to realize that every statement *could* be supported by an elaborate scaffolding of references.

Historians have for many years shown the importance of trying to sift a mass of evidence into the 'truth'. One could cite many a historian pointing out that people do not study history to learn historical facts but to acquire historical judgement. Behind every historical text lies not only a quantity of primary material and secondary sources but hours spent in sifting evidence, in making it into a coherent whole, in knowing what is significant and what is not. No one accuses the historian of 'generalization'. The text is the result of making many judgements about all the accumulated evidence of the past. The quality of the work shows itself partly in the truthfulness of the insights gained when all the evidence has been weighed, and partly in their practical relevance.

The fact that this book tries to communicate clearly does not mean that it is not based on a wealth of data which could, in almost every chapter, generate many additional footnotes. Every statement could be hedged around with small caveats, possible exceptions, or the elaborate construction of similar conclusions. This book aims to demystify research and talk to teachers.[5] It is not always the fault of teachers if they do not read, given some of the material presented to them.

We, as teachers, deserve all the help we can get. There are two standard ways in which help is offered. The first is through a list of ideas – of 'tips' and methods, practices which have been tried. These can be helpful but very rarely work really well. They can help at odd moments but they do not, in themselves, address the art of teaching and learning. When large-scale curriculum materials in various subjects have been given to teachers, they have not been of much benefit.[6] This is because the teachers themselves never went through the process of development from which the materials were derived. They never had a sense of 'ownership' of the underlying ideas. Sharing practical ideas can be very beneficial, but this implies a dialogue between people. Copying the *results* of other people's thinking does not have the same effect.

The second way of trying to enhance the effectiveness of the teacher is through checklists of competencies. These have gained wide currency wherever practice in the workplace is important. Competency lists are essentially a simple means of assessment. Can the teacher be observed to do certain things? They can also be very crude. At the end of almost every list the observer has to add an extra, qualitative dimension which is more nebulous. The teacher can present material, keep order, be prepared, communicate with most of the children; but can he *teach*?

Whilst competency lists can be simple, they can become a more complex and useful means of profiling an individual's progress provided that the competencies are defined and acknowledged by the teacher himself. Such a list is no longer a catalogue of attainments, but a more qualitative self-assessment which leads to action, to progress.

Both 'tips' and 'competencies' – ideas and actions – depend on the understanding of the teacher. Only then are they useful. The understanding of the teacher can, however, be enhanced in different ways, and one of those ways is through the stimulation of reading and dialogue with colleagues. The teacher needs to reflect, but he also needs someone else with whom to share his reflections and material other than his own experience in order to understand that experience. In-service courses can be helpful, but teachers can feel very threatened by them.[7] A book should not be threatening.

This book is one half of a dialogue.[8] It is like a map that presents evidence but depends on the teacher to interpret it. As with all books, the reader's response is what gives it life. This does not take away any responsibility from the book. On the contrary, the book needs to demonstrate that what it says is worthy of dialogue, even if it invites disagreement, and that every statement is no mere personal assertion but a conclusion to which the first response should at least be understanding so that there is a basis for argument.

It is always possible to learn to be a more effective teacher. It is the mark of the good teacher to pursue learning. And, as every teacher knows, learning includes being taught: not just imbibing facts, but receiving material on which to reflect. It is hoped that the material this book contains and the evidence it presents will stimulate, help and even surprise teachers. They deserve no less.

Chapter 1

The First Day

'With a good teacher you can get on better, but with a soft teacher you can't do much.'

(girl, 11)

Every day is like a first day. The experienced teacher approaches each day as a new beginning, a fresh approach to the interests and curiosities of human nature. He realizes the need to rethink the strategies of teaching and review the achievements of learning. Thinking of each day afresh concentrates the mind.

The experienced teacher can, however, take certain things for granted. To look back at the very first day of teaching, as if we were to start all over again, highlights many aspects of the nature of teaching. No one can quite forget what it was like at the very beginning. If we began again, what would we do differently? What would we want to have known that we did not know at the time?

> Over the years teachers change in their approach to their tasks. Their early concerns in coping and in managing a class are replaced by a greater interest in the content of what they are teaching. This interest, in turn, is replaced by a greater concern for understanding their pupils and the overall concepts that they are trying to teach. In so far as one can make a distinction, an interest in the practical is replaced by an interest in the 'theoretical'.[1]

Our first concern – the concern of all who are starting teaching – is simply to survive. How will we cope in the classroom? What do we need to know? What are we supposed to do? Fortunately it is possible to describe how to survive in the classroom. In that balance between personality and professionalism that makes the teacher there are a number of things we can learn in order to prepare for the first day.

For those who have yet to approach it, or for those who are going to teach a new class, there is some fear in the anticipation of the first lesson. There are two things that we are afraid of: ourselves and the reactions of the pupils. Our early fears of teaching arise out of insecurity and self-consciousness. We don't like so many people looking at us, although we are not so worried if they are 'only' children. We dislike colleagues watching us teach. We are afraid of the reactions of the class. Will they listen? Will they do what they are asked? Will they be bored?

> There are certain recurring nightmares that many teachers seem to experience. One such dream is of being confronted by an angry and noisy class who refuse to be quiet or obedient. The more the teacher shouts and the angrier he becomes the less effect he has. The children simply shout back.
>
> The other nightmare is of running out of things to say, like an actor who finds himself on stage before an audience, realizing that he is playing Hamlet when he hasn't even had a chance to read the play.

Fortunately the pupils are curious about a new teacher and try to anticipate what he will be like. Inevitably they wait to see what kind of style he will bring. This is fortunate because it means that pupils do not impose *their* will on the teacher, but react to what he does. This gives him the opportunity and the time to create the working conditions he wants. It is the teacher who sets the tone and the pupils who react to it, and try to test the teacher's will.

> Pupils in a classroom have one fundamental characteristic: that of accepting the basic conditions of the class, the role that they play against that of the teacher. They accept the essential authority a teacher possesses.
>
> Beyond that acceptance pupils differ in the way they think about the parts they play within their overall role. There are nearly always some 'jokers' – those children who see how much they can get away with, teasing the teacher to discover at what point he will impose order. These jokers are often amongst the liveliest and most gifted in the class. They stand out from the 'goodies' who quietly get on with their work and the 'gangs' who are more interested in their relationships with each other outside the class than in learning.[2]

The teacher therefore starts with an advantage, and he needs to know and believe that he has it. Pupils are not automatically antagonistic as a class. There is, as in any new job, a 'honeymoon' period at the beginning, even if it is sometimes a very short one. Before that first day, the teacher must be organized. There are some fundamental things to know. For every well-taught lesson the same amount of time as the lesson itself must be spent in preparation of one kind or another. Nothing gives teachers more confidence than knowing what they are doing.

> Every teacher has at one time or another, despite all the good advice received, run out of things to say or do, often towards the end of a lesson. The pupils have finished their task and the teacher desperately wishes the bell would ring. How do we keep the children occupied?
>
> We learn from experience that every moment is an opportunity to teach. We learn that there is never a shortage of material. On the contrary, we long for more time.
>
> But while teachers are still learning how to pace their lessons – for slow workers as well as fast ones – they cannot rely on their own inspiration, on instinctively knowing what to do. They need to have a lot of extra materials, just in case.

The first and fundamental way to cope is to be very well-prepared. This means:

1.   having an overall aim;
2.   having lots of ideas and materials; and
3.   having thought in detail about the lesson.

The Aims

By themselves, aims can be meaningless. At one time there was great interest in the distinction between 'aims', 'goals' and 'objectives', until these distinctions almost become a subject in their own right. But aims need to be translated into practice.[3] We need to work out what we wish to achieve and what the pupils should learn not just in terms of knowledge, but in terms of concepts and skills. Thinking about what we are trying to achieve focuses the mind on what matters most of all. We begin by having a broad and ambitious idea of what we want the children to achieve. We then work out practical ways of helping them to achieve it.

> There was a time when the whole of the primary curriculum was taught through 'topics'. A teacher would think of a theme – the weather, the local town, the Romans, change – and then try to relate every subject to it: history, geography, science, language, maths, technology and physical education. At best, this would produce some interesting ideas and good work, with connections of one subject to another. At worst, the children were not so much working as being kept occupied and given any task as long as it fitted into the topic. The difference between success and failure in using topics as a way of organizing work lay in whether the teacher had thought through the aims. Why are the pupils doing the work? What is it for?[4]

Ideas and Materials

There is nothing as useful as preparing too much, of having lots of things for children to do. These ideas and materials should not be vague or generalized. They need to be thought out in terms of actions and objects, in terms of stories and pictures, and in terms of activities. It is always wise to have several follow-up activities and a number of short five-minute teaching games so that you have something ready for every moment.

> One of the curious laws of teaching is that if one has prepared enough materials to last for the lesson one will inevitably find that some of the children get through it very fast, whereas if one has prepared a great deal too much the children will work more carefully and slowly. The more we prepare, the longer it lasts, not just because the children have more to do but because they go about it in a less hurried way. This is not because they know how much you have prepared, but because you know; there is a lack of anxiety and an interest in what the children are learning that is conveyed to them.

One of the advantages of thinking about topics is that one can remember many connected ideas. It is like making a Venn diagram where

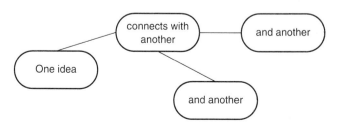

Teaching is not just dependent on general ideas but is informed by our equipment: a picture, or a piece of music, a model or a story. Preparation means, essentially, having a large number of things to do with the children: activities which are both stimulating and demanding, which show a new approach and are not just a matter of routine.

One does not need to try to use all that one has prepared for every lesson. The knowledge that we have plenty of extra ideas helps in two ways. First, we know that with so much to choose from we can select what will be appropriate and can adapt to the needs of the pupils. Secondly, knowing that we are really well-prepared gives us confidence.

Lesson Plans

It is helpful to imagine how we are going to start the lesson and how we will continue it, and even to rehearse the actual words we will use, even if we don't subsequently remember them! Some teachers even act out the way in which they will introduce a new subject.

> It is tempting for a teacher to start by trying to explain what he is going to do. It is tempting to give a long talk, outlining various aspects of the topic, and giving all the subject headings. This kind of approach sounds organized and logical. But from the children's point of view such an introduction can be very dull.[5]
>
> Think how much more interesting it is if the teacher puts a closed box on the table. The children think, 'What is in that box? Is it alive? What secret does the box contain?' This is how to capture the pupils' curiosity.

At the start of a lesson aims are quickly forgotten. We plan lessons around real events that we can translate easily into action.

The more we think of the practical aspects of a lesson the more ideas come into our minds about how we can extend it. Thinking of lessons creates new ideas. And the more we think about lessons, the less necessary it is for us to stick rigidly to our plans. We find ourselves thinking more about what concepts we are trying to teach.

> One might have thought that at the beginning of a lesson giving a clear outline of intentions, or an overall plan by way of introduction, would help. But in an experiment in primary schools two kinds of teachers were observed and the work of the children assessed. One kind of teacher gave a careful explanation of what he would be doing over the next day, outlining his intentions, the learning outcomes, the themes and the times allowed for each part. The other kind plunged straight into the subject. Which approach was more successful?
>
> Children responded far more positively, and did better work, for the second type of teacher than for the first. To them, the first type was like a speaker or a preacher who makes ten minutes of general comments like 'How nice it is to be here' before getting to the topic. During the time that the 'explainers' were taking, the children became bored and stopped listening. Far from anticipating delights to come, they felt time was being wasted.[6]

There are many skills that are displayed by the effective teacher that do not depend on knowledge. We know that understanding a subject is by no means the same thing as explaining it, let alone teaching it. But of course no teacher can do without knowledge. Understanding a subject underlies all the other skills of a teacher: the choice of material to match the needs of the pupils and the connection between key concepts and the examples which illustrate them. This book defines effective teaching, but the primary need for the knowledge of content, which has often been neglected, should not be forgotten.

In preparing for lessons, it is not enough to rely on knowing one's subject. It is necessary to think through what we are teaching, and how. This is why a detailed anticipation of what it will be like is important.[7]

Imagine, then, the first lesson. The first minutes are crucial. There is one essential fact for the new teacher to learn: the difference between the role of the teacher and the role of the individual personality. The teacher is concerned with the work and the welfare of the children. He is not concerned about being liked. Children know the difference between the teacher with authority and any other presence in the classroom.

> Children are very quick to recognize, and react to, the presence of a teacher. We have all seen how some people seem to have a natural authority; others seem to cause an immediate hysteria with ever-rising noise levels, including the teacher's shouting. Authority can be learned until it seems natural. It depends on believing in the role of the teacher.
>
> On the other hand there are some who never really like the role of the teacher. They crave for close personal relationships with individual children. They seek approval and cannot accept the authority of the teacher's role.

If there is a need to give just one word of advice to a new teacher, it is this, however easily parodied: 'be firm!' Once the rules have been made clear and insisted upon, then the teacher can relax. But the rules must be established first, and they must be made clear in detail.[8]

When a teacher gives an instruction he must mean it. This isn't as obvious as it sounds. Too often we hear the sound of 'Be quiet' being said or shouted loudly above all other sounds, and nothing happens. A teacher must insist that everything he says has a purpose, and is not redundant. We have good reasons for asking for quietness, so that such an instruction cannot be ignored.

> When children are asked about what they appreciate in a teacher they all say that one quality they rate highly is firmness: being strict and being fair. They do not like teachers who seem to want to be liked, and they resent teachers who are inconsistent (and don't mean what they say).
>
> Children also think that rules are necessary.[9]

Children need to have every instruction carefully explained. 'Line up by the door' can mean all kinds of things, including the adventures that can accompany every simple walk: kicking someone here, poking someone else there, seeing how fast the plants are growing, knocking over some bricks – all the everyday explorations that fill a child's life. What the teacher means by 'Line up by the door' is really '(1) Be quiet, (2) Put down your pens, (3) Sit up and fold your arms, (4) Table by table, stand up, tidy away your chairs, and line up quietly in order . . .' The children need to learn what the teacher requires in detail. Only when they have understood exactly what is expected can the teacher afford to give a more general signal.

> At first it is a surprise when children come for a conversation immediately after being told off. But they remain undisturbed by the teacher's annoyance or anger on a personal level. Children know that a teacher is in control, and anger comes from moral authority disappointed. There is nothing really personal about it. On a personal level relationships continue as normal.[10]

Discipline is crucial and it has a particular purpose. It is not imposed for the sake of imposition. That can be negative and lead to confrontation. Think of the real difficulties when a child refuses to do something. There is little the teacher can do about it either by sheer determination or by insistence. That kind of battle of wills needs to be avoided. Quietness without purpose, imposed for its own sake or to prove who is in command, can be like a vacuum. Insisting on high standards of behaviour is essential so that time can be used in a sensible way.

Always assume that the children want to learn, and that there is a purpose in learning. Very young children have no choice about learning; they have to make sense of their world, to understand it whether they are helped by adults or not.[11] Any sign that children are not learning, or do not want to learn, is not so much an indication that they cannot learn, as that they have acquired the distinct habit of not learning, of avoiding it. When the purpose of a subject is clear, and it relates to the real world of experience, then the basis of pleasure in learning is in place.[12] Nothing is more undermining than thinking that a subject is being taught, or learned, just because the teacher or the school says it must be. The individual teacher knows that what he is teaching is important in itself, but also that whatever the subject is, he is giving someone else a chance to develop and grow, by using skills. The alternative to learning is not play but decay.

> Think of the difference between the routine learning of simple sums, and the excitement of thinking mathematically. Mental arithmetic is often associated with routine tables, but at best it means thinking, predicting and analysing. The use of calculators illustrates the difference between the 'crunching' of numbers and the mathematics that everyone can take pleasure in. Calculators can take away the mindless part of maths.[13]

The teacher needs to be prepared, both psychologically and academically. This essential belief in the subject and the importance of teaching should carry anyone through. But there are some other practical steps that can be taken to be ready for the first lesson.

Get to know the classroom. How is it laid out? How can it be organized? Do we (and then the children) know where everything is kept? What kind of space can be used for displays? The way a classroom is used says a great deal about the teacher: the extent to which children know not only the routines but where things are stored ready for use, and the extent to which the teacher knows which resources are appropriate. One sign of discipline is the teacher's attention to details which include tidiness. This is not a trivial matter but a sign of real concern. A teacher can, from the beginning, turn any classroom into a symbol of the standards he expects.

> People who make regular visits to different schools, like inspectors and advisers, very quickly detect what is happening in a classroom, even when there are no children in it. They see how much litter there is on the floor, and whether the children's work is displayed as if it were important. They react against the clutter that covers desks, or the pile of half-empty, half-dried-up paints. And they can, like the children who are in the classroom, feel whether it is a pleasant place to be.

It is, of course, easier to create a personal space when, as is traditional in primary education, a teacher is in the same classroom for the greater part of the time. But it is also possible to make significant changes, even symbolically, to a classroom that has a variety of purposes. A teacher shows that the room itself has a purpose and is a real workplace that symbolizes the achievements of pupils.

> For many years the tradition of the primary school has been the tradition of the class teacher, alone with a group of children, teaching the whole of the curriculum from maths to art. But this role has been increasingly questioned. Can a teacher know so much? Shouldn't the teacher be more of a specialist?
>
> At the same time that the role of the single class teacher has been questioned it has been discovered that there is an increasing tendency for other people to be in the classroom: parents and other helpers, ancillaries and other teachers.
>
> The role of teachers is constantly changing, especially in the degree of autonomy and control over the curriculum.[14]

The teacher needs to know more than the classroom. To prepare properly, the teacher needs to know the school. This is because every school has its own ethos, and because every school is full of potential resources that the teacher can use.

'Ethos' is a difficult concept but an important one. It is a mixture of atmosphere and relationships. It can be detected in appearances and in behaviour. It comes about from a shared sense of purpose amongst the staff, and the influence of this on the pupils. Why do some schools do so much better than others?[15] Why do the children of some schools behave so much better, with more courtesy and kindness? It's not just a question of their home backgrounds. Some schools expect high standards of discipline and behaviour and do not tolerate untidiness or bullying. The teachers share a conviction that low standards are not acceptable. They plan the curriculum together but they also create a policy, an expectation of behaviour as well as of achievement.

> 'Ethos' is not such a vague concept that it cannot be studied. Two major research projects compared many schools and found there were some that were far more effective in helping their pupils achieve academic success. This was not dependent on the pupils' home or circumstances, or whether they were rich or poor. It depended on several factors, such as the quality of the headteacher, the sense of purpose in all teachers, parental involvement, good communication between teachers and pupils, intellectually challenging teaching, structured sessions and a work-centred environment.[16]

Understanding the school and how it works is clearly helpful. One of the qualities of a good school is the shared vision of the teachers. This comes about when people are willing to ask questions and seek advice. Many people prefer to give advice rather than receive it. But other teachers are a great source of helpful hints and ideas. This advice is not a matter of anecdotes about particular children – 'Watch him . . .' – but of techniques they have tried and sources they found helpful.

> One of the simplest ways of testing the ethos of a school is in listening to the dialogues in the staffroom. In one school one detects despair or exasperation covered by a sardonic humour: 'So and so's naughty yet again; it's typical of the family; her elder sister was just the same.' In another you might overhear a discussion about how to help a pupil overcome a learning problem.[17]

Finding out about a school and about its policies is a very important first step into preparing for teaching. No questions we ask can be too naive. The simplest questions are often the most difficult to answer. But it is also a good psychological step to show a willingness to ask and listen, and to seek help from others. It establishes credibility – the signal of a colleague who has respect for the professionalism of teaching.

> The school is like a microcosm of society. Its health depends on the shared vision of the people in it and on a shared sense of values, including school rules. The way in which children respond to individual teachers depends on the way they perceive teachers and other staff. Authority derives from an acceptance that society as a whole must regulate itself fairly and firmly.[18]

There are two ways in which colleagues can be particularly helpful: in ideas and in knowledge of the children. The most helpful ideas for a new colleague are the most practical. They consist of tasks which have been tried and found successful, in five-minute games that stimulate children's thinking. At first it can seem a chore to prepare detailed lesson plans, and easy to run out of ideas. But it soon becomes a habit to connect ideas and different parts of the curriculum. This is one of the reasons why topic work became so popular. It was not just a matter of seeing the curriculum as a whole from the children's point of view but a way of organizing its delivery. A theme, like 'travel' or 'housing' or 'weather', would enable teachers to think of all kinds of unexpected links, including science and history, geography and maths. Whilst the danger of not differentiating between subjects is often pointed out, the advantage at least of thinking about new ideas should not be forgotten. Topics are useful for teachers if not for children.

> When new teachers first try to evaluate their lessons they have a tendency to write general things not so much about the children but about themselves: 'The lesson went well; I felt happy with it.' Gradually we learn to look at the children, and what they learned; comments like 'They liked it' give place to 'They learned something new.'

The other information which colleagues can give is about the children. Here we must make a distinction between anecdote or gossip – 'Watch out for X; he's a sly one' – and assessment of the child's attainments. Each pupil has an individual learning style, and particular strengths and weaknesses. The sharing of a profile of a pupil – examples of work and indications of levels of achievement – makes teaching far more directed, and draws attention to the core professional attribute of a teacher: the ability to analyse the concepts children are learning.

> It is very easy to 'label' children. In what is called the 'Pygmalion effect', teachers are shown to judge children according to what they have previously been told about their ability. The children then perform according to the teacher's expectations. If a teacher is told that Mary is 'stupid' that is how she will turn out to be. If the teacher believes Mary to be clever, she will tend to be so.[19]
>
> In one research study teachers of children in reception classes were interviewed after the very first day of a new class. At the end of the day the teachers revealed they had something distinctive to say about each individual, pointing out which child was shy, which hard-working, and which might prove difficult. They showed very acute perceptions.
>
> At the end of the term the same teachers were asked once again to describe the children in their class. Everything that they said then was almost exactly the same as what they had said at the end of the first day. What does this suggest?[20]

Finding out about the pupils, what they have learned already, and what they bring to their learning also focuses attention on what should be at the centre of every teacher's concern: not the performance of the teacher but the performance of the children. This brings us back to the crucial role of the teacher – not just 'coping' but being able to evaluate and analyse.

Many people like learning but do not like being taught. The good teacher fosters in the pupils the ability to learn. What is being judged, in the end, is the way in which children make progress. The teacher can only do his best to help, and insist that pupils help themselves.

Remember two things. First, no teacher is ever perfect. Things can go wrong at any time – and often what goes wrong is hidden: a remark is misinterpreted or some impatience is revealed. A good teacher keeps trying and is willing to take risks. Secondly, every teacher brings something unique to teaching. Individual children respond differently to different personalities. Even if, as a beginner, we feel that what we have to offer seems inadequate, we are doing more good to some of the children than we know.

> One of the most difficult achievements for new teachers is to put into practice all the ideas about teaching and learning that are discussed on pre-service courses. The desire to 'cope', to survive the classroom, leads student teachers not to reflect on all the potential and actual skills that can be applied, but to revert to memories of their own schooling. Instead of a rational approach to planning, there is a tendency to think of their own life histories and their own 'latent cultures'.[21]

Whatever the personality we bring to the task, it is possible to develop into an effective teacher. What then are the effective teacher's special characteristics?

Chapter 2

The Characteristics of an Effective Teacher

'Learning your tables isn't fun but doing things is'.

(boy, 10)

We have all heard of someone who is described as a 'born teacher'. But are teachers born and not made? Is effective teaching really a matter of personality? Those who have been involved in educating teachers for many years will have seen thousands of different people become teachers. In the experience of a variety of different types of personality, they will have seen that there are a number of characteristics which all good teachers demonstrate, and which many different people, with their unique personalities, can learn.

There are of course some personal characteristics, like a concern for other people, and a willingness to work hard, that underlie the effectiveness of teachers. Personal charm helps. But many of these personal or moral characteristics can be developed. The variety of teachers' personal styles is enormous. It does not matter if the teacher has a flair for drama and likes to dominate with an ebullient presence, or whether he seems to be shy or retiring. Both can be effective. It does not signify if one teacher likes to have a variety of different activities taking place at the same time, and another likes to spend time on developing just one. Both can achieve the same success.

It is possible to describe some of the essential characteristics that effective teachers share. There is one aspect of personality that no teacher can do without: a willingness to learn and to reflect on teaching – a characteristic of anyone who is reading this. The result of such reflection is demonstrated not so much in the way the teacher presents himself but in the success of the pupils.

The signs of a good teacher can be detected in the way the classroom is run. The signs are:

- A shared working atmosphere.
- An awareness of the needs of each pupil.

- A purposeful, well-organized classroom.
- The celebration of successes.

Such signs can be detected very quickly on entering a classroom, but they take time to achieve. They do not appear as if by a miracle. The most telling signs lie not in the presence of the teacher but in the work that is being carried out by the pupils. If the teacher is working closely with one pupil it can even be difficult to see where he is when one first enters the classroom.

> There have been a number of research studies that have explored the effects of different teaching styles. Sometimes these have been motivated by a desire to prove the success, or lack of it, of a particular style. Beneath the definitions of differences – 'formal' or 'informal', for example, or *'laissez-faire'* or 'controlling' – there are clear signs of success lying in shared characteristics – a detailed knowledge of what children are doing, for example, and a strong sense of purpose.[1]

A teacher is not defined as a particular personality type. A teacher can be 'made' if he is willing to be made. In the great variety of people who become teachers there are, however, some who fail to achieve the necessary success. This failure is due not so much to a lack of intelligence as to one or two characteristics which are not personality defects but which are incompatible with the essential qualities of a professional teacher. These unsuccessful teachers are a very small minority but it is interesting to define exactly what they lack. One fundamental characteristic is a lack of self-awareness. They do not quite know what they are doing, whether it is right or wrong. A second factor is defensiveness. They cannot bear any criticism, however constructive. They react as if everyone else is to blame, especially those who observe them. If the work of the children is poor it is the children who are blamed. An interesting by-product of this blaming of children is the fact that the very same person will often want to be close to the children, will want their approval, not for what he is doing but for who he is. He desperately wants to be liked.

> There are now a number of schools where teachers share the job; one comes in the mornings and the other in the afternoons. Observing the children's behaviour, one can see how adaptable children are to different personalities and how quick they are to understand expectations about work and behaviour. The same class that one teacher finds difficult to manage can be the class that another teacher finds most rewarding. Children react to the differences in personality, but they *behave* according to the way the teacher carries out the professional role.[2]

Those rare cases of failure to teach or to understand what is wrong are the hardest to deal with. The teachers might be charming and well-meaning but all attempts to help them seem to fail because in certain important ways they seem to lack the ability to communicate on a professional level.

What, then, are the characteristics of the effective teacher? They are:

Integrity   The quality of someone who is doing his best, modestly and without self-consciousness. No teacher is ever perfect, but every teacher can try to do better. Often we are doing better than we think we are.

Learning   The quality of enjoying learning and sharing a sense of curiosity. The process of learning is similar at all stages; and the teacher is

	also involved in learning. Teaching is a chance to gain knowledge and insight.
Organization	The quality of managing a classroom, with good preparation, clear rules and expectations, attention to detail, the best use of the classroom facilities, as well as knowing when to teach the class as a whole, in groups, or individually.
Communication	The quality of showing an interest in other people, both pupils and colleagues, and being able to demonstrate that interest through ideas, and stories, as well as through shared values.
Humour	We need a sense of humour to survive and to avoid being burdened with all our other virtues.

All these qualities are central to effective teaching. They are developed through practice. Each deserves to be defined further.

Integrity

Integrity can be learned, for it arises from the way in which we deal with experience. We learn that however hard we try, and however much we think that what we do is perfect, other people do not share our views. There will always be some who are dissatisfied with what we do or wish that we did things differently. This does not prevent us from trying. But we acknowledge that all we can do is our best, to do as well as possible.

This is not an acceptance of second-rate standards. On the contrary, self-awareness, and an acknowledgement of our limitations, gives us an insight into how we can improve our performance. It suggests that we can always go on improving rather than attain a level plain of complacency.

> There is a book on the crucial role that parents play in the upbringing of their children. It describes how deeply parents affect their emotional as well as their intellectual and social lives. The book is designed to warn of all the damage parents can do, and to counsel them to be as sensitive and wise as possible. It sounds like the counsel of perfection but it is tellingly called *The Good Enough Parent*. In a similar way we wish to become 'good enough teachers'.[3]

Doing one's best implies self-awareness and a lack of self-consciousness. On the one hand we learn to accept and prize advice, even if we do not always like it. We learn to accept being observed carrying out our job. Neither is necessarily easy. We do not like having our weaknesses commented on, and nor do we like people coming into the classroom where we are teaching. We learn to accept both kinds of observation by remembering to separate the role of the teacher from the matter of personal style. We retain our personal style, whether we like it or not, and we do not pretend to be anyone other than the person we are. But as a teacher our concern is with what happens to the pupils, and that concern needs to be conveyed clearly and effectively.

The more that we reflect on teaching, the harder it seems to do a good job. The gap between what is and what could be becomes wider. Anyone can do a mediocre job and be unaware of it. The children can go through routine tasks without thinking.

They can be kept merely occupied. But once we pay attention to the concepts that we want children to think about, and recognize their ability to think about them, we begin to make more demands on ourselves. Instead of showing that we can cope in the classroom we begin to question what the children are learning and whether they could do more. And the answer is always that they 'could do better'. Instead of blaming them we then need to act on it, and work out strategies to help.

> In research studies that look at the work of children in classrooms, two themes often emerge. The first is how little time children spend 'on task', actually working. The second is how routine and undemanding much of the work is, for example doing repetitive sums like additions in maths. The deeper the analysis the more depressing it seems. The gap between reality and perfection seems so wide. But we must support ourselves with the realization that in the day-to-day realities of teaching it is impossible that there should be complete concentration by all the children all the time. Teachers need the occasional use of habit, just to survive. They also need to recognize what they are striving towards.[4]

The concern, then, is for others. There is a great distinction to be made between teaching and lecturing, a distinction observed years ago.[5] The *lecturer* deals with knowledge and shapes this knowledge into a 'work of art'. He addresses a mass. The component parts of his audience, the single minds with their difficulties, are nothing to him . . . The books and knowledge and skilful narrative are the sole business of the lecturer. The audience must take care of themselves.

Then on the other hand, 'The *teacher* makes the taught do the work, and occupies himself in showing them how to do it, and taking care that they do it.' The lecturer is caught up in his own performance. The teacher judges himself in the performance of his pupils. This does not mean that the teacher relies entirely on the pupils' learning, as if there were no place for the formalities of teaching. On the contrary, the teacher is concerned that what he presents is really effective, not for his sake but for theirs.

> One survey of teachers' attitudes found that they all agreed about the main ingredients of success, and what made their teaching effective. On this there was great unity.
> But observation of these teachers revealed that their replies had little or nothing to do with how they *actually* taught. There is often a gap between impressive statements and good intentions and the everyday reality of teaching. For this reason it is sometimes helpful to have an objective look at our own teaching, to analyse what actually happens.[6]

Concern for pupils is not the same as having designs on them. There is an important distinction between teaching and manipulation. Like any other art teaching combines the public and the private. In the 'public' domain one can see how 'mass' art can work like propaganda, trying to make its audience respond in particular ways. Propaganda has designs on the audience, with a view to creating an anticipated reaction. On the other hand one can see how 'private' art can be created just for the sake of the artist, as some form of personal therapy. True art communicates by avoiding either extreme. The same is true of the art of teaching.

> 'Knowledge is power' is a phrase that has many resonances around the world. In some countries it explains how teachers are viewed. Acquiring knowledge is seen in these places as a means to an end, to acquire power and money by having something that

> others want. This knowledge can be sold. But teachers are seen to give away knowledge freely, using it not for themselves but for others. In the countries where 'knowledge is power' this is puzzling.

The teacher, then, has a disinterested (as opposed to uninterested) concern for pupils, a concern that is for their sake rather than for their approval. The teacher does his best, not in competition with others but in collaboration with them. The effective teacher is consistent and clear. He does his best; and his best continues to improve.

Learning

The word 'learning' can be used in more than one sense. It describes the process of accumulation and change that marks our growing sense of knowledge and it also, as in 'man of learning', describes knowledge itself. The two must go together. It is impossible to teach without knowledge, even if some think it possible to acquire knowledge without thinking.

> It might seem obvious that teachers must possess a great deal of knowledge and know about the ways in which pupils learn. And yet, in one country at least, there have been constant arguments about which side of the teaching and learning processes are more important, to the exclusion of the one side or the other. On the one hand there is the idea of fostering child-centred education as if the teacher had only to give children opportunities to learn. On the other there is talk of teachers as 'deliverers of the curriculum' as if they had only to stand and present what they know.[7]

There have been times when a teacher's knowledge in primary schools in particular has been underrated. The primary teacher needs to understand all the complex skills of teaching, and the needs of individuals and groups as well as how children learn. The primary teacher also has to teach a wide range of subjects.

Learning is not a simple accumulation of knowledge or a steady accretion. It is an emotional experience, a difficult rite of passage that is demanding and can be stressful. Teachers often find it very difficult to go on challenging courses – for they have to 'unlearn', rethink, and question themselves about what they are doing.

It is a social fact that secondary schools are seen as more demanding because of the higher levels of subject knowledge. But secondary teachers, as well as primary teachers, need to understand the reactions of the individual as well as the subject. This understanding is merely more obvious in the primary schools as children develop their learning across a range of new subjects. Overall the primary teacher needs more knowledge, in terms of facts and concepts, than a teacher of other age ranges.

The crucial point is that the teacher cannot stop learning. This is not only because there is so much to know and understand that the teacher will never achieve all he wishes to, but because the desire for learning needs to become an ingrained habit. Nothing is more dull than the sense that there is nothing more to be known: 'I've done that', 'I've seen that'. Nothing is more stifling than a loss of curiosity. Children very quickly sense when the excitement has gone out of teaching, when the teacher is no longer curious about their learning or his own.

> Unfortunately, nearly all of us can remember at least one teacher relying on well-thumbed notes, reading out, yet again, all the things that he prepared years ago.
> This shows not just a lack of interest in pupils but a far deeper lack of interest in himself.

The excitement in teaching comes about when we see pupils making a breakthrough: showing renewed interest in a topic, wanting to share their newly acquired discoveries or being able to apply a new concept. But unless the teacher is also learning, his excitement will never be felt. A recognition of the learning process in others depends on the learning process in oneself, in being able to share new insights and discoveries, new materials and new techniques. The only way to avoid boring routine is to think of new things. This means that the teacher does not just learn new things for the next few lessons, but learns for learning's own sake. The teacher needs to have an interest in his subject, and to pursue his interest beyond the level of a hobby. While he plays the role of the teacher he is also a person with an inner life of his own, an interest in things beyond the world of the classroom. For the teacher as well as the children, education is concerned with making sense of the world, so that the individual can adapt to it and understand it, rather than be overwhelmed by it. For young children this is the driving force of their learning, and it needs to remain so.

> One of the most significant parts of a teacher's knowledge is his own experience. In bringing a topic to life there is nothing like an anecdote. For then children see the connections between the abstract fact and its reality. Teaching is then a function of narrative: 'teaching as story-telling', as one book calls it.[8]

Stress is placed on learning because it is possible to learn *not* to learn. In fact many people make a habit of this. They do not want to be disturbed by new evidence. They do not want to change their minds. They prefer to be frozen into a 'set', a series of habitual beliefs that will never change.[9] This refusal to learn is partly a matter of habit, of laziness or tiredness. It can also be quite deliberate. Prejudices arise because people feel more comfortable when well cushioned by stupidity. They like the languor of their own habitual rest, and justify the warmth they feel about people like themselves by hating anyone different. It comes to a point where they cannot even hear evidence that goes against their belief, let alone disagree with it. The final results of a refusal to learn are bigotry and cruelty to others, stemming from an initial break in the habit of learning.

> Politicians can be a good example of people deliberately not learning. They have their point of view to which they will stick in the face of overwhelming evidence to the contrary. They never admit to being wrong. One politician, for example, told me what a colleague was going to discover on a 'fact finding' trip to another country before he had even set out. Politicians' attitudes towards education and schools can sometimes be explained only by the fact that they base their opinions on some incident which often took place many years earlier. Personal anecdote overcomes all matters of factual evidence.

The excitement of learning is of two kinds. One is in our own learning, whatever the topic, and the other is in observing and sharing the learning of children. We cannot always detect when a child has learned something, but we can detect the results. We can see when they are making a new connection, or applying a skill to a new circumstance, or making use of a larger vocabulary. In any school there is not an *end* to learning.

There are many different ways of being effective.

- Teachers need not have identical styles. As long as the crucial points are acted upon it is worth remembering that there is no narrow definition of the good teacher.
- Teachers vary in a wide variety of personal and professional characteristics.
- Individual characteristics do not have a simple direct impact on pupils' achievements.[10]

Learning is not the province of the isolated scholar but something to be shared. The subjects which are being learned are always interesting at any stage. The young child is struggling with similar concepts to those that concern philosophers – why do people behave as they do? Children might struggle differently and sometimes more intensely but they share the same stuff of knowledge. It has been said that any concept can be taught to children of any age without losing intellectual integrity. This is because everyone is engaged in learning very similar things.

Teacher: Are you learning anything?
Pupil: No, I'm listening to you.

Organization

At the root of classroom management lies the matching of work to the needs of the individual. This is a complicated process. The teacher needs to cater for the skills, abilities and interests of each pupil, to avoid giving tasks that are impossible, and to avoid giving tasks so easy that pupils learn nothing. Catering for the gifted is never easy, nor is it easy to avoid some routine work.

Fortunately learning does not consist of a set of exact behavioural tasks, with one skill depending on another. There can be sudden leaps of understanding as well as plateaux of achievement. It is a successful device to give children some tasks which are far beyond them before demonstrating what they *can* do. If a teacher wishes the pupils to reach a certain standard, as he would for a test, it is important to aim beyond it.

Planning appropriate activities, and having plenty of them, is itself an interesting and crucial task so that there is no obvious mismatch between the children's abilities and the tasks they have been set. Planning is not just a matter of a broad scheme, but a detailed analysis of how to present material, so that all the children are not only occupied but sharing a sense of purpose.

'Time on task' describes those moments when children are actually engaged with their work, rather than getting up to find a pen, talking to a neighbour, dreaming, playing with a pencil, or just waiting for the teacher to give an instruction. This latter time can be described as 'waiting'. How much time do you think that a child spends waiting as a percentage of any school day, from the moment he arrives to the moment he leaves, including all the breaks for food and refreshment and play?

The most important aspect of organization is the management of time. It is very easy for children to spend their time waiting – waiting for signals from the teacher, or the bell, waiting for someone to reply to a question or waiting to begin work. Even if pupils are given a task to work on they spend a lot of time, not thinking or working, but looking for a pen or whispering to a friend. This is worrying, but it should worry us just as much when the work that they do is not interesting or stimulating, when they are copying something out or doing the same sum again and again. The first concern for the teacher is to recognize the dangers of wasted time and then avoid them.

> In several research studies where individual children were observed all day, the amount of time discovered to be spent 'off task' was disturbingly high: the amount of time children spent 'waiting' – not actually engaged in learning – was found to be around 75 per cent.[11]

The proper organization of time depends a great deal on planning, and on clearly set out routines in the classroom. The most important principle of organization is the authority of the teacher, the sharing of an agreed set of procedures that the teacher insists upon. Children need to know, and at first to be told, exactly how to behave, so that if they do not follow the agreed procedures there is a real sense of moral outrage. They need to know how to line up at the door, how not to interrupt someone else talking, how to keep the classroom tidy, and where all the equipment is kept. This means that the teacher has to insist that whatever is said is meant and adhered to. The teacher should not have to say 'quiet' more than once. If he does, then he has not meant it the first time. The teacher needs to give children clear signals, when they should stop what they are doing and listen, and when they should be carrying on with their work.

> There is one word used more than any other by teachers in English-speaking classrooms. When one asks teachers what that word might be they suggest 'Quiet' or 'Stop' or 'No' or 'Don't'. A few suggest 'Please' or 'Good'.
> The word used more than any other is 'Right'. On reflection this is not surprising as 'right' is a general utility word that can mean anything according to when it is used. It does not mean 'correct'. It is a word that depends on tone of voice. 'Right, stop what you are doing.' 'Right, now listen to me.' 'Right, you can get on with your work.' 'Right.'[12]

All rules in a school need to be clear and fair and consistently applied. Children both respect and need this. But in addition each teacher will create a particular set of routines within the classroom. The important factor is attention to detail. It includes a desire for tidiness, showing a respect for the environment and all that takes place in it. Knowing where everything is kept, and making sure that all is kept clean, is part of the underlying message to children about their work. At first it seems hard to insist on every detail, but it is essential. Just as a mother can find it so much easier and lazier not to pay constant attention to politeness and cleanliness in her children, so a teacher can be tempted not to bother. It is crucial to check every detail, each table and each piece of paper. After a time the children, knowing the teacher is observing all of them, all the time, do not need any more reminding.

> In a survey of teachers to find out which behaviours helped children learn there were some clear indications:[13]
>
> – Being clear and enthusiastic.
> – Using a variety of approaches and questions.
> – Not wasting time, yet not giving straight information.
> – Giving children opportunities to learn.
>
> There was one thing that did *not* help:
>
> – Being critical.

For the classroom to be a welcoming place with an atmosphere that supports work, it needs first and foremost to be kept clean and tidy. The teacher needs to work out how to make the best use of the space. This depends on the question of when the children should work individually and when in groups. Too often children are set in groups round a table and given their own task to do, without any proper thought of why they are working together (if they are) and why they are not doing the same kind of task as all the other children.[14] Group work is too often a matter of children merely sitting at the same table, without any planned discussion. Group work can be used to avoid having to provide multiple copies of the same material.

> Some classrooms are welcoming. There is work mounted on the wall, showing what the children have achieved. There are displays to be talked about, and things to be explored. The desks or tables are arranged according to the task in hand. The children know where all the paper and pens and books are kept and can organize themselves. The children are caught up in what they are doing.

Properly organized group work can be very important in children's learning. Children can often be good 'teachers' and clarify their own ideas by explaining them to others. They can explore their understandings, and elaborate their thoughts by talking constructively. But this doesn't necessarily happen by itself. The teacher needs to create the conditions for real group work.

The teacher also needs to create conditions in which he can help individuals, by following up earlier assessments and meeting particular needs. Planning the curriculum is accompanied by creating a classroom organization that can be constantly monitored. Once the children know what is expected of them and why, the teacher can concentrate on the real purpose of teaching.

> The teacher's most used phrase or word is 'Right'. But suppose we ask children what they think is the most used phrase? Would we be surprised?
> Teachers imagine that children would say that the most common phrases would be 'Don't' or 'Stop' or 'Be quiet'.
> In fact, as one survey discovered, children cited as the most used phrase that they associated with teachers: 'Do it again.'[15]

Communication

The ability to communicate derives from a curiosity about other people. It is not just a matter of being able to articulate, or demonstrate great wit. It is a two-way process, of listening as much as talking, of encouraging others to talk as much as talking oneself.

Fortunately children have an innate desire to communicate. They want to talk about things and respect our right to do so too. They are a ready-made audience. The classroom is the second most important place where communication skills are learned. It is second only to the home, where the first essential skills of making relationships and using languages are learned.

> So much depends on children's abilities to hold a conversation: to have a good working relationship with an individual adult. Whilst this matters most of all before they are 3 years old, it still remains an essential part of their school experience, and the more opportunities they have the better.[16]

Children like to talk and they like to talk in a variety of styles. They find it harder to listen. They must therefore learn all the skills of communication, being quiet when someone else is speaking, paying attention and understanding the signals that mean it is one's turn to speak. The most important example that children have is the teacher. It is the teacher who sets standards of communication, through the expectations of politeness and by giving everyone a chance to talk. The teacher is also the most important audience for the children.

Having something to communicate clearly helps. But everyone has something to say and can find the right words with which to say it. To learn to communicate is to learn the art of conversation and argument, to learn the skill of 'dialectics'. At the heart of the education process lies the development of logical skills, of sifting evidence and coming to conclusions. Long before children are aware that it is called 'philosophy' they are learning to argue points, to share and refine ideas. The chance to develop these skills can be deliberately provided by teachers, whenever groups are asked to work together. One has only to observe someone who can keep the 'conversational ball rolling' to see what a difference it makes to that person and to others.

> When children were asked to define the skills of the teacher that they most admired they mentioned a variety of them: firmness, for example, and fairness and consistency. But the greatest virtue that they found in teachers was their ability to explain, to clarify issues, and demonstrate how to understand them. This explaining included factors such as patience and not humiliating the children. Many skills centre on the idea of 'explanation'.[17]

Children see the teacher as an audience, but he is an audience of a particular kind. They want to please him and try to guess what it is he wants them to say. However hard teachers try to ask 'open' questions, to which any answer is reasonable – 'What did you think of the book?' – children will have an underlying sense that there is only one answer that the teacher is after. Every question to them is a 'closed' one: 'What is the capital of France?' Even the simplest question – 'How are you feeling?' – will give an immediate, if hidden, response: 'What is he after? Why is he asking me?' To ask 'open' questions, therefore, is not enough in itself. One must be aware of children's interpretations in such a way that one can demonstrate that they can answer by defining what they think rather than guessing what you want to hear. To encourage the speaker is also to create a listener.

> A priest came to a school to give his weekly lesson on the Scriptures. He asked a question which he expected 7-year-olds to answer: 'What is small and furry, has a bushy tail and eats nuts?' There was a complete silence. No one volunteered the answer. The priest was puzzled. At last he turned to the reliable Sophie who always answered questions. 'Can't you tell me?', he pleaded. 'Well,' she said, 'it's difficult. We know you want us to say, "Jesus Christ", but it sounds very much like a squirrel to me.'

Everyone has something to say that is important. And yet there remain some 'invisible' children who remain quiet and obscure and who are in danger of failing through sheer neglect. When we think back on classes that we have taught it is the difficult ones we remember or those who drew attention to themselves in one way or another, through talent or chance. But what about the rest? Can we recollect every child we taught? In every class there are groups which hang together – those who want to please the teacher and those who do not. But there are also those who know how to keep quiet, to keep out of trouble, and to keep away from learning without causing a fuss. Communication must be with every one.[18]

> From one study of classrooms, certain observations should give us pause for thought. The predominant feature in primary schools seemed to be writing practice. There was great emphasis on quantity and on simple punctuation. Most teacher–pupil exchanges were concerned with spelling.
>
> No wonder children associate teachers with saying 'Do it again' and 'Carry on where you left off'.[19]

Teachers do not only need the art of communicating with their pupils. They need to communicate with each other. This often calls for skills in diplomacy, but derives not just from the need for self-help, but from the needs of the school. A good school relies on a sense of shared purpose; and that means good communications.[20]

The skill of communicating with colleagues arises from a strong professional sense of purpose and a willingness to learn. The skill of communicating with pupils also depends on the ability to use appropriate language. This does not mean 'talking down'. On the contrary, it means heightening children's sense of language, but doing so by using new words in a context they can understand and using the extended vocabulary again and again. Children learn new words every day, not by having them defined, but by hearing them, guessing what they mean, and using them. The teacher can also share such explorations of vocabulary, for without new words we are left with little to say.

> Most of us will have experienced at least one teacher who, however limited in his everyday teaching, one day became inspired and talked about a subject he really knew and cared about – even if it wasn't on the formal curriculum. Suddenly he was communicating what he wanted to, and not just what he had to.

Humour

Humour is a serious subject. It is important for teachers not to take themselves too seriously: 'the gravity of the body to hide the defects of the mind'.[21] Teachers need humour in order to survive.

Why should humour be so important? Humour has little to do with formal jokes but more to do with a sense of irony. Teaching is a stressful job, not only in itself, but in the tensions that arise around it: lack of money or support, the expectations of parents and inspectors, and the abuse of politicians and journalists. Teaching does not always feel rewarded or rewarding. A sense of humour then is a serious factor, a knowledge that we are only doing our best. Humour is a kind of self-awareness.

Humour is also an important part of the repertoire of teaching. Children appreciate teachers using it. They want to see how far teachers can take it, and keep testing the parameters of behaviour. Humour is also part of a teacher's charisma, a sign that he is also an approachable personality, to whom children can relate.

> It is a sign of grace in people that they do take humour seriously. Thus, if you mention to teachers the word 'humour' you can be guaranteed to see them all smile – to demonstrate they possess it.

Humour also reminds us that we cannot force children to learn. There are other more subtle means of helping them, by diverting rather than confronting.

But most of all, humour is part of integrity. It is a sense of irony, an understanding of the complexities of circumstances, and an acceptance of them which does not sacrifice a sense of purpose.

Chapter 3

What Children Should Learn

'To get a job you have to know English, science, history, maths and spelling.'

(boy, 10)

'Without vision the people perish.' The vital spark of education is a sense of purpose. There must be a reason for teaching, a reason for creating a whole system of education. Without a sense of purpose no teacher can be really effective. And yet the sense of vision is often lacking. Why?

Many people have a suspicion of what seems like missionary instincts, and a dread of the optimistic. It can appear mawkish to talk earnestly about the underlying purposes of education. Many people also fear the political exploitation of education and assume that purposes can be too narrowly defined. There are those who think that a belief in the transforming power of education implies a disbelief in religion or the power of fate. And it is simply unfashionable to express a sense of purpose, for we live in a pessimistic age.

Even if we do not express it, we all have an inner purpose for what we are doing. It could be merely to earn enough so that we can eat, and drink, and go to social events. If some purposes are anything but idealistic, they are still strong. If people are not motivated by high ideals, they will still be motivated by greed or envy or hatred. It is impossible to be utterly unmotivated or utterly neutral. If this is true of every individual it is just as true of the education system.

The aims of education are talked about, by some, in general philosophical terms. The question of the content of education is also addressed as a preliminary to statements about the curriculum. But rarely are the two put together and more rarely thought about by teachers. It is as if we took these things for granted. Perhaps we feel they do not need elaborating. But defining what we are doing helps us teach. Thinking about what children should learn, and why, is very practical.

The sense of purpose that affects the teacher is a personal one; it does not have to be elaborated. It is based on an essential belief that education makes a difference, for better or worse, and that something can be done to improve things. One has to accept the fact that there are many teachers who don't really care if they make much difference, and 'deliver' the curriculum simply because it is their job. They too are giving clear signals to the children.

> One of the reasons for a lack of belief in education is the fact that we live in a conservative time. This refers not to any political party but to an underlying sense that people will always remain as they are and there is little that can be done about it. This conservatism is expressed in the instinctive belief that criminals are born to be as they are and that the only solution to crime is prevention with more police and more prisons, more burglar alarms and more punishment. Education, on the other hand, offers solutions based on the belief that people are 'made' as well as born.

Definitions of what children should learn are often no more than vague lists, either of subjects or of general fields of thought, like the aesthetic, the moral, the spiritual, the cognitive, and the physical. When national curricula are defined and imposed they tend to be seen in terms of traditional subjects with clearly defined boundaries between them. There might be heated arguments at the edges: what is the distinction between science and technology? what does environmental education cover? is information technology a subject? ... But for the most part the central acceptance of subjects is complete. What makes the arguments about subject boundaries or content interesting is that they unleash all the underlying ideas about the purposes of learning. Thus one person will say, 'Drama is the most important subject of all', and another, 'Only through history can you understand.' It is at this point that a real discussion of purposes is attained.

Any national curriculum is bound to be a monument to blandness, partly for fear that a curriculum might be used for political propaganda. It is, however, possible to share convictions without having designs on people, and even a national curriculum will reveal the half-hidden purposes of those who propose it. From the point of view of any government, for example, there are some clear requirements for the education system to produce people who have certain skills so that they can contribute to a manufacturing economy in competition with others. The vocational – producing engineers and programmers, designers and physicists – must be at the heart of a government's purpose. But even this is not really thought out, and does not affect the still-traditional subject boundaries of assessments. Nor does it much affect what takes place in universities. It is almost as if there were a fear of working out too clearly the implications of the curriculum.

> In more than one survey of school leavers, especially of those who had not gone on to university, it was clear that they look back on their school experience with regret and disappointment. To some extent they blame themselves for not working harder and wish they had a second chance. But most of all, school leavers regretted what they had been given in school. They all felt the curriculum lacked one vital ingredient. They did not merely say the teachers were dull or anything like that. They said that what was missing was a sense of purpose. No one told them why they were there, and no one talked about their futures, about contemporary issues, about politics or society. That is what the young people missed.[1]

What people should learn and what they wish to learn are, often, very different. The Swedish programme of offering mature students the chance of further study when they were already well into their careers as scientists and accountants revealed a desire not for further vocational qualifications, but for subjects like the arts, philosophy and anthropology. The earliest desire expressed by young children, to understand, was being reaffirmed by the mature.[2]

We live in a time when there is a strong movement to think of education in terms of 'competencies'. Individuals are measured against attainment targets. Teachers are assessed against a checklist of performance indicators. The problem with 'competencies' is that they can be very limiting, like small behavioural tasks. Defining specific skills cannot capture the inner convictions, the reflectiveness, which underlie observable practice. The effective teacher cannot be defined in a series of competencies.

> For young children the connection between what they are doing in school and what they will do afterwards is always in their minds. When asked what school is for they will tell you that it is to help them acquire a job. But this idea is rarely explained to them in school, so they have to make their own minds up about how a school subject relates to their later lives. The one connection they all make is with their prospects of future employment.
> 'What do you want to be when you grow up?'
> 'I want to be a speller, because I'm good at spelling.'[3]

When we talk about what children should learn we clearly include skills as well as content. Thinking is a skill much prized in every profession. It is natural to wish to find means of assessing it, against clear attainment targets. And yet such standard assessments can have an inhibiting effect on enterprise by gearing what is to be learned towards what is easily measured. They rarely suggest that a child is capable of asking the really difficult questions, of the kind that involve choices and decisions. In every subject, as in geography, for example, there are crucial political issues. To what extent should coal be exploited or other forms of energy sought? What effect would such decisions have on the local populations? When teachers discuss what children should learn, however, they tend to assume that children of 6 or 7 cannot understand such issues and indeed should not. There is a fear that discussion might lead to exploitation. The problem is that exploitation of attitudes arises out of ignorance. By not looking at political issues (with a small 'p'), children are the more exposed to manipulation by Politicians (with a big 'P').

> Sometimes children have a surprising view of what a 'subject' is. Some think of 'spelling' or 'writing' as a subject. Some children in infant schools know that 'history' is a subject and that they do not do it. For most children a 'subject' is what the teacher tells them to do. They learn the labels that teachers give them. 'Hello, what are you writing about?'
> 'I'm doing English.'[4]

Children are learning all the time, even if they are not always learning what we want them to. They are observing other people's behaviour, they are watching television, listening to songs, reading magazines and discussing ideas with each other. They are taking on the moral outlook of their peers and analysing their environment. This is not a conscious policy, of course, any more than it is a school subject. It is an innate need, one which is quite obvious when they are very young but becomes less so as their learning processes are overlaid with a formal curriculum. Children understand how society functions from observing social behaviours in school. What they do at school and the way they are led to behave has an impact on the rest of their lives.[5]

> In recent years there has been a growing awareness of, and concern for, instances of bullying in school. Although some schools would prefer to deny it, there is no school

completely free of bullying, verbal if not physical. Even if some children are never either bullies or victims, they are nevertheless observers of such behaviour. Bullying is a worrying phenomenon, especially because there is a very strong correlation between bullying in school and later criminal behaviour.[6]

Children bring to school a need to learn. But they can become bewildered at what actually happens at school. We have already noted how much time is spent waiting for things to happen. That is an odd experience in itself but it comes about because of the need for order. The school is a social centre. It contains clear hierarchies with people of widely differing status and power. These hierarchies include not only teachers, governors and cleaners, but children, especially dependent on their age and size. This is one of the factors that underlies bullying. From the child's point of view the school presents a very firm impression of the way that societies work, with rules and regulations, sanctions and punishments, marvellous moments and terrible half-hours.[7]

To a child, a school also seems to have a social identity of its own, one which remains slightly obscure. It is as if a child were always to some degree undergoing the first day at a new school. We can all remember the bewilderment of not knowing the routine, or not understanding what people were doing. Now and again each of us will have suddenly forgotten a rule, or wondered if we were in the right place, and suffered from intense bewilderment and worry. That feeling of the first day remains because few schools ever explain their purpose. They say a lot about expectations, about how hard people should work and how they should behave. But it is as if it is taken for granted that whatever the school does, including a wide variety of subjects, is an acknowledged and shared set of standards rather than values. You learn maths and learn to read. You learn about other countries. Some people learn Latin. No one learns anthropology, at least not under that heading. You study people, but not psychology or sociology. And the importance of certain subjects is demonstrated not by explanation but by the amount of time they take up.

All the attention paid to the 'core curriculum' – the need for mathematics and reading and writing – suggests that these subjects are missing. In fact they dominate, with more than three-quarters of the time spent on them. Children understand the differences in importance between subjects by *when* they take them. Mathematics, for example, is always done in the mornings and never in the afternoon. It is the mornings that matter for 'real' work. The afternoon is for the more playful subjects, like art.[8]

Successful schools have an ethos of their own. Every school has a moral expectation in terms of standards of behaviour. Each school should have clear rules and policies. But these are rarely related to the academic curriculum. The child is there to accept what he is given. He doesn't accept everything quite equally. There are some subjects that he prefers, depending on taste and the qualities of the teacher. Gradually he learns to construct a picture of the academic world which is slanted to things easy to do, or things that must be done, subjects that have prestige and those with none.

Parent: 'That is a wonderful painting; you must have spent hours doing it. It must have been rewarding. What did you get out of doing that?'
Pupil: 'Seven out of ten.'

The content of the curriculum remains largely unexplained. Children are there simply to learn what is presented to them. Meanwhile there is another world of speculation that takes place beneath the formalities of the classroom. The school is a social centre, a testing ground for friendships and enmities. This is where children learn about relationships.[9] They also learn to form their views of the world, not through the explanations given to them by teachers but through their own conversations. Almost as a by-product of their work or their games, they exchange information and prejudices. They imbibe attitudes and repeat facts, even if they are inaccurate. It is an odd phenomenon that the discussion of fundamental issues is often left to children to deal with amongst themselves.

The question is whether this part of the curriculum should be left hidden. We ask what children should learn, but begin to accept that we have little control over it. We don't even try. And yet we have a clear picture of what we would like the children to become just as we have a powerful image of ourselves.

The vision that drives us on in teaching is one that affects both how we think of ourselves and how we think of pupils. We want to help each individual fulfil all his talents. But we are more than enablers, doing so much according to the different levels of ability. We have a picture of what everyone *should* achieve as well as a recognition of what many *will* achieve. Beyond the idiosyncrasies of personality, which we cannot change, we must have at least some idea of what everyone should know.

We want pupils to have in their grasp all the attributes of a civilized person. These attributes are a mixture of skills, knowledge, understanding and behaviour. But why does such a statement seem so bold and so rarely expressed? Is it so obvious that it doesn't need stating, or so idealistic that it cannot be attained? Or is it so contentious because no one can agree what 'civilized' means?

> 'What do you think of Western civilization, Mr Gandhi?'
> 'I think it sounds like a good idea, worth trying one day.'

Teachers have expectations and hopes for their pupils. This is not the same as saying that they want them to fit into prearranged stereotypes, but they are capable of disappointment when expectations are not met. It matters how a person behaves.

Behaviour is part of knowledge. Children have to learn and continually refine their sensitivity to others. They need to learn to respect others of different cultures or gender. Their awareness of equality of opportunity needs constant attention, because it is possible to be inadvertently insensitive. Ignorance can hurt. And attitudes to gender, class and 'race' need to be explored and explained, rather than ignored.

> Mr Patel arrives in an office for an interview. The secretary looks up and, seeing him, says: 'Your name is not on this list.'
> 'But I haven't given you my name yet.'

The person truly sensitive to others and self-aware expresses not just a battery of skills but an awareness of his place, and other people's place, in the environment. What makes us (and them) as we are? We can fully understand that only if we explore all the circumstances of time and place that make each person unique.

> Bertrand Russell formulated a social grammar of 'I, you and he'. This was to draw attention to the subtle, almost subconscious way in which people can discriminate in their judgement of themselves, their acquaintances and others. For example:
>
> 'I have a hint of that mysterious aroma of the Orient.'

> **'You've** rather overdone it, dear.'
>
> **'She** stinks.'

No one can know everything, but everyone should be aware of what he does not know. Any subject, approached in the spirit of wanting to know why, constantly expands, for knowledge is limitless. But with the accumulation of knowledge comes coherence. The more a subject is known, the more sense it makes, and the more it takes in an awareness of other subjects.

Let us take some examples. To know why things are as they are must include a knowledge of history. History is sometimes seen to be, and taught as, a dull subject. 'Oh no; it's the Romans (or the Anglo-Saxons) again!' But if one starts from where we are now, rather than at the 'beginning', and ask why things are as they are we begin to realize that we cannot understand the modern world without knowing about the Second World War. How do we explain the existence of concentration camps? The rise of anti-semitism? How do dictators come into being? There is a great deal of explaining to be done and none of it is easy. One then realizes that it is not possible to understand the Second World War and the rise of the dictatorships of the fascist and communist varieties without understanding the First World War. And one cannot understand that without exploring the rise of nationalism . . .

> The sense of a lack of purpose in schools cannot be explained only on the basis that children might find the curriculum 'boring'. When we look at schools we see that there is often a great emphasis on quantity, and that most teacher–pupil exchanges are concerned with spelling and punctuation. Is 'neat work' really the most important element in the school curriculum?[10]

We could go on and on with many such examples. What drives the desire to know is the need to understand. History is not just a list of what did happen, but an attempt to understand why. It is also driven by the same curiosity that makes people study social psychology. Why could a State impose such systematic wickedness on people? Why did they become part of it? And the 'they' of history means us, means you and me.

There are some who would say that young children are not ready for such advanced and difficult subjects. Why, of all things, even mention the Holocaust, even if it is as alarming socially as the 'greenhouse' effect? The fact is that children cannot escape from knowledge by innocence. First of all they see and hear a series of images on the media. They are regular witnesses of the news. There are few children who have never been frightened by a programme – whether they relished their fear or not. And there are few children who have not witnessed cruelty of one kind or another in their surroundings. The question remains. What makes some people like that? How can we prevent it?

> What are children to think when they see on the news the confrontational aspects of parliamentary politics? One man or woman stands up and says that the person before him is a boundless villain, incompetent and destructive. This person then states, by way of reply, that the person who said that is not only a liar but a more loathsome creature than ever walked or crawled on the face of the earth. If what they are both saying is true then that is devastating. If it is not true they are both lying. No wonder people shrug their shoulders and say, 'Politicians!'

The first need is to understand. Children are capable of dealing with difficult subject matter, provided it is treated both seriously and delicately. Children see the news – and how much of that is innocent? They are presented with a picture of the world that is anything but positive. The people most in the news, the politicians, keep reminding us how dreadful all the others are; how stupid and untrustworthy. Are children to believe everything they say? Of course children are more sophisticated than that – and more indifferent. They therefore receive a mass of information from which they put together a kaleidoscopic vision of the world. The idea of history is to help out sort the details and make them into a coherent whole.

> Children are far more capable of learning about the past than they have been given credit for. They have, in fact, a mature historical sense and do not need to be given lots of 'familiar' or parochial material. But they do not learn history through contextual knowledge; they need to be taught.[11]

History enables children to understand why things are as they are, why there are political parties and why society is run as it is. It therefore has a strongly 'political' dimension. So does geography, where 'politics' is not a matter of parties but a matter of decisions. When human beings organize themselves, as in a school, and when they make choices they are being political. 'Politics' is the everyday; it is human dialogue; and hence Socrates' great interest and concern. It is not the debasement of decisions into party slogans and party political slanging matches. And yet the two have been so closely associated that 'politics' has come to mean for many people 'parties' and movements; the stranglehold over, rather than the freedom of, thought. And out of this fear has come the avoidance of all mention of politics in school, thereby depriving children of that central issue that makes them social beings, able to make decisions, to participate, and to respect what other people think.

Geography can be a very dull subject or an ill-defined one. But when its purpose is to give evidence upon which ideas are based, when the understanding of other people and the interaction between humankind and the environment is at the core, then it begins to present its evidence as central and important. Then all those school-leavers who find the curriculum so meaningless would no longer need to complain.

> Children are always aware of the importance of school and look forward to secondary school specialisms. They are also aware that success, or failure, lies in their own hands. The reasons for their giving up, or becoming disillusioned, are therefore not simple. They hope that there is a connection between the subjects they do and their subsequent lives, but gradually realize that there is not. Whatever their own efforts they become thwarted. Their energy then is turned *against* learning.[12]

The issues that confront very young children remain the same issues that concern us into old age. The difference is that as we get older we learn to accommodate the issues or ignore them. They might be treated differently, and presented in a more controlled way, but control also brings a narrowness of vision. For a young child the world is confused and complicated, and he does not have the means to present his thoughts about it. But he is nevertheless trying to make sense of it, and is always asking 'Why?' There is a need to know.

> Many people take a great delight in the open-minded questioning of young children. But they also find themselves having to answer questions which seem impossible to answer. Why is this? It is not because young children ask naive questions. Nor is it because we do not have the words or think children will not understand. It is because we ourselves

haven't always addressed the answer: we ignore it. And so children are often given silly answers: a sign of the adult avoiding responsibility. 'It's the storks . . .' 'It's Father Christmas . . .' It is curious how often adults give fantastic answers to direct questions, as if they cannot take children seriously.

Despite children's need to know, knowledge is often denied them. This might seem a strange statement to make. But the knowledge that is needed for understanding is different from the accumulation of facts: it is derived from evidence, from having opinions and ideas that are based on facts. Knowledge, in the real sense, is based on dialogue, on reaching understanding by reason.

Knowledge has been an underrated commodity. For many years the skills of thinking, like an intelligence 'quotient', have been promoted as if ability could be made abstract and applied. The simple knowledge that is a matter of memory, or the accumulation of facts, is not enough in itself. Knowledge for its own sake is pedantry. Real knowledge is the basis on which thinking skills are based.

There is a television show, popular for many years, called 'Mastermind'. It is based on the assumptions that cleverness lies in memory, in being able to know all the facts about a particular subject. Naturally the excitement and appeal of the programme lie not only in its element of competition, but in the visible unfairness of the questions and arbitrariness of chance. But it still presents a myth that memory of facts equals cleverness.

For many years there has been extensive research into information technology and artificial intelligence. What makes a computer different from the human brain, given the enormous power, the 'megabytes', of computers? Is it the infinite flexibility of the brain? Is it its ability to guess as well as to be logical? One would have thought that a computer could be constructed that would, avoiding guesses, work out answers so swiftly and logically that the brain would seem by comparison a feeble machine. And yet the human brain is always (despite the best endeavours) superior. It is ironic that the latest attempt to explain this phenomenon centres on the fact that people possess knowledge. They have evidence stored at a variety of levels on which they can draw.

There is always a tension between the skills of thinking and the accumulation of knowledge. Both depend on each other. To have one and not the other is to make a person a bore or a pedant. To understand what children should learn one must acknowledge that there are two principles to learning:

1. *People accumulate facts.* This cannot be helped. We are all witnessing, overhearing, seeing new facts all the time. Much of the process of growing up is the acquisition of knowledge: not always formal, but constant. We might seem to forget as much as we absorb. Can we recall all the items we heard on the news this morning? But we still have heard them, and we experience new things all the time. Many of the items will have been heard but then forgotten. Young children are particularly good at combining experience and memory. They learn new words (and concepts) every day.

2. *Organization.* Bombarded with so much information, we need to deal with it. It can be ignored. Alternatively, information can be simplified, or it can be organized. There is a natural organizing tendency in any learning. This process is a constant one. The more information that is acquired but not organized, the more difficult it is to recall. Organization is a means of understanding, of fitting new knowledge into place.

> A lot of what we remember depends on the attention we paid in the first place. If you have listened to several items on the news last night or this morning you will probably be surprised at how little, beyond two or three headlines, you can easily recall. If, however, you know that someone will ask you this question and you prepare yourself for it, as for an exam, you will listen in quite a different way.[13]

The accumulation and ordering of knowledge depend on each other. But how often are they seen together? How often are people expected to do one – learn the important dates; remember the scientific principles – without the other? It is through the complementary attention paid to purpose and evidence that accompanies knowledge that knowledge becomes useful.

The principle of what children should learn could have been addressed by giving a list of major subjects or facts or even the one hundred best books. But this is not the best way. The principle underlying what children should learn is one which each teacher should make his own. It is a principle that 'in-forms' the accumulated knowledge and organizes it in a way which supports not just one argument but many.

> The divide between academic subjects and vocational ones has long been with us, however artificial this divide seems. New subjects or approaches, like 'rural studies' or 'environmental education', tend to be rejected after a time, partly because of the strong academic tradition of a set pattern of subjects.[14]

In the Socratic ideal of education the idea of 'rhetoric' was central. This was no verbal display of politicians but an understanding of dialogue, of presenting a case in the face of opposition. The reason for having knowledge is not to display oneself but to make good use of it – to open knowledge rather than hide it. The skill of using language is at the heart of education. We wish to give pupils the ability to argue fairly, kindly and lucidly.

It is fundamental to children's learning that they know they have a lot to learn. They should also learn that they have something to say. It is only through this sense of purpose that knowledge makes sense. For knowledge is a coping skill, the need to survive.

> We have all experienced the person whose mind has been closed against learning; whose idea of argument is to say the same thing, only more loudly. At the heart of that 'unlearning' lies the inability to change or grow or adapt. The person who cannot bear advice not only ceases to grow but decays.

Chapter 4

How Children Learn to Think

'Sometimes you're finding things out in your mind and searching your mind.'

(girl, 10)

Learning begins as an involuntary activity from the moment a child is born. A young child needs to learn. The fact that learning is involuntary does not mean that it is inactive. Learning is not a matter of accumulating information. It is not a passive process. Learning is a need.[1]

The first principle for all teachers to take in is that all children are capable of learning something and that they are learning something all the time. A secondary principle of learning is that what children learn is not all automatically good. Children can also learn not to learn, to narrow their ideas into prejudice and to refuse to take in new information.

If a pupil is not learning new ideas, and not making any progress – by wasting time, or trying to distract himself – then he is not doing nothing. He is actively unlearning, forgetting, getting into lazy habits, and becoming accustomed not to use his mind.

Learning, in one sense or another, takes place all the time. Learning is not always formal. It does not belong just to the school or to periods of concentration. Children are constantly making connections, overhearing opinions, forming new ideas. It is only the formal, academic levels of learning that cannot be maintained all the time. Learning in the full sense takes place continuously.

> If you think back on some of the most significant things you have learned you will discover (a) how hard it is to work out what is 'significant', and (b) how difficult it is to isolate any particular moment.
>
> But if you think further and remember a moment when you suddenly said to yourself, 'Now I understand' or 'This really interests me', you will often find yourself remembering an informal circumstance: not a response to someone's speech, but your own thought processes; the ownership of the experience.

The principles that we are learning all the time and can learn to forget as well as to remember give an insight into the nature of learning that should inform all our teaching. There have been some very simplistic notions of learning. One has been that what people are taught is what they learn, as if they remembered all the information they are given. Some people would say, 'Would that it were so!' They could then manipulate others. Think how often politicians behave as if anyone who listens to them should believe them. Think how easy it would be for a teacher if pupils responded automatically and understood and remembered all they hear. Of course we know this is impossible but there is nevertheless the temptation in many people to view learning in terms of a simple model of 'stimulus' and 'response', treating the human mind like a computer.[2]

There are many people who believe that if only people would listen to them, those people would change. The worry is that those who believe this, if asked if *they* are ever changed by the views of others, will deny the fact. Other people can be manipulated but not themselves. It is odd how many people think of themselves as 'self-made' and of others as products of their circumstances.

There is another over-simple notion of learning. It is the idea that it consists of fixed stages, as if children are not capable of thinking when they are very young and that they only slowly acquire the same mental capacities as you and me.[3] This is untrue. The fact is that the capacity is there, if not the experience.

> One of the signs of the mismatch between belief about others and belief about ourselves is demonstrated in the debates about the effect of television. Some people believe that television has a powerful effect for good, especially if it is their own programme that people watch. They forget it is one programme out of the hundreds the audience sees.[4] Others believe that television programmes do great harm, as if to see a particular programme is to be damaged. If this is true, the same people must have seen the programmes they criticize. Have they therefore been harmed? No.
>
> Children are similar in this respect. Ask them 'What's your favourite programme?' and they are likely to name a thriller. Ask them what programme they would not let their younger sister or brother see because it might do them harm, and they are likely to name the same one. 'Other people might be damaged or influenced but not me.'[5]

Learning is an active and idiosyncratic process. Learning is the human mind at work at a variety of levels. We can understand the principles of all learning and understanding in young children by seeing how learning begins. These principles, whilst described in children, are true of all ages.

Learning is the interaction between the individual and the environment. It is not the complete control of one over the other, but the tension between the two. This is why there has been the age-old discussion of the relationship between 'nature' and 'nurture'. Only the pathologically ill are dominated either by their individual vision without reference to the world they are in, or formed entirely by their surroundings. Only those who might wish to dominate and control would suggest that other people's behaviour is formed by either their genetic make-up ('a born criminal . . .') or their circumstances ('it's not his fault').

When a child is born we observe the shock of the first moments of liberation, the opening of the eyes and the very first attempts to understand. From the very first moments of consciousness the infant not only sees and hears and feels but tries to make sense of all the experiences. What we know (and the child does not) is that he is trying to put the world into a defined form – into a concept.[6]

> Every part of a child's world is crowded with information. If, for example, you are concentrating on reading you will have prevented your ears from attending to all the sounds

around you. But stop. What can you hear? The splash of rain? The drone of the aeroplane? The buzz of the fly on the window? The wind? The fan?

The young child has to learn to concentrate, to ignore all the other sounds that still continue, and then to tune in to one voice.

It is like being at a party of people talking. You are listening to one person, but the babble of conversation that you are ignoring is still taking place.

Let us consider how the child defines the world step by step. Two of the first sensations of new experience are sight and sound. There are many different levels of sound but only by experience and definition do some of them make sense. By experience we know what sounds are; the rustle of leaves, for example. By definition we know what sounds means, like those unique sounds that make up the sound of the voice. One of the first steps of learning is the realization that sounds have a source and that some, like the voice of the father, begin to carry meaning.[7]

The detection of the significance in sounds is balanced by the same development of vision. In our experience we take for granted objects in relation to each other. We know perspective. We understand that a chair is a chair from whatever angle it is seen. We know that when an object comes towards us it seems to get bigger. But all these aspects of the visual world that make it coherent need to be worked out by children. They need to separate the different elements of what begins to seem one vast blur of colours. They need to explore edges and shapes and they spend hours looking, gazing at faces or anything that is visually complicated.[8]

The first learning task, then, is to define the separateness of things, seen and heard and touched. This intellectual task of defining categories is one that is constantly being developed, for children need to understand the meanings in what they see and hear. This is more sophisticated than comprehending more and more; it means learning to discard certain elements for the sake of the essential meaning. Let us take two examples. The world might be crowded with different sounds; it is also full of different voices. Each voice is unique, and yet despite the different tones and despite accents and dialects children can pick out those sounds that carry meaning. They recognize a familiar voice, and they recognize those sound patterns – phonemes – that convey meaning. Whether a person speaks in one accent or another, in one pitch or another, at one speed or another, phonemes are the significant sounds. It is like hearing the same script which, when read aloud, sounds different according to the person reading, but still understanding the same word whatever the accent. When we hear a new language we cannot make any sense of it because we don't know which parts of what we hear are words or letters or sentences. Gradually we learn to recognize what matters. Children go through the same experience without any previous knowledge or outside help.

Children's understanding of visual clues has been demonstrated by the following experiment. Young children are put on a flat board that consists both of patterned wood and glass:

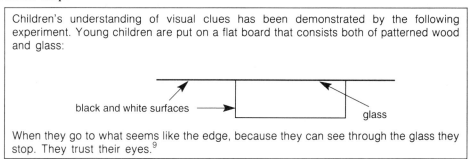

black and white surfaces ⟶

glass

When they go to what seems like the edge, because they can see through the glass they stop. They trust their eyes.[9]

Children learn to pick out the significant from a mass of detail. This means that they are learning to categorize, to make choices, to impose meaning on what they experience. Gradually they learn to connect certain events or objects. The world becomes simpler to understand, as well as more complicated, through language. All 'dogs' have a label as well as an individuality but can be thought about as well as described. Children learn to use the essential categories of distinctions.[10]

Sometimes experience can impose meaning on what we see, to the extent that it is hard not to be influenced by previous knowledge. For instance it is difficult, without our knowledge of parallel lines, not to think of one horizontal line being longer than another.

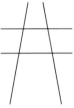

Knowledge of shadows tells us if there is a dent

or a bulge.

We can even make choices of how we see something. In this 'Neckar cube' can the box be seen, if we look at the dot, as going from the left to the right or right to left?

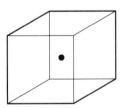

The learning of concepts is not at first a 'conscious' process. It is the need to store memories, to simplify new information so that there are connections with what is already known. The active mind imposes meaning on new things. It forms a series of associations, through guesses, through trial and error and through experience. Even the simplest things are learned, like the discovery that the teddy bear hidden behind a cushion can be found again.[11] And the process of learning is active. Even the baby in a pram needs and desires rich visual stimuli, like pictures, to look at, rather than a blank black wall.

The principle of learning is that a series of connections is being made between things which are seen as significant. The child has to impose meaning on experience. This involves learning how to simplify new meanings so that they can be understood.

Gradually the mind learns what to expect. Just as the strength of learning lies in the forming of concepts, so can this process become its weakness. To understand learning fully we need to remember this. When they are older and as part of their experience of school, children can learn not to 'unfreeze' their mental 'set' and not to let in new information. The most public example of such a process can be seen in the behaviour of some politicians, who cannot let evidence disturb their prejudices. Advice from experts which might deflect the minister from his political goals is therefore rejected, sometimes deliberately and sometimes flagrantly. But this is not just a matter of the doctrinaire overcoming the rational. It is an aspect of self-deception when individuals cannot see, let alone understand, that they might be mistaken.

> We seem to be mentioning politicians quite often; perhaps this is a sign of the times we live in. We should apologize for using them as a symbol of the human species. Another example we could have chosen is religious leaders of a certain kind; they too do not like to see their beliefs challenged. Besides, they draw attention to themselves, are often on television or in newspapers. And they do have power over us.

It is not only politicians who have the capacity not to learn. We have all heard people using the phrase: 'I know what I think', or: 'Nothing will make me change my mind.' Being absolutely certain about a set of prejudices is for many people a comfortable state of mind and one which they would hate to change. To say that they are well-padded with stupidity is to miss the important fact that intelligent people – like politicians, like ourselves – can also become accustomed to be set in our ways, to learn how not to think as well as to think.

It is in the nature of learning to simplify, at first from need and then from habit. It is, after all, very easy to run the mind away from demands, to seek something easier to do, and even to refuse to think. For teachers this is one of the central dilemmas of schools. It is difficult, if not impossible, to force pupils to think and to concentrate. A significant proportion of their energies is taken up by avoiding thinking and even by inventing means of doing so. Every teacher has seen how 'creative' pupils can be in finding different ways of avoiding learning.

> There is no child who does not develop some kind of interest. Sometimes one can despair at meeting the person to whom everything in school is boring – nothing but 'work'. But there will be some interest of some kind – in something like motorcycles or horses – that is supported by a lot of information.
>
> One of the first tasks of a teacher confronted by a child who seems to refuse to learn is to find something that is that child's hobby – something that he or she would choose to spend time on, like a sport, and which, also like a sport, has a great number of facts and statistics that can be associated with it.

The moment that learning is associated with drudgery, the task of education becomes that much more difficult. The most satisfying pleasures are quite demanding – of our responses and thoughts. Shallow and easy entertainment does not linger in the mind. But if the world is too easily divided into the extremes of work and play, both suffer and remain unfulfilled.

Young children need to learn. It is a natural desire to acquire language, to accumulate evidence and make sense of it. But we see children in schools who seem to have lost this need. How, and when, does this happen? It happens in a series of stages. Before children go to school they have rarely been wholly prejudiced against learning. They still see no distinction between work and play, in manipulating paints and making sense of stories.[12] But even if they are willing to learn they might have already been denied the means of doing so, because they have never had a chance to develop the sense of dialogue: questions and answers and the curiosity of exploring shared feelings and opinions. For every child needs not only the experience of explorations – books and materials – but a person to whom they can narrate that experience.

> The desire to seek out a relationship and a form of communication can be observed in different ways. Babies not only show a fascination with studying faces and other complex forms but learn to copy facial gestures made to them – like sticking out a tongue. As young children learn to use language they will begin to ask the more difficult, seemingly inconsequential, questions, or give a piece of information to the person standing close as a starting point for reflection – a starting point an adult doesn't always know how to take further![14]

Learning depends, therefore, on the ability to share it with others, especially through language. This is where the influence of the peer group can be very strong. When they enter school, children will reinforce each other's attitudes and learn what can be got away with. By the time they are 8 children will have discovered the difference between ability and achievement – how some do well without trying and how others, despite their utmost efforts, are less successful.[13] This 'success' or otherwise is measured against the criteria of expectations set by the school. It can be very traumatic for a child to discover the different manifestations of ability which are not distributed evenly. But then some children can deliberately not extend themselves because they do not want to offend their peers. Laziness can be deliberate as well as catching.[15]

The secret for all involved in education is to turn the need to learn into curiosity. The mental capacity of young children is strong and exhausting. There are all kinds of questions that they want answered. But the moment this curiosity is ignored, or diverted into tasks that do not seem to carry meaning, it is damaged. An earlier chapter explained the importance of having a purpose. This purpose is the connection between need and curiosity. A young child's engagement with the world is not an idle one. He must learn language, must learn distinctions . . . indeed these needs are as strong as physical ones.[16]

> One way of tracing children's development of mind is based on Plato:[17]
>
> | | | |
> |---|---|---|
> | 1. | *Mythic thinking*: | security |
> | | | binary opposites (good and bad) |
> | | | stories |
> | 2. | *Romantic stage*: | excitement about outside world |
> | | | love of facts |
> | | | idea of adventure |
> | 3. | *Philosophic stage*: | craving for generality |
> | | | moral sense |
> | | | impatience with world |
> | 4. | *Ironic stage*: | when people are more forgiving of themselves and others |

The process of learning develops through a number of different stages. At first children seek to understand the world in such a way that it makes unambiguous sense. They will seek to simplify and try to discover clear solutions to questions. They will want to recognize a clear distinction between good and bad. The first and simplest categories are, after all, the binary opposites.

There are many mythologies still current about the limitations of young children – that they are not able to reason or understand the subtleties of thought. Piaget, for example, said that young children believed that natural things are created by people. This is untrue. By the age of 4 children are aware of the distinction between man-made change and natural causes. They can identify specific kinds of natural causes, like growth, and understand the links between internal parts, like bones, and activity.[18]

When children have sorted out their sense of inner structure they will then wish to accumulate as much information as they can. This is at a number of levels. It includes the stage of developing hobbies, of making collections. It includes the desire to know facts, and collect technical data. It includes the conscious interest in lists and the subconscious accumulation of myths and stories. One should add that it is possible for some people never to progress much beyond this stage. They remain wedded to particular narrow interests, such as a fan club, and cease to show the same interest in reading.

But most children progress to the stage of trying to make coherent all the facts they will have acquired by pursuing distinct moral causes. They will want to explore issues about which they will have strong opinions – about the environment, or hunting, or whales. They will want the whole world to conform to their opinions and will find it difficult to accept that others might not agree. Again, this can be a stage at which people cease to develop, locked into a passionately narrow prejudice and unwilling to accept any alternative, even unable clearly to present their point of view.

Not only can children think about issues, they can think and reason about thinking; they have what is called a 'theory of mind'. They are like amateur scientists, constantly exploring and contrasting mental states and public entities. The 'theory of mind' is demonstrated in their ability to understand lies, deceptions, pretences and intentions. By the age of 7 they already conceive the mind as an active interpreter of information rather than as a passive receiver of ideas and images.[19]

By the time the individual's learning matures it will be a more complex matter. It will retain features of the individual's past: a sense of moral clarity, a sense of adventure and deep-seated feelings. But it will also comprehend the irony of the world, the fact that good intentions can have unfortunate outcomes, the existence of unfairness, the many differences of passionately held and contradictory opinions, as well as the forgiving nature of understanding.

Seeing someone learn something new is a great excitement. Sometimes learning happens without anything visible occurring.[20] It is rare to have that moment in the bath when one shouts 'Eureka!' at a sudden inspiration, and even that moment is probably undeliberate and unplanned. Learning is not always a deliberate matter. We never quite know at what point we learned something, or the moment when all made sense. It is only afterwards that we realize what people have learned: a new concept or a new idea, as well as new words and their meanings.

There are many reasoning processes that children need in order to understand their environments. These can be broken down into various categories. However complex they sound they apply equally to the young child and to the adult: classifications, equilibrium, abstract models, probability, correlations, ratios, variables, proportional thinking.[21]

While learning is visible in actions and in outcomes, and difficult to analyse, we nevertheless recognize that there are certain stages that we all go through at whatever age in approaching any new subject, and teachers need to be aware of this.[22] The very first response to a new subject is a lack of understanding of what the subject is about, allied with a disbelief that it makes any sense at all. It will seem to be obvious, lacking any real meaning or point. The new subject will seem to use words in an unnecessarily complex way and seem little more than common sense. Thereafter a new subject will seem to be a simple matter and easy to understand until, gradually and insidiously, it will accumulate more and more pieces of information until the student realizes that, far from being simple, the subject is nothing but a vast mass of contradictory and uncontainable facts. It will seem impossible to order all this into a coherence that both recognizes the facts as they are and creates a body of knowledge. Only when it is possible to master the subject, to know enough, will it be possible to make it lucid, to know which are the most salient facts. Only those who have a deep understanding of their subject will know how to explain it truthfully and simply.[23]

> The reasons that children's powers of mind were not noticed were that people did not want to notice, or that they were sentimental about children, or that they were brought up to think that ability is like the accumulation of knowledge. Children are able to think in ways not easily measured in traditional scientific experiments. Indeed, children acquire new concepts far more readily in an everyday context than in the laboratory. '$x + y = 2$. No x = No 2' is not as comprehensible as 'A man and a woman = marriage. No man = no marriage.'[24]

Simplification comes at both the beginning and at the end of learning, but it is of a very different quality. Whilst the process of learning has a consistent underlying structure that all should recognize, it does not mean that all people learn in the same way. On the contrary, just as there are many ways of storing information – on paper, books, file cards or computers – so there are many ways of internalizing information. Some people are good at spotting the essential point, and others need to go through carefully and steadily before coming to any judgement about what they read. Some will meticulously read a passage through line by line; others will scan it for its concepts before returning to the detail. Some make their memories serve them like a well-organized index; others will rely on associations.[25]

Underlying all the distinctions between styles of learning is the one between those who are 'serial' learners and those who are 'holistic'.[26] The former try to understand new information in the order in which it is presented. The latter reconstruct new information in new ways. The former go for surface details, and the latter try to make coherent what is presented, even if idiosyncratically.

> Children can be helped to learn by having their abilities acknowledged by others. Their awareness of learning is helped significantly when they are in a group that includes dialogue about learning as well as about the context in which they are learning.[27]

Look at a class of children and reflect. Which are 'divergent' learners, thinking of strange or far-fetched connections? Which are reflective and which impulsive? Which understand best through images, and which through language? Which are doers and which theorists? Which are over-cautious in making a judgement and which impulsive? Which try to come to a conclusion as quickly as possible and which only want to describe what they read? Which merely reproduce what they've read and which try to make it their own in a new way? The more you look at the way in which pupils learn the more you see how differently they do so. Recognizing that fact and diagnosing the style of each pupil is at the heart of true assessment and individual help.[28]

Children appreciate teachers who can 'explain'.[29] This reveals something about their desire to understand. The infants' need to make sense of things develops into a motivation to learn, but, as we can observe in many classrooms, this motivation is not automatic, and not equally applied. The way in which children approach work in school depends heavily on their early relationships and the quality and style of their dialogue with adults.[30] But there are few children who, on entering school, do not still possess a strong curiosity. This is because the desire to understand is not self-conscious. Each child assumes that he or she will work, and will share work and play with anyone. But around the age of 8 a change can be seen to take place in many children. This is the time when they realize two fundamental facts.

The first realization is that there is no automatic link between effort and achievement. Children begin to realize that some of them work very hard but do not always do as well as the others. They then notice that some children seem to grasp new concepts or produce work without even seeming to try.[31]

> 'I'm quite happy here because Mrs P likes me and she likes giving me responsibility. That's how I know she likes me and she doesn't shout at me a lot when I've done something wrong. She tells me off but that's not too bad. She explains why I shouldn't do it.' (girl, 10)

The second realization that faces children is that their work is compared, and that in some way or other they are in competition. Even when a school tries to avoid too great a stress on competitiveness, children will know there are distinctions and labels. 'Don't talk to me; I'm one of the stupid ones'; 'Ask her; she's clever.'

Children who realize that all their efforts do not result in the same achievements as those of others are tempted to give up. Those who realize that they can do far better than their peer group are also tempted not to bother. There can be a variety of causes for a lack of strong motivation. It is quite possible for children to apply their minds to other things or not apply their minds at all.[32]

It is not easy for children to concentrate for hours on end. If you observe them on a task, like writing, you will notice how much time is spent in distractions, in daydreaming and looking out of the window. But even when the task is being attended to, the mind wanders, for we think at a variety of levels. Even as you read this there will be other things 'at the back of your mind'. You will rarely be exclusively caught up in what you are doing.

Children learn how not to apply their mind, to cease listening carefully. Sometimes this is out of a fear of learning. Let us take reading as an example. The teacher is asking the pupil to read a sentence. Under that pressure of expectation the child often does the opposite of what is expected; instead of thinking, he or she looks away, waiting for, or hoping for, some external intervention, inspiration from heaven, or simply makes a wild guess. The task has become too much, too frightening, and the child wants simply to escape.

> The more we study individual children at an early age the more apparent it is that their abilities are very great. Virtually all children start by being 'gifted'. What happens to them after that often prevents their continuing their giftedness: their relationships with others who do not encourage their development of language or whatever. But it is important to

keep in mind the great potential of all children. Giftedness should not be the exception. The belief that it is the rule transforms teachers and schools.[33]

Every learning task can be undermined by fear, by the fear of not knowing where to begin and by the fear of being found out, or trapped. This is why confidence is such a powerful factor in learning, and why it should be fostered. There are many subtle ways of doing this but they all centre on two things.

The first is the encouragement of a child to talk. This depends on nurturing 'open' questions, questions to which there can be wrong answers. 'What do you think about this picture?' can elicit a range of responses from the simplest 'I like it' to a very complex account. When children talk they develop their ideas, and they learn the important conventions of dialogue, of talking as well as listening. Talking is the expression of confidence.

The second way of fostering confidence is through giving children a sense of 'ownership' over what they do. They need to learn to produce work of which they are proud and which is worthy of an audience. This means more than automatic praise. It means that the child will have thought of the difference between a first draft and the finished result and will, in the process, have used the task as a means of exploring and developing ideas.[34]

Children are not always aware of their own processes of learning. They discover what they have learned when they look back on their earlier work. They sometimes make great leaps of the imagination, and sometimes seem to make little progress on the surface. But the important developments are conceptual and the more teachers concentrate on concepts, the more they can help.

When we look at what children are learning we are often surprised to find gaps in their conceptual learning. They might reveal a misunderstanding of height and width, or leaves and petals. They might not understand the differences between odd and even, or the unitary system in mathematics. They will certainly show some idiosyncratic concepts in science, not even believing a teacher's explanation.[35] At one stage they will have their own views on volume and displacement. At another they will reveal many different versions of how electricity works.

The problem for children is that many concepts remain unexplored and their idiosyncrasies undetected. Children can learn them and be interested. But it takes both curiosity and the ability to analyse what a concept is, to grasp both the excitement and the reality of learning.

Chapter 5

How Children Learn Language

'I hate French because it's a different language, and some of the things they do
in the country seem really soppy.'

(boy, 11)

Human beings are unique in their use of language. Animals can communicate, and
give signals. Some possess a sense of humour. Bees can signal directions. Chimpanzees
can paint and solve simple physical problems. But only human beings define and communicate ideas. Language is such a central human activity that some linguists have
termed infants 'language acquisition devices' or LADs.[1] This stress on the ability to
learn language is partly in contrast to an earlier tendency by psychologists to see all
learning in terms of simple imprinting, as if everything were merely copied.[2] The fact
is that the learning of a language is clearly a matter of interaction between the innate
abilities of the child and the influence of his or her environment. 'LADs', after all,
speak the language of their country, but they never merely copy what they hear.

> Caliban to Prospero:
> 'You taught me language; and my profit on't
> Is, I know how to curse; the red plague rid you
> For learning me your language!'
>
> Shakespeare, *Tempest*, Act I, scene ii

Children learn language from the moment they are born. As they struggle to understand the many new sensations that bombard them, they learn the distinct sounds of
the human voice and associate it with certain pleasures. Even before the language that
they hear makes sense to them they understand differences in tone, between the
soothing sounds that are meant for them, and other adult conversations. Just as they
learn to parody facial expressions so they learn to parody the sound of words. They
even practise making sounds. If you overhear a baby 'babbling' in his cot you will
notice how consistently babies try out particular sounds, sounds that are close to the
central sounds of language, anything but arbitrary.[3]

There have been many studies of early child development designed to discover what it is that makes a difference to each individual's subsequent academic success. The question keeps being asked: Is this due to innate intelligence? Is the crucial factor the wealth and status of the parent? Is it important to be in a large family, or a small one?[4]

In all the research there is one central factor about which all agree, a factor which goes beyond questions of income and class: the chief factor that underlies subsequent academic success is the quality of the conversational experience a young child has with adults.[5]

The first sounds that children learn to pick out as significant are phonemes. There are all kinds of sounds one can make with the human voice but only certain combinations of teeth and tongue make linguistic sense. These sounds are called 'phonemes': the 44 different sounds in English that are distinct from each other. Each language has a slightly different sound pattern and each relies on children's detecting the significant sounds out of a mass of different voices. After all, each person has a different voice, to the extent that a machine can detect the individual sound patterns of each one. Out of all these individual differences infants need to understand the phonemes that all people have in common.

Different languages have their own slightly different patterns of 'phonemes'. There are a number of tired old jokes about Chinese waiters offering 'Flied Lice'. The fact is that in Cantonese there is no distinction between L and R; they are the same phoneme. In Bengali P and B are the same phoneme; even to those who speak English they are very similar. In some languages the L in 'feel' and 'leaf' are distinct. If you pronounce them and notice where your tongue is placed you will see that they are different.

Mandarin and Cantonese are very complex in sound. The word 'Ta' can be three different words depending on intonation: whether spoken with a rising sound ↗ or a descending sound ↘:

Ta Ta or Ta

The active intelligence of young children is engaged in picking out meaningful sounds. This is a sophisticated activity. We all know the phoneme 'd' and yet the same machine that records voice patterns cannot isolate the 'd' sound from the sound that follows it: De or Da or Do ... Once the first meaningful sounds are learned – like 'Da' as in 'Dada' – the child has grasped the sound pattern of language. He has also understood the meaning of tone.

When we learn a new language we recognize how important it is to understand how to make a distinction between the sounds of words, and letters, and between different tones. If we overhear a conversation in a new language, we have no idea where even sentences begin and end, let alone words, which seem to flow into each other. After all, we don't pause between words when we speak.

The child learns phonemes because he or she is searching for meaning in sounds. It seems like an instinctive understanding that language is communicating not just actions, like requests, but definitions: not just 'I want a drink' but 'This is a book'. The same sophistication in learning sounds is attached to realizing all the different types of meaning conveyed by words, from labelling – 'Dada' – to definitions. The remarkable fact is that children learn the meaning of words – that words carry meaning – from context and not from definition. At an early age it is clear that one cannot explain a new word. Children acquire a vocabulary by guesswork and by use.

Studies of the way children acquire language consistently demonstrate how quickly they learn new words. When one looks at how many words children know when they are 16 years old and divides them into all the days of their life since they first started to talk, or when one measures the knowledge of an 'average' child at 6 and then at 8, the increase in vocabulary is several new words each *day*. One study concluded that at the point of the most rapid expansion of language children actually learn 21 new words a day. They do this by listening to the context in which words are used.[6]

The ability to understand the meaning of a word is remarkable because words are a convention that can cover a variety of objects and meanings. It is no wonder that children make revealing mistakes. For example, they can use one word as if it were only to be used in relation to one object. The word 'dog' might refer only to their own pet and not be extended to all the other creatures they see on leads every day. Or again they might think of the word 'chair' not only as labels for a particular kind of seat but something that extends to include 'sofa', 'bench' or 'bed'. Every mistake the child makes reveals a desire to grasp the limits and the extent of words' meanings, and the distinctions between them. Even in simple terms this isn't always easy. When is a 'girl' no longer 'girl'? When does the word 'cat' include a panther? What is the distinction of the word 'tree' when it is part of a hedge, an oak, or a large bush?[7]

In one sense all words are generalizations. We know what we mean by 'snow', and those who love skiing will, in particular, know the difference between wet snow and powder snow. But those to whom it really matters, like the Inuit in northern Canada, there are (allegedly) 28 different words for snow.

Red is a simple colour. But can we define the difference between crimson, salmon pink or orange? People living in the Kalahari have many words for what we would in the narrowest definition call 'red'.[8]

Children learn to extract the meaning by noting features that are shared by different words. They also learn, in morphemes, that some changes of meaning which are crucial come in small sizes. The 's' at the end of the word that denotes plural makes a big difference to the meaning. It is defined as a 'morpheme'. Words are not just labels but units of meaning. They can be constructed out of parts. Just as children like to invent new words so they like to explore how to use words. It is as if language were a kind of game. But it is a game which is also very serious.

There used to be a favourite way of illustrating the formation of 'morphemes' – the smallest units of meaning - by looking at one of the longest words in English:

Dis establish ment ar ian ism

How many morphemes are there in this, like 'ism'?

Some languages, like German, continually make new words by putting several words into one, creating a new meaning out of the combination.

The understanding of the meaning of words and their operation is an impressive achievement and one that needs to be extended and encouraged throughout schooling. The rapid acquisition of a large vocabulary in the early years is not always suitably developed. Some people have far larger vocabularies than others. And yet a knowledge of words is essential to express meaning. Seeing how narrow is the range of words used by some people reminds us of how easily we stop learning later in life. This is not because we do not want to seem too erudite or because we do not want to show off but because are rarely encouraged to seek new meanings. A rich vocabulary carries meaning and we deprive ourselves of meaning by not extending it. Children learn language fast but need that ability to be fostered.

If children are adept at learning words they are also quick at understanding syntax, which is the structure of grammar of language. There was a time when people tried to relate all European languages back to Latin, as if parts of speech and declensions were more significant than order. But long before children can be muddled by the definitions of grammar, their actual use of syntax – the structure of language in noun phrases and verb phrases – is quite sophisticated. Again, even the mistakes they make reveal how quick children are to grasp the point. They understand some ground rules, like '-ed' for the past tense. They even show their understanding for the rules by misapplying them as in 'He hitted me.'

But children also understand the basis of syntax long before they are able to demonstrate complex constructions. Their early utterances are like a string of the essential points – sometimes called telegraphese – leaving out the inessential connections as in 'Daddy go car' where we understand the implied words that are left out.[9] The fact that they can combine two words to create a meaning as in 'Teddy come' is already a sign that they have grasped the essentials of syntax.

> Whatever their limitations in vocabulary, it is noticeable that most people remain very adept at syntax, even to the point of playing with it.
> Those who use the same dull swear-word so often can nevertheless embroider words in a sophisticated way: 'It was absobloodylutely awful.'

After all, a whole sentence can be contained in one word: 'No' [i.e. 'No, I do not want to come outside into the garden': 'No' in response to a question].

We observe young children rapidly acquiring language through a combination of insight, guesses and experiments. This process should not come to an end. We can understand a great deal about helping children in school by understanding the processes that very young children go through. Some of the developments in their understanding are paralleled by later ones. Very young children, for example, find it much easier to grasp a concept like 'cold' in a directly physical sense than in a metaphorical sense: 'It is a cold day' rather than 'He is a cold person.' They also grasp more quickly words of action than words of description.[10]

> When professional actors rehearse their parts for a new play they need to find the right 'tone' to make sure that they balance exaggeration with reality, that they heighten characteristics whilst not losing sight of the context of the part they play. To achieve this they often first read the play in the most boring everyday manner. Later they play the part with all the exaggeration they can muster, really overdoing it until even the serious parts are funny. In the end they settle into the right balance, heightening the tension without merely playing to the audience. This process is not unlike children's experiments with language, and expresses the delight in language that teachers could exploit.

There is a pattern in the learning of language that derives from the fact that some things are clearly simpler to understand than others. Saying 'Da' and 'Pa' both come early because they come easily. But children both understand what they hear and develop their own way of learning. Children retain their own versions of meaning or pronunciations even when talking to others. A child who says 'w-w' for 'flower' can have a conversation with an adult in which he knows perfectly well that the other person is trying to say 'w-w' when he says 'flower'. And if the child could articulate it, he would point out that he couldn't pronounce 'flower'.[11]

Even meanings of words, whilst shared with others, carry their own idiosyncratic differences. When children are accumulating a vocabulary so rapidly, picking new words up from clues about their usage, they are bound to make mistakes. They make more misinterpretations of words than others would necessarily recognize. To some extent the meaning of words always remains personal. There are one's own nuances of meaning that surround each word. It is not just personal associations of names with people that give the name a 'tone'. Every word has its complex, hidden associations, layered over by the sheer number of times it was used.

Children find 'active' words easier to learn than abstract ones. It is therefore amazing how quickly children understand the meaning of a word like 'thought'.[12] Nothing could seem more abstract than that. How do you define it? The child has grasped the concept of that word by the age of 5. He 'thinks' and 'is'. The fact that this ability is evident at so early an age suggests the huge potential of children, often left unused.

The learning of language is not just a steady acquisition of new words. So much depends on how words are used. Children do not just learn one language. They learn a variety of language uses: according to the situation, a language for their siblings, another for teachers.[13] They learn that words explain as well as describe. They learn that words are symbolic, that words create ideas. It is through words that children learn to think.

It is easy to notice differences in the way people speak. The world is divided by different dialects, between the sounds of one region or another, or by the sounds associated with status. But these differences are superficial compared with the way language is used to structure and explain ideas. The ways in which children learn to use language have an important bearing on their education.

> It helps children to be aware of their own learning, to check what they have learned and be given circumstances in which they can use it. This is true of their learning of language. There was a time when attention was drawn to lists of words: 'Extend your vocabulary'. The crucial point is, however, to have language in *use*; not just to check a knowledge of words but to demonstrate their utility.[14]

Each person has his own way of using language, his individual 'dialect'. But the types of language necessary for school are not always used by children in their home environment. We have already noted how important are the earliest relationships which children make. One of the reasons that relationships play such a crucial role is that they depend on an extended use of language. It is possible to have a perfectly normal life using an unextended language, with a limited vocabulary. But this becomes a barrier to learning in school. It does not mean that the person with limited language cannot think or have subtle ideas on a variety of subjects, but it does mean that that person cannot always use language in the way that education, and schools in particular, demand.[15]

Several studies have revealed how important is the early extension of language. All reveal the close connection between extended conversation with adults before the age of 3, and subsequent academic achievement. At the heart of education lies the ability to use language rather than be used by it.

One study, which was carried out in the United States, sought to explore why some children from poorer backgrounds did far worse than others from a richer part of town.[16] The school took in pupils from two different communities, labelled 'Trackton' and 'Roadville'. 'Trackton – the 'wrong side of the tracks' – was the poorer community. Both were studied to find where the differences lay. These were not found to be significant in terms of emotional security or depth of feeling, in innate ability or the amount of language used. What was different was the way language was used. In Trackton the children were told stories and expressed their feelings, but they were not made to explain and define like the children of Roadville. It was the language of definition, that used in schools, that was missing.

> In one study, which illustrates very simply, if crudely, the differences in using language, children of pre-school age were observed and recorded waiting outside a headteacher's study. In the room were several toys. Some parents, when the children asked, 'What is this?', would say immediately, 'Don't touch it! Keep still!' Or they would ignore the question. Others would do the opposite. When a child pointed to a train and said, 'What is this chimney?', the parent would begin a dialogue: 'We call that a funnel ... Do you remember when we went on a train?'
> One can imagine which children found settling into school easier, and which had the better chance to do well.[17]

When one observes different children in school it is noticeable that many children use language to say whatever is on their minds, that they are highly volatile. They do not know how to listen, how to tune in to what others are saying or how to use language as a means of shared exploration. For these children all kinds of work in school, let alone social awareness, are far harder. Learning language therefore is both a more subtle matter than a question of accumulation and far more important.

A look at the early stages of learning language reminds us very clearly what lies behind this complex process. This learning is an analogy not only for the learning that continues throughout life, but for what can be done to foster growth. The ability each child brings to the mastery of language shows how active is the mind in perceiving what is necessary to be learned: which sound or visual clues are significant, and which communicate. It also shows how much each person needs language.

It is because of the need to communicate that a first language can be so much easier to learn than a second. Once one language is firmly embedded the need to communicate is fulfilled. Another language will never have the same force. Indeed, a first language can get in the way of learning a second one. Reminding ourselves of the difference between one and the other can clarify how we can bring some of the techniques of one to the other. In learning a first language children realize that they have something to communicate and that others have something to say to them; they learn by using language, listening, predicting and guessing. It is a very different style from translation – from looking at grammar from the outside and finding verbal equivalents. To learn a language one really needs to get inside it.

> Humpty-Dumpty was sitting on his wall when Alice came along. They had a long and absurd conversation which ended like this:
>
> *Humpty-Dumpty*: 'That's glory for you!'
> *Alice*: 'What do you mean by "glory"?'
> *Humpty-Dumpty*: 'I mean – that's a nice knock-down argument for you.'
> *Alice*: 'But "glory" doesn't mean "nice knock-down argument".'
> *Humpty-Dumpty*: 'When I use a word it means what I want it to mean, no more and no less.'
> *Alice*: 'The question is whether you can use words in that way?'
> *Humpty-Dumpty*: 'The question is who is to be master? That's all.'[18]

For a teacher the question is how we can create the same conditions in which children learn language so rapidly, the conditions in which their desire to learn is met with encouragement and where the circumstances are stimulating. There is a basic rule that needs to be acknowledged and that is that language is learned only through its use. This means that we need to seize every opportunity to give children the chance to experience dialogue; not just talking but listening, not just listening but responding. They need to learn to express themselves to an audience; not only talking but writing. They need to have the confidence that what they say matters because they are expressing something and not merely fulfilling the task set by the teacher.

> There is the expression 'keeping the conversational ball rolling'. It is noticeable that some people are much better at this than others, at asking questions, showing a curiosity about what other people might say, at exploring ideas in a stimulating way, at thinking of things to say. It is an art that needs to be learned.

One of the most lively ways of learning is through simulations, putting oneself in real-life circumstances, and having to invent what one would say. This can be done in simple drama but it can also be far more demanding. Suppose a group of pupils were asked to put together a local news programme on the radio. One pupil is the news editor, another a reporter, another a guest, another an interviewer, and another someone interviewed. They are given items of local news to choose from to make an interesting fifteen-minute programme, and once on the air they mustn't have any gaps; it must all run smoothly and professionally. They are given just ten minutes to get it prepared – to decide who will play which part, and which are the most important stories. And this is done as the news keeps coming in, even when they are 'on the air'.

It is when language is put to use and the mind is challenged to be inventive that children learn best. When we think of the way in which children initially learn language we can detect means of helping them. Children need to be able to guess, to find the right word for what they want to say. Children also need to experience, to draft ideas without being too overwhelmed by trying to avoid mistakes. They learn what is right by seeing the differences between mistakes and corrections. They can only learn what is 'right' by knowing what is 'wrong'.

> Children can understand the point of language and interpret it even when they cannot use it properly, i.e.
>
> *Father:* 'Say "Jump."'
> *Child:* 'Dup.'
> *Father:* 'Jump.'
> *Child:* 'Dup.'
> *Father:* 'No – "Jump".'
> *Child:* 'Only Daddy can say "Dup".'[19]

The easiest part of their first language for children to learn is the syntax; and yet this can be the most difficult in a second language. This is partly because syntax serves the other sides of language; it does not come before them. The most significant development in learning a language is through its meaning, and that means fostering vocabulary. It is through the awareness of an ever-increasing array of words that children learn what to do with them. Children need to be encouraged to extend their range, to discover how much more subtle meanings can be given to things once there are words for them. Then that spectacular advance in their learning of words can be continued.

There is a story about the playwright George Bernard Shaw. It is said that he never spoke a word until he was about 6 years old. His parents were very worried and assumed there must be something wrong with him. Then, one morning at breakfast, they heard him say:

'Please pass the marmalade!'

'Bernard! You spoke,' said his parents in surprise and delight. 'Why haven't you spoken before?'

'Until now the service has been perfectly satisfactory.'

Chapter 6

The Development of Reading Skills

'I get fed up with reading because I've read the book so many times – the same one.'

(girl, 10)

Reading is not just a task for infants that, once mastered, can be taken for granted. It is an art which needs constant development and practice. Reading is never simple but it lies at the heart of the learning process and deserves attention throughout school.

The way we learn how to read also serves as a very potent analogy for learning generally. It is not something that we can neglect or cease to learn. To do that is to regress. Reading is not something which can be done superficially. It is something that at one level seems purely instinctive, as unselfconscious as the ability to ride a bicycle. At another level it is very demanding. It is at once simple and complicated and something that too many people never fully master.

The way in which we learn how to read remains something of a puzzle. What is there about such an essential act which is so difficult for some to master? Why can it remain a barrier rather than become the most central of means to learn? It is because reading difficulties are not always well understood, and because the process by which the majority learn such a complex task is obscure, that reading is so often a central political issue. At the heart of the debate about reading, which affects all teachers, lie several contradictions. These contradictions take various forms and are often expressed in simple opposites. Should one use formal reading schemes or real books? Is it more important to encourage children's pleasure in books or make sure they understand the letter–sound correlations which are called 'phonics'? Do children learn to read through developing their perceptual abilities or their understanding of context?[1]

Children who are not very good at reading, or generally low attainers at school, associate reading with:

1. Saying words aloud.
2. School work.

3. A source of status.

Children who read well and are high attainers associate reading with:

1. A way to learn things.
2. Private pleasures.
3. Social activities.[2]

All the arguments which take place about reading centre on the central dichotomy of all learning. Do children learn to read by themselves, whatever the teacher does, or do they need to be taught formally? Again, it is the tension between learning and teaching; between 'nature' and 'nurture'.

Children need to be taught; and teachers need to understand that children are actively engaged in learning. The two things go together. But when one reads some of the accounts of the debates about reading it appears that at different times people are determined to forget either one or the other. In the 1960s a large number of experiments were carried out in different techniques of teaching, each of which was supposed to be the answer to all difficulties. Large sums of money were spent on different schemes, on books and games and colour codings, as if the key to learning reading were the brilliant teaching methods delivered by teachers.[3]

One example of the resources poured into teaching methods was the initial teaching alphabet – i t a. This was introduced into a number of schools, based on the belief that the difficulty of reading could be overcome if only there were a simple correspondence between the letters (of which there are 26) and the sounds – the phonemes (of which there are 44 in English). This meant that children learned a script that looked vaguely normal and then, having learned through using this method, at the age of 8 would have to transfer to the 'normal' method of spelling: 'Traditional Orthography'.[4]

There was a natural reaction to all this methodology. Seeing the peculiar difficulties that children faced in elaborate schemes, researchers again discovered that children bring their own intelligence to bear, that some are very quick to understand the point and techniques of reading, and even those who are slower reveal intelligence at work.[5] A study of how children think about reading showed that even the mistakes they make, like their grammatical errors, actually indicate intelligence. Reading was then called a 'psycholinguistic guessing game' since children were seen to learn how to read through making conceptual leaps.[6]

This research aided the understanding of the reading process. Unfortunately it also led to a neglect of teaching, as if all teachers could do was to interfere and even prevent children progressing. The use of techniques of teaching other than the strict phonic methods became associated with sloppiness, a lack of perception and even indifference. More recently it has been acknowledged (yet again – the wheel is come full circle) that reading is something both taught and learned, and there are many things a teacher can do to help, whether in a subtle or an obvious way.

It must be said that some of the most mechanistic of reading schemes, with repeated words and either simple or non-existent stories, could be off-putting, making children associate reading with an unpleasant task.
   What should one make of sentences like 'I can fan a tan man', 'Can I fan a sad man?' or the hackneyed: 'See, Janet, see. Dora has Jane. Run, Nip, run. It will get well. I am Fluff the Cat. I can fan a bad man . . .'?[7]

It is important to understand what the task of reading means to children and where the possible difficulties lie. Suppose we were suddenly confronted with a set of symbols:

ᒪᑫ ᕌ ᒐᒡ ᓬ ᒡ ᕊ ᓬ ᐃᒐ

How would we begin to decode them? We would first need to know whether these symbols stood for words or sounds, and whether the word (or the sentence) was to be 'read' from the left or from the right. Even with all our knowledge of reading we wouldn't know where to begin and would be as helpless as with ancient scripts – until some breakthrough, like the discovery of a Rosetta Stone giving the same message in three languages, came to our aid.

Central to the mastery of reading, both in the earliest stages and later, is the secret of knowing which clues to recognize and which ones to ignore. Personal experience and the confidence to guess are important, but all are subtly prepared by a series of insights. Children need to understand that at one level reading is a matter of a few simple conventions, that a letter stands for a sound. But at another level there are many difficulties to do with inconsistencies. The same letter is not always the same sound.

> The peculiar difficulties of the alphabetic system in English are shown up by a contrast with Chinese. The new simplified Chinese script consists of 515 characters with an average of 8.16 strokes each. This must seem a huge amount to learn, and yet Chinese children find this comparatively easy: they learn the characters as fast as words.
>
> In one experiment, American children who were having great difficulties mastering reading were given Chinese characters to learn. Then found that this was as easy as the orthography of English was difficult.

Even before they approach the decoding of script children will need to have learned a great deal. They will clearly need to have a strong grasp of language, know how words work, and how sentences are constructed. They will have observed their parents' habits of reading, and associated books with consistent stories and with pleasure. They will have noticed that the book and its pictures run from left to right and noticed that the same words were spoken on the same page (and complained if the parent got it wrong!). Even before they pick up a book of their own, therefore, children should have learned something about the way reading combines 'knowing that' and 'knowing how'.

> English is not a consistent code; it is sometimes exact and sometimes 'sloppy'. Children need to learn not to try to work out each separate element (letters, syllables) as they try to understand the clues they meet.[8]

For many children the great barrier to learning to read, and developing their skills, is that reading is not associated with pleasure. Children in school can value reading and see it as one of the most important tasks, but the more they value it the less pleasure they have in it. It is a chore, a series of difficulties, many barriers rather than delights. It is for this reason that the home environment can be such a help, demonstrating the value of books and the idea of the story. Parents play a crucial role in all learning.

There are many skills to be learned about the peripheries of reading, like a context in which reading is placed. The more attention that is paid to these skills the easier it is to learn how to read. Children need, for example, to tune their ears to the exact sound of words. Many spelling mistakes subsequently emerge because children haven't listened properly. For this reason rhyme is not only helpful but essential in preparing children for the systems of writing. All those days spent on rhythms and nursery rhymes are days well spent. Tuning in to the sound systems of language means homing in on reading.

> Great importance was once attached to what was called 'reading readiness', as if there were one moment when at last the child should start learning, and as if anything done too early would be wasted. It actually resulted in many children being held back when they were longing to read. Clearly there are some essential prerequisites – like language – but one cannot isolate a particular age or stage as the critical one.

The developing of the ear needs to be accompanied by the sense of growing visual discrimination, the ability to separate one visual symbol from another. After all, children will be learning both similarities – that 'A' and 'a'; are the same letter, even in a different handwriting – and differences as small as that between 'q' and 'g' or 'b' and 'd'. There are many visual games they need to play to be able to pick out those clues that are significant. For example, Figure 6.1 shows how what at first appears as a whole can be observed to have distinct parts. The same is true of a word.

> We are not always aware of what we do when we read; it seems as if we are following script from left to right, and then from left to right on the next line, and so on. In fact our eyes make what are called 'saccadic jumps'; they move backwards and forwards over words and sentences, scanning larger areas or smaller. The eyes are never still.

Figure 6.1

There are many other subtle skills behind reading, beyond understanding the text. Certain concepts which are afterwards taken for granted, like up and down, top and bottom, need to be learned, and we often discover the necessity of these concepts when, to our surprise, it is revealed that a child has never thought about them as concepts. Some of the skills that precede and surround reading include balance and coordination, categorization and the understanding of signs and symbols.

The learning of the spelling systems and the reading process is easier in many languages than in English, because English is not only alphabetic, a phonetic system, but inconsistently so. Nevertheless one of the useful pre-reading skills in addition to language, sight and sound, and the 'mechanical' processes like left-to-right orientation, is the understanding of signs. There are all kinds of significances in symbols, from those that are in common use to those generated by children. Signs range from the traffic-light values of red and green to the warnings given by

shields, or the pictures within them! Children also naturally generate their own symbols as they learn to make pictures, recognizing simple representations:

as well as understanding what is meant as they create simple stick figures, where a round shape and some long lines can represent their parents.

All these indicate at once the early development of symbolic understanding and the sophisticated international acceptance of the use of signs. The process of recognition is linked with children's awareness of what particular marks stand for. The idea of a symbol is that of being able to generalize. The same mark in different circumstances carries the same meaning. This contrasts with the uniqueness of each object, whether a person, pet or toy.

Children need to learn the language of categories, of being able to apply opposites to a range of experiences. If one says that one object is bigger than another the same difference could be applied to a wide range of dimensions. One mountain is bigger than another. One coin is bigger than another, as well as one mountain always being bigger than a coin. Children learn to make categories in their experience, and they develop this through their language. Without language, reading is clearly meaningless; but to read, the children need to learn more than language. They need to learn the particular code in which language is carried and learn its particular consistencies. The same word is the same whether written large or small.

> For many years one of the mythologies about reading was that it could not be taught, that the child would learn to read despite the teacher. This mythology was partly a reaction to a series of very intrusive teaching techniques that suggested that only one approach would work.
>
> In all the research that has taken place on how children learn to read – and there is a lot of it – there is always one conclusion: the more direct help a child gets, the better; and this instruction is best concentrated on letter sounds and names.[9]

Being able to detail differences, as well as consistencies, is important. These small but significant differences are those of sound and sight. Knowing how words are pronounced implies the ability to detect the value of particular sounds – again, the difference between phonemes, knowing the differences between 'f' and 'th' and 'b' and 'p'. Children also need to practise a particular form of visual discrimination between marks, like:

so that they can be aware of the importance of knowing how to pick out one letter from another, from the clearly different to the similar:

o x o x o x o x o

p p p p b p p p p

d d d b d d d d d

A child's interest in the idea of reading, in its rewards and satisfactions, needs to be combined with particular skills. Motivation is not enough in itself, for there are many clues that can be given to children to help them. And they need help because although English is a language which is learned comparatively easily it is also a language which has peculiar problems in the way it is read. The problem can be expressed quite simply in terms of its spelling system. The relationship between sight and sound can be fluid. We all know an 'a' when we see one. We know what it sounds like in the alphabet. But when we see 'a' in context we realize that it can be pronounced in a variety of ways: 'all', 'any', 'want', 'at', 'calm'. The child learns both a letter – easily done – and that it cannot be quite trusted, which makes life somewhat difficult. Similarly we know the way 'i' sounds in a word like 'child'. That vowel is often used. But we find that same sound produced in a variety of different ways, from 'child' to 'aisle', 'height, 'lie', 'sign', 'high', 'island', 'guide', 'buy', 'dye', 'by' ... It is because of this that attempts have been made to change the way the language is written.[10]

> Children can approach reading in a way that actually prevents them from reading well. If they associate reading solely with a task that is carried out in school they even learn to avoid books. Children who believe reading consists of 'saying the words' – in other words, reading aloud to be tested – do far less well than children who believe reading is a private pleasure or a way to learn things. Some children associate reading solely with social status: 'Look at me!'[11]

We should not, however, exaggerate the difficulties that some children face, even whilst we are sensitive towards them. The way the language is written is, after all, at least 80 per cent consistent. The difficulties are the exceptions to rules. Children do not find the essential principle of sound and sight correspondence difficult. They understand an alphabet of figures from 'Annie Apple' to 'Inky Imp' with some ease. They become accustomed to the idea of an alphabet. What they need to understand in addition is that 'C' 'A' 'T' (see-ay-tee) when pronounced as in the alphabet does not spell 'cat' – or 'cuh ... a ... te'!

> 'Once I was trying to read a word and I couldn't find out what this word was and I went to Miss. It was "the" and because I couldn't read it I was ever so frightened because she kept going on and on and on.' (boy, 9)

Learning single letters is one stage in the art of reading. But just as sound cannot be easily divided into simple segments, so one cannot properly read until one has learned to blend one letter with another. The secret of reading lies in being able to carry out several actions at the same time. One is to recognize how some letters make a unit when joined together – a 'digraph', as in 'th' or 'ch'. Another is to learn how letters blend into each other, as in 'bl' or 'ng', and a third is to see how a letter at the end of the word (like the 'hidden "e"') can change the sound and meaning of the whole word: 'hat' or 'hate'; 'bit' or 'bite'.

What seems at first sight a simple matter becomes more complicated as the different mental processes are analysed. It is no surprise that so many books and so much research are devoted to trying to find out both how the mind copes with learning to read and how the individual can be helped. Reading is a question of knowing how to balance motivation and desire to learn with a peculiar skill. But its importance does not lie only in the early stages. The early stages underpin the later ability (or inability) to spell and understand the structure of words (like 'morphemes'). And once one has mastered the ability to 'read' a text slowly, one needs to master the ability to read in a true sense: a mastery of whatever material is presented, even if it looks difficult at first.

> When children's early reading is analysed – or their spelling patterns looked at – one detects the fact that even their mistakes show logic. It might be misapplied, but it explains why reading is a 'guessing game'. Children can read their own texts.[12]

In the end, true reading involves an understanding of complex texts. This is not just a product of hard work or massive brain power, but of interest, excitement and the desire to learn. But this is 'in the end'. On the way to true reading remain barriers that some people find hard to overcome. It is because reading is a matter of knowing the complexities of language on the one hand, and focusing on particular clues on the other, that some people have a peculiar difficulty that, as with spelling, can last a lifetime. For most people who do not read the cause is simply a matter of indifference, but for some there are difficulties that are based on a physical cause. This 'physical' cause is not just an obvious disability – not seeing clearly, needing coloured lenses – but a difficulty in making particular connections of sight and sound. After all, the fluent reader is able to detect clues in a way that does not make much logical sense:

'If y ar a flt reodor y will hav no difflucky readg this.'

The fluent reader brings all kinds of abilities to bear; whilst the eyes scan line after line, the mind anticipates what might happen next. The ability to learn to read, slowly and painfully, is different from reading fast. Indeed, it is almost as if 'speed reading' were a skill of its own. To carry out speed reading in the real sense, as opposed to reading rapidly, or scanning, requires the ability to dissociate the ears from the eyes; for it is the 'sound' of words, even when read, that holds us up. It is possible to flit the eyes over a text and gain a knowledge of the central structural points.

> There has been a great deal of controversy about 'dyslexia'. Some have denied its existence, saying that it is an excuse to cover reading failures. But whilst one wishes all people to read well, the term does at least highlight (a) that a simple desire to read isn't enough, (b) that people have not been properly helped in their learning at an early stage, and (c) that reading reminds us of the complex processes of the brain.

But that is 'speed' reading, not fluent reading. It leaves out all those parts of language that are to do with sounds: poetry, the human voice, and all the ways in which the depth and ambiguities of the human experience can be conveyed. Fluent reading is reading for meaning, not just the structures of an argument.

There have been a number of experiments in helping a slow or backward reader that involve using coloured lenses. Whilst it appears that coloured filters can help in some cases, this could be due to the fact that the child is gaining individual attention. The child's confidence is increased and the reading difficulties are no longer attributed to stupidity. There is a general lesson here.[13]

There is, of course, a great difference between learning the mechanics of reading and learning to read fluently. One of the problems with reading is that the two almost seem to have little to do with each other. Fluent readers are so accustomed to their style of reading that they can encounter their own difficulties. For example, a beginning reader will find one sentence easier to read than another:

'Go back must word you your on not.'

'You must not go back on your word.'

The fluent reader will 'stumble' over the first. It says something about the early 'mechanical' stages of reading that the early reader will find the second more difficult, or equally so.

The fluent reader anticipates and predicts and does not necessarily notice details, like mis-spellings. The fluent reader looks for meaning. Reading is a tool rather than an end in itself. When there are two levels of meaning difficulties can occur until one level is translated into another. For example certain barriers need to be overcome to be able to read:

'When they herd bear feat in the haul the buoy tolled hymn he had scene a none.'

In order to help children we need to remember the difficulties of the different styles of reading, and be patient about the physical and mental complexities of the process as well as bearing in mind that we are aiming to teach the use of reading for pleasure and information. Reading is a synthesis of many elements, of attitudes and skills, visual and aural. The process has sometimes been likened to an orchestra: a whole made up of many delicate parts.

There are many different ways of reading fluently, and responding to the text. Some readers are dominated by the text, whilst others predict what response they will make even before they approach the text. They seek gratification. Some readers actually look for bits of the text to pick out of their context. Reading is always an interactive rather than a passive process.[14]

The teacher needs to be able both to diagnose any specific difficulties a pupil might have and to inspire a taste for all the different uses of literacy. A concern for pleasure in texts should be present throughout. Reading 'texts' means reading in a variety of ways, from illustrative stories and comic strips to novels and encyclopedias. There are as many ways of reading as there are types of text, including maps and music, dictionaries and timetables. Once pupils understand the idea of *format*, of what is being presented and why, they are able to translate that understanding into fluency; they connect different techniques of presentation with the purpose of the message. It is like understanding once again the need for and the power of signs.

To enable pupils to extend their reading, we need to bear in mind their various needs. These exist at various levels, and must be harmonized. They include:

1. The understanding of the pleasure and reward of reading. It is too easy to turn reading from a set task into a powerful barrier, to make the pupil so conscious of the act of reading and of its difficulties that the underlying purpose is com-

pletely lost. Some books are clearly more attractive than others, both to look at and to read. Imagine being confronted with nothing but dry, complex texts and compare them to the relish with which other books can be approached, and think what a difference this can make for the young reader.

2. The confidence to go on trying. A reader must be unafraid to make mistakes, since reading consists of guesses and predictions, anticipations and scanning. If a pupil is fearful of trying to work out what a sentence might say, he becomes stuck behind the hurdle rather than surmounting it.

3. The persistence to go on trying. Mental laziness or fatigue can happen in many different ways. The young pupil might so fear failure in reading that he just wants to run away from the problem. The older pupil might resent the effort of tackling a text which makes demands. Both need the persistence, and the confidence, to go on concentrating. In the end this persistence is a matter of habit.

4. The knowledge of all the conventions of writing. These include an awareness of language and its sounds as well as the formation of words and sentences. Some of these conventions are agreed systems, like writing from left to right, or right to left, and some are attempts to find ways of isolating necessary clues, like phonemes.

5. The knowledge of common spelling patterns, and not just the more famous inconsistencies.

6. The willingness to engage in practice. Nothing succeeds so fast, with persistence, and confidence, as actually trying to extend the habit of reading. This practice can include parents and other people willing to share in the process.

> When one looks at the books that children read as beginners there are some surprises in the pictures that children receive of the world. In the texts children tend to ask questions, especially of adults. Most sentences are declarative, and in the present tense. The language is that spoken by young children rather than the language they hear. And the adults in the story tend to collude in a construction of 'child-like playfulness': 'Naughty Daddy!'[15]

If there are certain needs that a pupil has in developing reading skills, this implies a number of roles that a teacher can play. These include:

1. *Diagnosis.* The teacher will observe and record the idiosyncratic mistakes of each pupil, for they are often consistent – like mistaking certain letter blends, or omitting certain words. Without the ability to look closely and quite formally at a pupil's progress, the teacher will not be able to demonstrate that there is help at hand and that difficulties can and will be overcome.

2. *Organization.* The teacher is the provider of a range of experiences and a variety of materials. Finding the right time for reading and the suitable texts means keeping one's eyes open for a lot of 'extra' input, and not sticking purely to one scheme or text.

3. *A partner.* The teacher is also a reader, and as such a model for the pupils. When children learn to read they learn alongside someone, like a parent, who is sharing in the story and who is demonstrating how reading takes place. The teacher can join in the pleasures of reading, as companion as well as guide.

After all, think of all the rewards we derive from reading!

Chapter 7

The Development of Writing

'I like creative writing. It sharpens your skills. It makes you want to be a poet.

(girl, 10)

We are sometimes tempted to think of education as a one-way process. In devising the curriculum and working out teaching strategies and assessments it is too easy to think of the pupil purely as a passive recipient of knowledge. Clearly the individual is going to learn from whatever experience is offered or gained. To think of the child learning all he is told or witnesses is to be as unrealistic as believing that all learning comes from within. We need to remind ourselves that learning is a balance between the individual and experience.

The two-way process of learning language involves the child's need to speak as much as the child's need to understand. Some have even suggested that the child's first utterances are cries for help, that the expression of a want comes before detecting the connection between that and the reply.[1] When we observe young children experimenting with language we see them try out sounds that gradually become more like the sounds they hear. The desire to make their voice heard is as strong as the desire to listen.[2]

The same drive to understand speech underlies the written form of language. Children do not learn to read and then, belatedly, to write. The two go together. The idea of script needs to be understood in action and not merely recognized. Children often begin to learn to read by trying out pictures and then scribbles. When we follow the development of children's drawings we see first the love of colour, and then the formation of outlines that emerge from the colours – houses and windows, and then people. These drawings are symbolic; the children know exactly what they mean and can interpret them for us. And although they know the difference between writing and scribbling – 'I can't write, Daddy, I can only scribble' – they recognize that there is a purpose, even if they do not know how to use it.[3]

Gradually the 'scribble' that children make can be seen to emulate the patterns of letters. Just as they will want to copy the sounds they hear in their own way, so they will begin to parody the way in which script works, long before they can read. They practise the ideas of making marks, of directions, of being able to communicate ideas through signs as well as sounds. Children learn to read as much by being engaged in writing as in being read to. We therefore find them making parodies of letter shapes, and then making characters stand for syllables.

> Whenever people analyse some of the essential differences between the ways in which people learn, they mention one great distinction: between those who learn through verbal means and those who learn through images. Many children who are not very good at definitions in language are very capable of expressing themselves through drawing, and this ability can be used to help them communicate in other ways.[4]

One of the first words that children ever attempt is their own name. This is significant. Writing gives people a means of leaving their mark as nothing else can. They can label what they have done. In a true sense their name spells ownership. Young children seem to understand early this reason for writing. But 'ownership' is a lot more than personal autograph.[5]

There are four essential principles of writing that need to be understood, and that remain valid, at every stage of development. There are practical implications in each of them.

Ownership

This word is used in the sense of personal responsibility and individual pride. If you want someone to believe in an idea you must make him believe it is his own. If you want a teacher to put a great deal of time and effort into trying out a new idea you must help him re-create it as his own. Anyone will work harder if they are personally engaged in the work, and not doing it simply to respond to someone else's request (or demand).

The concept of ownership used in this way is not a question of taking over someone else's individual property. It is meant in the sense of personal individual achievement that underlies motivation. In terms of writing it draws attention to the crucial need of the individual writer to feel in command of what he is doing, to make it his own, to be satisfied by his individuality. 'It might not be very much, but it is my own.'

Ownership is also personal responsibility and pride in what has been achieved. Every piece of writing should give the individual a sense of doing the best he can to master a subject and communicate it. It is no longer a routine, done to keep the teacher or examiner quiet, but done essentially for its own sake, and for the sake of the writer. Every original piece of writing gives the sense that the writer had to write it.[6]

Self-Exploration

'No-one likes writing,' to quote Conrad, 'but one likes what one gets from writing; the chance to know oneself.' It is the ability of the pen to explore and discover tracts of experience that would otherwise lie undetected. To brood or to think one is thinking is not enough. Even to talk, to stumble over words in an attempt to communicate, is only a half-measure. True, the need to articulate means that we have to define what we want to say. But writing forces a deeper contemplation about meaning. It forces us to look for, if not find, the right word, to tease out exactly what we want to say.

Children have strong feelings about different parts of the curriculum. They express their satisfaction in carrying out interesting experiments, and they know where they are with their maths. But they all say very clearly that one of the things they do not like doing is 'writing'. This is because writing is used as an exercise. It is associated with copying things out, or with boring repetitions – anything but what writing should be used for.[7]

It might seem at first glance far-fetched to expect children to undertake some form of self-analysis. But just as children like to experiment with sounds and signs and language generally, so they like to explore ideas. Writing, seen as exploration, is for children a landscape in which they are involved, not with self-consciousness, but with self-discovery. They make what they write their own when they see how much they can experiment. Children's abilities in creating stories are demonstrated again and again. Children's ability to reflect on ideas is revealed when they write material which goes beyond copying, and in which they are truly engaged.

Self-Correcting

The worst writing is carried out simply because it has to be done, and the author has no interest in it. Children can produce some very boring work: short, careless and scrappy. It does not need to be like this. For if writing is an exploration it is also an experiment. Writing includes ideas, notes and lists. It means planning. And yet, think how often pupils are expected to produce a good piece of work first time. They are told to do an exercise in their 'best' handwriting and the result is treated as if their first thoughts were the same as their last.

Writing is an instrument to help thought as well as being the final form of that thought. When pupils start to see that they can write more than one draft, and that their first draft does not have to be perfect, they begin to understand two things. First, they understand the utility of writing, that it can help them. Secondly, they realize that even if the final product isn't perfect, they have improved what they are doing by thinking about it.

Children have a surprising facility for drawing and have clear ideas about what they mean by their drawing even if one cannot detect any connection between the explanation and the visual representation. Furthermore, even infants are sensitive to aesthetic criteria.

It is worth remembering the underlying aesthetic of drawing whilst we observe children going through stages, from scribbling to unrepresentational designs, to 'tadpole' schemes and so on.[8]

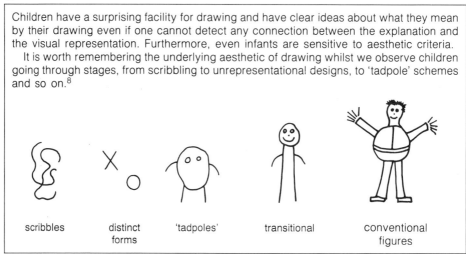

| scribbles | distinct forms | 'tadpoles' | transitional | conventional figures |

Re-drafting requires the pupils to look at their own work, analyse it and find out where its particular qualities lie. There is no fear of making mistakes, for these can be corrected. From being a hurdle to be surmounted, the task becomes something that will always be attainable.[9]

Re-drafting work is not a routine task. Even when it is applied to spelling and simple sentences children much prefer to be responsible for self-corrections than for their work to be simply ticked 'right' or 'wrong'. When they know the difference between notes and ideas and the finished texts, they can use writing in ways which are creative. They begin to realize what is meant by 'style'.

The Audience

Writing is always carried out for an audience, even if the audience is oneself. Self-exploration is not self-indulgence (at least, it shouldn't be). People who are so caught up with themselves that they forget those with whom they are trying to communicate soon cease to create anything worthwhile. They assume their gnomic utterances will somehow be explored, or that they do not matter. Those who entirely forget the audience are as ineffective as those for whom manipulation of the audience is all that matters.

An audience makes writing real. But what is an audience? For many children the audience is the requirement of the teacher.[10] The audience is not even the teacher as a reader, but as a taskmaster. But the 'audience' should always be something greater. Except in the case of a personal letter, the audience is a combination of those who will understand and those who will not; and the audience will always vary. Writing for the audience is writing with a purpose.

When children read and learn they are part of an audience; it is a sign of their growing understanding that they see the difference between one text and another. They realize that they are critics, and can see that some texts are dull and others are stimulating. Awareness of an audience makes children realize how differently people react to the same text, and they begin to develop their personal taste.

> Children exhibit their tastes at an early age, and yet are often taught, in schools, to be uncritical, as if they should not be able to distinguish between one book and another, one set of exercises and another, or one scheme and another. No wonder they revert to the negative – 'it's boring' – if they are given no critical choices.
> The poet Robert Graves, at university just after the First World War, was called to see his tutor. 'Mr Graves,' he heard, 'it seems that you are showing signs of great eccentricity and idiosyncrasy ... Indeed, it seems you prefer some books to others ...'.
> What was once a canon of taste is now often presented to children as exercises to which they cannot react in a normal way; as if all books presented to them were equally valuable.

A sense of an audience allows children to discover that what is produced can often be bettered. They know that to succeed in writing is to communicate, in the best possible way, and once they have succeeded in doing that they have also discovered applause, for the audience does not only criticize; it appreciates. Then, what the children produce, re-drafted, carefully researched, their own, is celebrated; and that is worth doing.

Mentioning the importance of an audience reminds us of the usefulness and the utility of writing. Teachers need to remember this since it is too easy (as a member of the audience) to rely over-much on what has been called the 'creativity' of children. For many teachers, writing can be divided into note-taking (putting together information and copying exercises) and the spontaneous outburst of powerful feelings ('creative' writing). This means that for children, virtually all of the writing they have to do is singularly uncreative – a routine task to fill the time, whether it is an exercise or a story.

> There is much debate on what can be deemed to be creative, and the more exhaustively this is discussed the more unhelpful the term becomes. In any real sense of expressing original ideas in original ways, only a very small minority of children is 'creative'.
>
> One would like to think that unselfconscious instincts and fresh naive responses are 'creative', but we often mistake our delight in the attempt for the real thing. Children can be more genuinely creative than we give them credit for.

The perceived gap between 'transactional' and 'poetic' writing puts particular pressures on children.[11] Indeed, it is this false distinction that partly explains why children find writing 'boring'. For them both are routine exercises that seem to have little to do with their experience as readers or observers. It is very easy to give children exercises that carry no meaning, and yet seem to.

For example, consider this exercise:

Sentence: The squidly nitch flummelled in the snobe.
Question 1: Where did the nitch flummel?
Question 2: What kind of nitch was it?
Question 3: What did the nitch do?

The sentence is meaningless, yet all the questions are easily answered. Think how often children have carried out similar tasks. Did they make more sense than this?

On the other hand, giving children a subject to write about – 'Write a poem about a butterfly' – is just as quickly seen by them as routine. Many children are asked to write 'stories' or a series of stories. But what kind of story can one write on one or two sides of paper? Even if they write at some length and really take trouble, the stories they produce as work bear no resemblance to the stories that they encounter in real books. Even the shortest of short stories, except for picture stories written for the very young, go on for several pages. The 'creative' endeavours of children are therefore only to do with the school, and not to do with their actual experiences.

> One way of overcoming this problem is to set a different kind of task. Instead of saying 'Write a story' (would you expect them to write a novel?), give out pictures, postcards, on all kinds of subjects and explain that these are illustrations from books. Each pupil imagines what the picture illustrates. He has to write just one page from the book from which the illustration comes. He can start in the middle of a sentence, near the beginning of the story or the end. He has to work out what characters are involved, what has been happening and what might happen.
>
> The result is that the page he has written looks like a page from a real book. He has to think of the literary experience he has had, and at the same time he will have imaginatively explored a real novel, with all the ambiguities, the suspense and the development of character.

If we were given some of the tasks that we give to our pupils we would find them at least very difficult. To write a coherent, sensible story with characters, a beginning, middle and end, that is interesting, in two hundred words is an amazing as well as an unrealistic task. It is more demanding than saying: 'Talk for one minute on the following subject.' One can learn to do it, but it is a task for panel games and competitions, and not part of the normal experience of many people.

So what do we do to help? The first thing we do is to remember that the children are engaged in experiencing a real world – a world of books that explores the realities of human emotions and thoughts on an individual level, and a world of images taken from television and newspapers that describes the politics of what people do to each other. What they do in school must not be divorced from their real world. Instead of having to carry out tasks in the vacuum of school, they should understand, even analyse, the ways in which people actually communicate with each other.

> There are many subjects that should have a clear sense of purpose. The ability to write well, to communicate and to understand language should be an obvious priority. And yet it seems that the majority of pupils in secondary schools do not see any purpose in English, finding that teachers have contradictory attitudes towards grammar, with some insisting on 'correctness' and others indifferent to it. The result is that they feel uncertain about the subject and come to resent anything to do with it, like writing. But writing is not the favourite activity of primary school children, either.[12]

Children need to be aware of style. One might think that such a concept is too sophisticated for children; but style is, at its most basic, the recognition of what is appropriate. Newspapers differ from each other. People use language according to the circumstances. In order to help children develop their own sense of the personal and of what is unique to them we need to let them learn how other people write. The truly creative never comes from a complete vacuum but from a great deal of observation and a great deal of practice. Children can only develop their own voice by listening to others, their own way of self-expression by seeing how others express themselves. All that they do in school should enrich their sense of themselves, of their audience and, above all, of what writing, in the greater context, actually is.

The uniqueness and the idiosyncrasy of each piece of writing that the pupil is motivated to produce has been stressed. But any creative endeavour does not appear out of nothing. No artist is 'born' as opposed to being 'made'. Each child learns by being engaged in understanding, is actively involved in discerning those clues in the environment that make sense to him. We must constantly remind ourselves of the creative tensions between the learner and his surroundings because this has a strong influence on the practice of teaching.

> There is no time by which pupils – or indeed adults – have learned all there is to learn about writing. Language acquisition is a continuing process in the secondary years, but thereafter pupils continue to refine their style, learning how to adapt what they read to their own purposes. They often try out ideas in writing before doing so in speech – because there is more time.[13]

One way of expressing the way the pupil learns, in practical terms, is in the word 'parody'. A child does not learn by pure imitation, taking in all the teacher says or imbibing information. As every teacher knows, sometimes with regret, no pupil remembers all he is told. Even when he is trying to learn something the memory will distort the information, will focus on those points that are of greatest interest and discard other points that do not make the same connections. The process of response is an idiosyncratic one. Even when the pupil tries to imitate, he brings something of his own.

This fact can be exploited by the deliberate use of parody. Every pupil is aware of the variety of uses of language in written, as well as spoken, form. Children meet newspapers and magazines, as well as books, and see the differences between them. This is print in everyday reality, and the tasks that the pupils carry out should be related to this reality. Each pupil is able to see the difference of approach to the same story by different people. The question is: how can they express what they see?

To ask a pupil to define stylistic differences is difficult. Children do not automatically possess a critical vocabulary. They will revert to a defensive: 'I know what I like.' But what they can do is to parody style. By making their own versions of what they read they will be made aware of the singularity of texts. Even very young children have their favourites: as they get older children become more aware why they like and dislike different texts. The materials that a teacher can use are around all the time, and are at a great remove from the school text or scheme. What the teacher needs to know is how to match the task to the interest and knowledge of the pupils.

> One of the useful means of helping children to understand the purpose of writing and its development has been called 'instructional scaffolding', which sounds grand. It means drawing attention to the nature of writing itself, through planning and discussion, through revision and rewriting. Writing needs to be seen as a meaningful task, with an end-product that is worthy of attention.[14]

The most practical way of enabling children to understand written language is in encouraging them to make things. This can be done either individually or in collaboration. Suppose the task is to make a class newspaper. This can give different children several roles to play: gathering news stories, editing, designing, creating advertisements. The stories can be their own experiences or their versions of typical newspaper stories. They can study the way in which advertisements are worded and construct their own. They can experience the way that space is used, what decisions are made about publishing, what to leave out as well as what to include, and what headlines to use. All the time they are using writing in a 'real' way as well as at a level which is appropriate to them. I have seen newspapers successfully put together by 6-year-olds as well as by older children.

Children can also make their own versions of other forms of literature that they encounter, including magazines and comics. Nothing makes them more aware of the level of demand and expectation (or lack of it) in popular journals than making their own versions of them. Let us take comic strips as an example. These use stilted stories and very odd language. Usually when children read comics they scarcely bother with the words. They hardly ever remember what they have read since they paid so little attention at the time. They simply recognize that they have read a particular comic when they come across it again. They will not have looked at it closely, but on doing so they examine, at a deeper level, what is actually being written and they become more critical. A parody of a comic strip is probably more demanding of drawing skill than of vocabulary.

We have already mentioned the difficulties for children in writing stories that relate to their experience as readers. There are many ways in which they can produce worthwhile work. They can concentrate on particular aspects of a story, like a convincing opening; they can provide what they think would make an interesting outline for a book, chapter by chapter, and give a sample chapter; and they can produce a short book designed for younger readers. Having looked at story-books with illustrations, they can produce their own and try them out on their intended audience, bearing in mind the levels of vocabulary, the relationship of text to illustration, and those elements of a story that make it interesting to younger readers.

> Writing might be seen by children as a chore, but it is an activity that is never finally mastered and they must realize that it is not a static, unchanging activity. It is important to ensure that pupils see writing as the most powerful way of helping them discover what they know, rather than as a means of confirming that they know less than we do.

In all these kinds of activity, each one of which could be greatly elaborated, lie some common themes. There is a sense of an audience, so that what is written is meant to be read, not only by a teacher, but by people that the writer has borne in mind. There is a sense of producing something real, worth writing for its own sake. And there is the sense that what is being produced needs working on; it needs planning, thought, and the willingness and ability to have second thoughts.

The principles that underlie the development of writing include the notion of 'parody' and re-drafting. In order to produce something that has a sense of purpose and is worth producing, the pupil needs to be aware of the audience and of the kinds of written material already available. This means that what is written is not just a response to a test, or to demonstrate knowledge. It means that the words themselves are interesting, that the pupil thinks of how to say things as well as what to say. The ability to reshape material, to plan and change and correct, gives many benefits in addition to a more splendid result. It gives the pupil that sense of ownership, of personal command, that should affect all his learning.

Re-drafting also teaches the differences in the ways in which people write. Sometimes writing is a matter of note-taking, of jotting down ideas as they come. Writing can be a personal affair, with an audience restricted to oneself. Encouraging children to keep diaries as a kind of compendium of notes that they are keeping for themselves adds an extra dimension to their learning. They learn that they can write for their own sakes, keeping something that is just for them without the weight of expectation of producing something public. They learn the difference between the private and the public, and the respect which is due to the finished article. They also learn that writing can be exploratory and analytical, can define feelings, and can relieve anxiety. The diary does not have to be anything more than a collection of ideas and notes – like the artist's sketch pad of words and pictures. But it gives a personal identity to the idea of writing.

Writing is, therefore, from the beginning, an essential tool of learning. By using writing at a variety of levels, children become more aware of the world of print which includes, but is much wider than, the texts used in school. They become more critically aware of the processes of publishing and marketing, of the ways in which facts are presented, and of themselves both as readers and as learners.

Chapter 8

Talking and Listening Skills

'I like dinner time really, because you can sit next to your friends and have a little chat and that makes it nice'.

(girl, 10)

It is a basic truth about human nature that people like to talk. In fact, as any overheard conversation will reveal, people like to talk rather more than they like to listen. Remember the conversations on the bus, when two people are talking at once: 'And I said to Mrs P; you remember her don't you, her with that funny cousin, Fred, who reminds me of Sally's boy, him with the squint, I never did like that, it makes me not know where to look, and I think there's something shifty, like I feel with Mr A . . .' It is as if talking through their free associations were all that mattered. Bring up the subject of illness and everyone will want to tell you about their own experience.

There is a primary need to express oneself. But to communicate demands an audience. This explains the importance of early relationships and their effect on subsequent intellectual performance. There is a need to talk, but also a need for someone to listen. We might think that two people talking at once or listening only long enough to know when it is their turn to speak is just a sign of the garrulous. But every conversation gives clues of the two principles that underlie them: the place of talk in forming ideas, and learning the skills of detecting the moment when to talk.[1]

> Different styles of conversation can be likened to the distinction between recall and recognition. Much is learned through recognizing what we have seen before, putting a fact into a new context. We know what we have seen. It is more difficult to remember all that we want to at will. A lazy conversation is like a series of recognitions: making automatic connections between one idea and another according to previous experiences. True conversation means to have control: giving shape and substance to what is said.[2]

Talking might be a need, but the skills of talking and listening need to be learned. It always takes at least two people together to learn the skill and it is not easy to create the circumstances in which it can be learned. The very simplest abilities that we take for granted (knowing the signals of when someone has finished talking – signals that are usually visual but can be, as on a telephone, through the tone of voice) are abilities that are in constant need of refinement.

It is important to be reminded of the almost mechanistic skills of talking and listening because they underlie the intellectual feat of conversation. At one level we see the reasoning behind dialogue. Conversation is at the heart of Socratic thinking, of arguing so that one can refine one's thought. It depends on understanding what is being said – 'Yes' – and being able to take the argument further – 'but'. An acceptance of what the other person is trying to say precedes the chance to make a counterargument. Reasoning lies at the heart of the true conversation.

Reasoning is also an art that can be learned. But to achieve the ability to argue logically requires a knowledge of all the attributes that underlie argument: patience and courtesy. Conversation needs a framework that teachers can set up, the willingness to play to the rules, the most essential of which is to know when to listen.

> The ability of two people to share non-verbal signals is revealed not so much in the expressions on their faces or the body movements, but in the way they behave on the telephone. One can detect when the conversation is coming to an end: the voice changes, there are small verbal gestures, more in the tone of the voice than 'Well it's been nice talking . . .', and the pauses become slightly longer. Both people recognize the signals.

But there are many small gestures that people learn to make to 'keep the conversational ball rolling'. The point is that the ability to hold a conversation reveals a great deal about a person; curiosity in others and knowledge. Great things can be learned in small stages, as young children reveal.

The more often children are given the opportunity to practise the skills of conversation the better. For many children, however, this will be something new. When they come to school they bring with them a variety of experiences at home. They will have become used to dialogue, or they will have become accustomed to statements made for them or to them but without demanding a reply. Teachers who have taught in a variety of schools, from inner cities to rural areas, will quickly recognize the difference in children's approaches to conversation.[3] Some children will know very well the importance of listening; others will have a far more volatile sense of talk, assuming that they can say anything that comes to mind. The differences between pupils' approaches to the classroom come about because of their earliest experience. Of all the attributes that children bring with them to school, perhaps the most crucial is the knowledge of how to make relationships. This depends on talk.

> It can be difficult for children to realize when a teacher is asking genuinely 'open' questions. They are so used to questions being presented as a form of test, to make sure that they have understood something. Year after year, children have understood that the prime function of questions is not to stimulate thought so much as to train them to think in certain accepted ways. This can make it hard for teachers to open up genuine discussions. The most often heard question is, after all, 'Will you close that door?', which isn't really a question at all.[4]

From the teacher's point of view the most important of all dialogues are between teacher and pupil, between the teacher and the class. No one can allow opportunities for conversation without creating the conditions of authority. Conversation depends on self-discipline. Opportunities depend on the disciplines of the classroom, of each pupil knowing two things: that he will have a chance to talk and that he has to wait for it.

The organization of a classroom is made coherent in the authority of the teacher. The teacher gives the crucial example when to talk and when to listen. The teacher who talks too much is like a teacher who adds to general noise and babble. Sometimes, when children are all chattering away, the teacher starts shouting things like 'Keep quiet'; this can merely cause the children to ignore the sound and talk more loudly. Just as conversation means listening, so the teacher must insist on quiet. Children have to learn to listen, and listen carefully. This means quietness.

Teachers also listen. To find time to do so to individuals is not easy. The most extended dialogues need to take place between pupils so that they have defined subjects to discuss. The kinds of listening skills that the teacher demonstrates are, in the classroom, of a more formal kind. They depend first on the framework of discipline so that all pupils accept the importance of recognizing the teacher's signals, and the need to listen when any one person is talking. The teacher is like a conductor who is bringing sounds out of each individual. The sounds that matter are not just those that concentrate on getting an answer right, but those that show reflection. Every moment is a potential teaching moment, at the start and end of every session. There are often some 'stray' minutes when the tasks have been completed and pupils are ready to go out to lunch. It is those moments that the teacher can use to explore further the issues the class has been discussing, or to remind pupils what they have been learning.

> Although teachers recognize the importance of getting to know each pupil and having extended conversations with each of them, this is not an easy matter to achieve in the normal classroom. Observation of teachers has shown that on average a teacher spends just two minutes every week with a pupil who is in the class the whole time. This is hardly extended conversation. The quality is also different. Compare the snatched conversation in the classroom with the kinds of conversations that take place on school outings where quite different aspects of personality are revealed.[5]

Teachers can practise the art of asking interesting questions however simple the subject. Suppose a child has a strong desire to tell the rest of the class about something of importance to her. Her parents have acquired a dog. She wants to tell everyone about this: others will respond by revealing that they too have pets. The question for the teacher is whether he can encourage the interest of all children. The fact might be interesting in itself to all children. The fact might be interesting in itself, but what can be taught from it? Any subject is the starting point for any number of explorations: what type of dog is it? What kinds of dog are there? What have dogs always been used for? What happens at dog shows? What are the best examples of useful dogs, like sheep-dogs and guide-dogs? And what other kinds of pet are there? The point is that one doesn't just accept a statement as read. One needs to make it interesting.

> In a study of school lessons, when both the reflections of the pupils and the quality of their work were taken into account, the most highly rated lessons had:
>
> 1. A lot of talk by the teacher.
> 2. This talk directed towards how the children should do a task.
> 3. A focus on mental skills.

> The talk included examples of problem-solving, and embedded new concepts in ones already known. Most importantly, the teachers talked to make the pupils think; they gave them responsibility.[6]

There is one important and simple technique that the teacher needs to use to help children listen. That is to make them realize that they might have to answer a question at any moment. It is too easy to rely on the same child, his hand held high, straining to be unleashed. It is too easy to be automatically responsive, to answer to anything called out, so that it is the children who are controlling the session. The professional teacher cannot allow interruptions even if it is a normal adult behaviour pattern to respond to what people are saying. In the classroom the individual must wait his turn.

Allowing the same children to dominate a collective conversation allows the majority to withdraw into an inattentive silence. We have all observed children sitting on the carpet around the teacher (sitting on the one comfortable chair) whilst using up their time in gently poking at each other, or seeing if they can make a book fall off a shelf, essentially waiting for something to happen. Questions need to be directed by the teacher to include all the children. If one child has not said anything for three occasions it is almost bound to be his turn next. At first children who are unaccustomed to this seem reluctant to respond: they are used to their silences. Even adults in seminars prefer not to say anything and almost resent a question. But in the end the ability and confidence to articulate an idea is the mark of the successful pupil and student.

> Children are known to be full of curiosity, and we expect them to ask difficult questions. But in school their experience is dominated not by asking questions but by being asked questions. Teachers use questions as a means of imparting information and sometimes children can find this off-putting.
>
> It was found in one survey that the teachers who asked the most questions were the least likely to receive questions back from the children, as if they couldn't get a word in for themselves. Furthermore the teachers who asked the most questions were the least likely to encourage children to make spontaneous comments on other kinds of contribution. Questions can be used in such a dogmatic way that they inhibit children even from elaborating their answers.[7]
>
> It all depends, of course, on the way questions are used. The problem for many teachers is that they give the impression of not being real questions but ways of testing what children don't know.
>
> The quality of questioning is more important than the amount.[8] And it is important to allow time for answers.

There is a way of asking questions which gives everyone the chance to get the answer 'right' and to add to the general dialogue. Often the teacher will take up a simple point that a shy child has made, and elaborate it. If, to the teacher's question 'What kinds of dog are there? . . . Simon?', Simon says 'Wolf', the teacher has a choice. Technically he could say 'No, what nonsense, that's a wild animal, I mean kind of dog, like Alsatian . . .', which would discourage Simon from venturing forth with anything thereafter. But the good teacher uses every answer, however difficult it might seem to be. 'Ah, now that's interesting. The dog family covers a lot of animals as well as pets . . .' The teacher then opens up a more extended discussion on the differences between animals – in any of a number of directions; and Simon has genuinely contributed to the learning.

Again, the secret of talking and listening lies in the courtesy of accepting an answer. It might not be the answer you were looking for, or what you expected, and you might not agree with it. But the worst thing anyone can do is issue a flat contradiction. Those children who in early childhood find themselves receiving bald instructions without explanation: 'Stop doing that! Come here! Have an ice cream!' face a very difficult task in school in learning how to make an argument, in fulfilling those tasks of presentation that lie at the heart of the educational system.

The conversation that the teacher directs is of a collective nature, and includes all the children. The skills they learn are of contributing to shared knowledge and awareness, of bearing in mind what has been said, and seeing the direction in which the argument is going. The teacher uses what children contribute. This is clearly not the same as the face-to-face (or ear-to-ear) dialogue. Whilst there might be moments when the teacher can have a conversation with an individual these moments are rare and normally dominated by the need to explain, either by the children – such as a domestic problem – or by the teacher – such as a new skill the child finds difficult.

The opportunity for extended dialogue lies in the pupils themselves. They are the ones who have the time. But to make these interactions fruitful takes careful planning. The group or the pair will need to have either a distinct problem that they can only work out if they think it through, or an opportunity to teach each other something new. Fortunately most children make good teachers.[9] They can be patient and understand learning difficulties. They also accept learning from each other. For the 'explainer' as well as the learner there are the added benefits of learning how to use language, of checking whether the other has understood. This kind of dialogue develops the communication skills in both. Also, children find that talking through a problem eases it; just as in adult life a full discussion precedes a decision, so it needs to be in school.[10]

This suggests the ethos of collaboration. Sometimes schools can contrast too greatly with adult life, to the detriment of the pupil's work. The striving for individualism, and for competition, can easily make children back away from learning as they strive harder. Talking through a set task implies that the task is interesting: a genuine problem, like how to design a structure of paper that will be strong enough to support a weight, rather than regurgitating information that is stored in a book.

> In many classrooms the week begins with the sharing of news. What did people do over the weekend? What do they want to share with each other? This might seem a time when children are free to bring their own personal experience to bear in school. In fact children often treat these news sessions as formally as everything else, defining the teacher as the key receiver and announcer of news, and adapting what they say to the official school curriculum.[11]

Whatever the situation that the teacher arranges, children need to have the confidence to speak. For young children in a secure environment this should be little problem, but everyone has their shyness and embarrassment. Some people overcome it, ruthlessly. But for the majority shyness remains and for some acutely so. There are a number of ways in which they can be helped, beyond the encouragement of making what they say worthwhile by listening attentively.

The easiest way to encourage children to talk to the whole class without embarrassment is to give them a task that each of them can perform easily. The easiest task is to let them do a parody of something they have heard and seen. The safest forms of parody that encourage the ability to talk are directed at the media. Just as children's work is developed through imitation of other people's style, so children can learn to analyse and make their own the curiosities of voice and gesture as seen and heard on television or radio. Let us take one simple example. Asking a child to take part in drama, to improvise or learn a part, could be quite demanding. But there is no child who has not seen an advertisement and known how it works. It is the simplest of tasks to do enough of an act to indicate which advertisement they are referring to. They can imitate the particular vocabulary that becomes the advertisement's trademark. They can make this simple or sophisticated according to their ability. But they can all do it.

> Think of questions from the children's point of view: it is the teacher who asks the questions. It is the teacher who knows the answers. Therefore, repeated questions imply wrong answers.[12]

This notion of performance has been suggested because of its support in giving children the confidence to speak in public – to be listened to by an audience. But such techniques do more than that. They help children listen carefully to what is being said and the way it is being said. They learn about different accents and voices, about tricks of speech. They learn about the idiosyncrasies of speech, from counting how many times the teacher uses the word 'right' during a day, to noting the uses of accent to make a pompous effect. And they also begin to analyse what kinds of designs different people have on an audience, from the advertiser to the politician.

> Children might be born with the desire to ask questions but it is an art that needs to be developed and learned. They are not very good at drawing out inferences through asking questions because they respond to ambiguous messages by guessing rather than by seeking clarification.
> Fortunately there are tasks like 'Twenty Questions' that help children to learn how to ask questions to discover things and to keep asking, rather than guessing and allowing what they hear to remain obscure.[13]

Knowing about dialogue helps people use it. There are many circumstances surrounding interviews that can be recorded and analysed. One can see the way different interviewers bring different responses from those they interview. Some are aggressive and lead the interviewee into silence. Others are patronizing and make the interviewee exasperated. It is not difficult to put together a dossier of 'bad' interviewers: they reveal very succinctly the difficult and delicate nature of human interaction.

The skills of talking and listening are not to be seen as an extra, or an afterthought, once the essential and prestigious tasks of writing and arithmetic are carried out. They are the means of developing logic and reason. There was a time when 'rhetoric' was an essential part of the curriculum, defined not just narrowly as making speeches, but as understanding the ways in which people communicate. Socrates drew attention to the importance of human dialogue through discussion, and not through writing. He was concerned with a constant, shared advance in understanding and feared being held back by written 'tablets of stone'.[14]

Preparing a short speech is a very different task from drafting written work. The awareness of the audience is of a different kind. The way the speech is structured needs to be attuned to the way in which an audience reacts: and a speech gives its maker the advantage of seeing and helping the audience react. There are questions which are not purely rhetorical. To make a speech interesting is an intellectual challenge; it is more than a game. Think of how often people need to make presentations, to stimulate interest and organize. It is not only teachers who need presentation skills.

There is one technique in talking, however, that is more like a game, even if it is also intellectually challenging. Imagine being asked to talk for one minute non-stop on any given subject. The need to put together an anecdote, a fact, an opinion brings out not just whatever the person knows about the subject – try 'Coal' – but the way in which facts hang lucidly together. There is, of course, a panel game on the radio on which people perform this task (with a few extra rules to trip them up) for a living.

> When children are themselves asked about their conceptions of good listening they reveal some interesting developing characteristics. Older children rely much more than younger children on attempts to comprehend rather than on behaviour. They understand that appropriate responses depend on the circumstances. They understand the need to question and to listen carefully. But as they get older, children also become more negative; they learn to be suspicious of the speaker. They also tend to remember best those things they hear that do not fit: the unusual, the mistake or the incongruent fact.[15]

When children learn to read they need to know some basic facts about language, like the formation of words. They also need to understand rhyme.[16] This implies the ability to analyse sound. But this is, like reading, an art that continues to develop. The ability to take in oral information is not an automatic one. You only need to rehearse what you heard on the news this morning to realize how much went in one ear and came out of the other. The voices chattered on but were ignored. Children receive a great deal of information that they ignore. All the entertainments of television become easily likened to the background noises of school. To concentrate, to learn, is harder work.

It is sometimes difficult for children to listen carefully because they are so accustomed to shutting out sounds. Their attention span is at best fairly short. Even when trying to take in what the teacher says they will find part of their minds wandering, with their own associations drifting into and out of the task in hand. For this reason, it is worth teaching children to analyse a dialogue or a speech they hear; not just to recall the facts, but think of the ways they were put. It is after all possible to listen spellbound to a brilliant orator and then afterwards find it impossible to remember what he said.

> The mind being such a crowded place, full of words and pieces of stray information, it is not surprising that a number of private and personal associations are triggered off even in the act of concentrated listening (or reading). It is like a vast network of connections, where the routes through are not altogether cut off from their surroundings.
>
> The fact that the mind hears what it wants to hear, to make sense of what it hears, even when trying hard to listen, is illustrated by the party game of Chinese Whispers. Invariably the very clear message that is passed from one person to the next will be distorted during its passage. The final message will make some kind of sense: but it won't be the same as the one first heard. This is not because no one is listening, but because they are listening too hard.

Those who have been brought up in an oral tradition demonstrate great powers of memory. The art of story-telling depended on the ability to know not only the essential outlines of the myths, but on a detailed expectation of hearing the same words. Young children also have this power of remembering, knowing when a word in a story-book is misplaced. They want to make the story their own, and do so by remembering each word.

The advance of literacy has meant that people rely on different systems to store information. It seems, to some, that people have lost as much as they have gained from learning to rely on visual rather than oral codes. File cards, books and computers can seem to provide access to many things no longer kept in the brain. But the fact is that usable information does not depend solely on knowing where to find it; the really usable still needs such speed of access that it can only serve in the memory.[17]

> Children often play with talk as they would play with a piano. They will explore ideas in their head, or aloud, acting out a part of an argument, and will talk with each other for hours.
>
> At the same time there will be moments when they do not want to talk, or respond to the demand of a teacher, when they clam up and say, 'I don't know.' This is a refusal rather than ignorance, a desire to hide in the subjective, with inner dialogue, rather than the objective demands of school.

The connection between oracy and memory is a close one. For this reason there are two themes that underlie the development of talk. One is the importance of remembering what information is to hand in order to make a speech: this is the memory for what is significant. The other is the sense of ownership that comes from 'knowing' the words. There have been times when remembering poetry has been used not so much as a pleasure as a punishment. Memorizing Shakespeare speeches has, indeed, often been used as if one could combine retribution with 'doing them good'. But there is a real sense of pleasure in knowing poems, understanding the words and their rhythms, and bringing them in tune with personal feelings. Quotations are apt not just for their use in illustrating a point, but also in illuminating personal understandings. Poems can be remembered for the pleasure they give.

In all the different tasks of talking and listening that can be given to children it is important to consider the time frame. It is important to make distinctions between those tasks that have to be carried out quickly, like simulations, and those for which there is plenty of time. There are times when it is a positive advantage to hurry things along so that pupils almost do not have any time to reflect, or brood. You concentrate on speed of response, on leaps of the imagination, on guesswork and experiment. At other times it is important to make sure pupils have enough time and space to follow a project through. Management of time depends on variety.

> In one study, teachers were asked to increase the use of private praise: the result was that the minimal use of private reprimands and the use of private praise improved the on-task behaviour of secondary children by 20 per cent.[18]

Chapter 9

The Social Skills of Children

'If you didn't meet anybody else you wouldn't be socialized.'

(boy, 10)

Children closely observe their surroundings. The younger they are, the more time they have to do so. They long for visual stimulation and the more they have, the more they puzzle over it. Their first social observations are of individuals and explore individual relationships. Their observations are the means of making relationships: learning to detect mood, imitating gestures and seeking a response. We have already noted how gifted children are in playing their part in the dialogue of relationships, but they badly need other people in order to develop this gift. Social skills might seem the birthright of human beings, but, as we see in the worst forms of social unrest, these skills are not something that happens automatically.

> Children's natural giftedness in seeking out relationships is revealed in a number of ways, and research over the past few years has shown first how early children learn and secondly how rich their understanding of social habits is. How else can one explain how babies imitate facial gestures, and how children before the age of 3 can actually compensate for the limitations of others? We know that children fully understand the social concepts of truth and falsehood, blame and guilt before they are 5. They already possess a 'concept of mind'.[1]

Social skills need to be fostered and refined. The first crucial help that can be given to children is to develop their ability to make relationships, not only showing sensitivity to other people's needs, as well as their own, but extending their relationships through the complexities of dialogue. A true relationship goes beyond being able to manipulate or negotiate the feelings of others. It includes the ability to share in a discussion about those feelings. Many children are not given the opportunity to define what they think, and are given few explanations for the rules of behaviour. These are the children who will always find the demands of any social organization, like a school, difficult.[2]

The first task for children, and for those who teach them, is to develop individual relationships, understanding not only the reactions to mood, to warmth or coldness, but the reasons behind different patterns of behaviour. Children wish to understand and are capable of understanding. To deny them the explanations is to inhibit their social development.

Children explore their relationships. They also closely observe the way people behave to each other.[3] Individual dialogue is reinforced by seeing the ways in which people keep to certain standards of conduct, of manners and courtesy. For this reason alone, explanations of behaviour are not enough in themselves. It is frustrating for the child to be treated as if there were no given framework which guides behaviour.[4] Treating a child as if he or she will come automatically to the correct conclusions is a form of spoiling. One of the first social habits that children need to learn is the way in which all relationships depend on rules.

It is sometimes difficult to know exactly what effect observation has on a child. We know clearly that children are deeply affected by the breakdown of relationships in the case of divorcing parents. Children feel so closely involved through their witnessing that they feel guilty for the quarrels and arguments of their parents. But even in less extreme cases of difficulties between adults, children overhear and inwardly digest what they observe. Sometimes they can brood over an event they observed, or a remark they misunderstood, for years. When they see a relationship break down they feel personally involved because of their need to feel that they have their own clear part in the framework of relationships.

> All research on young children's development shows not only their mental abilities but their social skills. Far from being egocentric, children of 2 and 3 show great sensitivity in understanding arguments and the need for rules of fair behaviour. They are willing to cooperate in play and help each other, understanding other people's needs as well as their own.
> Even babies comfort each other.[5]

Children like the security of clear rules. They need explanations but these explanations include the fact that there are certain expectations of behaviour which are sacrosanct, including obedience. Again, there is a close analogy between what happens in the home and what happens in the school. Children cannot do whatever they feel like doing, interrupt because something has occurred to them, or tell easy lies which parents are tempted to accept because it is harder work to do something about it. 'Have you washed your hands?' 'Yes.' It is easier to accept the answer, or even not to ask, than to pay attention to the real truth.

Children make and observe relationships with adults but they also witness and create relationships with other children. They are performers as well as observers. They explore, in playgroup or kindergarten, in school and out of it, all the possibilities of sharing and choosing toys, the negotiations involved in taking turns, the frustrations of having things snatched away. Everywhere, as in school, children instinctively seek out the security afforded by clear social control. Their own experience of the misery afforded by bad behaviour leads to their sense of the need of reinforcement of a shared and collaborative set of standards.

It is important to understand children's need for rules, for this affects the way in which schools operate. When children are asked about school rules – whether they are necessary or fair – they are adamant that discipline should be clear and firm.[6] Far from wanting fewer rules, children wish to see more. Far from appreciating the lenient teacher, they like teachers to be very firm, as well as fair. In that context they know where they stand. Children see schools as the most important place where social discipline is learned, and there are many parents who share that view.[7] This implies that schools have, with parents, a duty to develop the social disciplines of children and not merely to create a discipline in which learning takes place.

> Children hold conservative views about human nature, and tend to assume that the older a person gets the more likely he is to be depraved. They therefore say that rules and sanctions become ever more important as they progress through their school careers. They stress the importance of rules rather than the autonomy of the individual in having personal freedom and making personal decisions.
>   This desire for social codes can be used by teachers and should always be remembered.

There is a fundamental reason for having rules. Nothing creative or useful could happen without them. But in addition to their necessity, rules are also a study in their own right. Much of children's theoretical learning is about human behaviour. How have people organized themselves over the years? Are there differences in custom and manners between one culture and another? What are the most significant structures in a constitution? Where does one draw the line between freedom to publish and libel? The big educational questions are fundamentally social.

> When children are in school they spend a lot of time with each other. This forces them into friendships whether they like it or not – into alliances and groups. When children are left alone by adults and when in new circumstances, friendships are both more important and more brittle. This is why friendships seem fickle, with quarrels as well as reconciliations. Friendships are for the exploration of interpersonal relationships and are ways of maintaining order in children's social world. Some are contingency friends; others change according to the manoeuvres going on. All this is natural.[8]

Differences in behaviour can be observed early. There is a connection between the forming of individual relationships and behaviour to strangers. Inhibited children who cling to their parents find it difficult to relate to new people.[9] Children clearly respond to the stimulus of others, to attention that is given all the time rather than as a response to a demand. Seeing young children playing with each other shows how they will often try to defy some rules if it is to their advantage. They are not just obedient but have an urge to test rules. Boys in these circumstances tend to be far more rumbustious. They are the ones who take over the big mobile toys in a playground, like carts and scooters, and their greater physicality is made apparent early on.[10]

For this reason the quality of playgroups depends clearly on two factors; the willingness of adults to give time and quality of dialogue to individuals, and the demonstrably clear expectations of behaviour.[11]

Children reflect what they observe; they parody what they see. This emphasizes the importance of good models of behaviour: not only the issuing of commands, but the demonstration of politeness and fairness. The more one analyses behaviour, the more complex it becomes.[12] When we look at the language teachers tend to use with children we see that they ask questions or make demands that would be considered most impolite with adults. Children see and resent the differences between the expectations placed on them – like saying 'please' – and the behaviour of teachers. Firmness does not need to be shrill or rude. On the contrary, children expect teachers to maintain high standards.

> Children learn by modelling themselves on children they perceive to be like themselves. Self-confidence can be improved if children observe others, like themselves, develop from lacking self-confidence to gaining it. Their own self-confidence is not helped by seeing previously self-confident pupils continue to demonstrate self-confidence.[13]

Sometimes social behaviour can hurt inadvertently, and what some have called 'innocent' racism reveals deep-seated prejudices that are not meant to hurt but do. Again children are quick to spot inequalities, like the different treatment of boys and girls. Both genders resent the fact that it is the boys who tend to be singled out for attention – often negative.[14] And yet we note how early some stereotypes are set up: 'Girls, line up . . . Boys, stack away the chairs.' Equality of opportunity, however, goes beyond overcoming stereotypes; we are concerned with sensitivity of behaviour to all individuals. Being aware of what might hurt is the first stage towards refining behaviour to individuals. Can racism ever be 'innocent'?

One of the useful means of joining rules with individual expectations is the drawing up of 'contracts'. These can be made with whole classes or with individuals. The important point about them is that they are agreed by everyone involved. They might not always be obeyed but at least the agreement means the rules are understood and acknowledged. Contracts place emphasis on rewards for good behaviour and high expectations, rather than on a reliance on sanctions. When we look at the way that authority works in society as a whole we see how it depends on a social contract, on the acceptance by all involved of shared standards of respect for others.

Even when the importance of shared expectations and a clear social code has been accepted, it does not mean that more subtle forms of social learning do not continue. The ways in which children are expected to work teaches them a lot about collaboration, about individual initiatives and the way in which problems can be shared. There has, for example, always been a tradition in Great Britain of 'doing your own thing', exemplified in the fact that children are expected to work by and for themselves. There is a certain irony in this in so far as children are individually placed in groups. One hardly ever sees rows of desks. Instead five or six children sit around a table. This doesn't mean, however, that they collaborate.

> An American researcher explored the ways in which children worked in school in a number of countries. Some of the findings were surprising. In the then Soviet Union the emphasis in schools was on children helping each other – in giving extended explanations to others who had not yet understood. In the democratic countries there was observed to be far more emphasis on individuality and competition.[15]

Children understand their careers in school as some kind of competition. From an early age they recognize that they go to school to be prepared for future employment, and they see that some children are far more successful than others. They know whether they are above or below average, not against a series of criteria, but against a set of norms. They do not want to 'come last'. That is more significant than doing well, like running fast. The way in which a class is arranged with rewards and observed failures reinforces children's understanding of hierarchy. Even if a teacher tries to disguise differences of achievement children will still label each other.[16]

> Children seem to find it easier to help each other when the one who is acting as a 'peer-tutor' works with another who is not a close friend. To change a relationship from that of friend to tutor is to change roles significantly, and that is difficult.[17]

Children do not label each other only in the classroom. They share collective attitudes to individuals in playtime. Once a child has a particular reputation, that reputation will be reinforced by others' behaviour. The social relationships of children are subtle and complex.

The social skills of children can be negative as well as positive. One of the worrying things about schools is that children take for granted that there will be a lot of bullying. Opportunities abound. The movements along corridors or the crowded playgrounds all present the chance to jostle or push, tease or argue. Children seem to think that this is all part and parcel of social life – that cruelty is as natural and widespread as kindness.

Bullying comes in many forms, from subtle verbal harassment to physical abuse. It can consist of ignoring individuals as well as drawing overt attention to some physical peculiarity. Bullying is worrying not only because of the suffering of the victims but because there is a strong correlation between bullying in schools and subsequent criminal behaviour in adults.[18]

> Everyone wants approval from others, and much of children's lives is spent seeking it. But they do not always know how to go about getting it, having to guess what would please. This is partly because adults do not necessarily know how to express support.
>
> From the children's point of view we have already noted that the phrase they associate with teachers is 'Do it again.' The phrase they associate with parents is 'Come on.' Parents want their children to do better and better, and cajole them into action.[19]

The problem is that many children are involved in some form of bullying, whether as witness, bully or victim. They find bullying difficult to define and realize that it does not consist only of the extremes of physical violence. It is the problem of definition and the hidden nature of much bullying that make it so difficult for teachers to deal with. Bullying in the classroom can be spotted quite easily and cases of harassment made into a moral lesson. But bullying is kept for the most part private by the children and they do not think that teachers really care about it or want to be involved in preventing it. Up to a point they are correct. Teachers are busy people. Dealing with cases of bullying takes time. Many people have to be interviewed. And some schools, associating bullying with an extreme lack of social discipline, prefer to deny its existence.[20]

The answer to bullying is to see it as widespread and subtle, and not only as extreme pathological behaviour. It is, whether we like it or not, one aspect of peer-group behaviour. It is not confined to certain 'types' who like to inflict pain on others, or victims who almost seek out, with a terrible fascination, the attention of bullies. The answer to bullying lies in the witnesses, the behaviour of onlookers and their support of, or reaction against, different forms of cruelty.

Children are very skilled at detecting weaknesses in others. They can feel sorry for them or take advantage of them. Some children are also adept at seeking out the weaknesses of teachers, as well as understanding their strengths. In every class there will be jokers who see how far they can go with a teacher; to what extent is the teacher willing to share a joke?[21] To what extent will the teacher allow individuals to get away with bad behaviour? The classroom is one of the testing grounds for social behaviour where children share with each other ways of usurping imposed authority.

> When children direct their attention to things other than work – like counting the number of times a teacher uses a phrase – they can come up with elaborate games. One class

of children decided to see how much time could be 'wasted' in a lesson by seeing if the teacher could be diverted from the subject and made to talk about other things. One or two children were employed as independent observers because there were bets being exchanged as to how much time could be totted up as 'wasted' by the end of the week. The problem with these bets was that the use of time could be diverted according to individual requirements. Those who had started on a low figure tried to keep the teacher 'on task'. Those who betted high did all they could to distract him.[22]

Much of children's attention in school is not on the task in hand. This is not only because so much time is spent in organizing or waiting for the bell or day-dreaming. It is because children share an interest in talk. There are other things to do in addition to the task in hand. As much intellectual energy can be used up in finding short cuts or avoiding work as in doing it. The classroom is fertile ground for a variety of experiments.

We must not underestimate the influence of the peer group, for good or bad. At worst a group of children can encourage each other in causing disruption, in creating an ethos in which work is of the least interest. Every class has an incipient 'gang' which can cause difficulties in the playground as well as in lessons. They create their own standards and their own heroes. They go in the opposite direction from those who joke and negotiate with the teacher. They are concerned with alienation, in avoiding rather than manipulating the demands of the school. The problem with gangs is that they feed off each other, creating their own separate social culture. They are at the extreme end of the forming of peer groups.

Peer groups can also be creative. Much of what a child learns about the environment is learned from discussion. What is learned is often anecdotal and strictly inaccurate, but it is in discussions that children learn all those things that teachers hardly mention: intimate relations, families, jobs, prisons, distant relations, holidays, God, the meaning of life ... Children bolster each other's belief system in conversations, through anecdotes that they pass on. Their awareness of society comes about not only through their behaviour and observation but through discussion. It is a pity if such conversations are left entirely up to children.

'Play' remains a very important element in learning throughout childhood, even if it is more hidden from teachers' eyes as pupils get older. Play is important because it is essentially an intellectual activity: children play with ideas and with rules, they use games to practise and to recapitulate. In play they express their personalities and explore their relationships with others.[23]

Many children want to learn whatever the teacher allows them to. We have all seen them straining to be good, sitting upright, faces taut with concentration, trying to catch the teacher's eye so that they will be the first to go out, or the first to answer the question. It is a competitive kind of goodness and it is welcomed by teachers. But teachers also need to be aware of the difference between the desire to please the teacher and the desire to learn. It is possible for children to be so adept at anticipating what the teacher wants that they actually disguise the fact that they are doing little real work.

Nothing is easier for a teacher than to be able to assume that children are quietly getting on with tasks, without needing constant supervision. Attention is easily directed only at those children who make the most demands. It is more difficult to make sure that all children are receiving enough interest in their learning. Children are very skilled at avoiding too much notice. Having observed the disparity between ability and success they decide to go for an easy and undemanding life. They know just how little work they can get away with. The gap between what they could achieve and what they succeed in doing inevitably widens.[24]

> When teachers reflect back over the different classes of children they have encountered, there will always be those who come readily to mind, years later. Try it: think of some of the children you have taught, and notice that what makes them memorable is that they were often outstanding – often for bad reasons as much as for good ones. But they stood out.
>   But what about the rest, the forgotten ones, the 'invisible' children? What happened to them? Did they have the same amount of attention at the time that your memory now gives to them in comparison with the outstanding ones?[25]

From the teacher's point of view it is, of course, difficult to pay constant attention to every individual, and therefore a great temptation to concentrate on the difficult ones. But often teachers do not realize what is happening because the social skills being deployed are so subtle. Teachers should not allow interruptions if they want to create a dialogue which involves all the children. But they need to bolster this by insisting on behaviour which draws all children together. Some children will always volunteer information and their hands will shoot up at every opportunity – even before they know the question. But the others, the 'goodies', are also demonstrating advanced social behaviour. They keep still, they look as if they are paying attention without catching you in the eye. They look as if they are working steadily but somehow produce work which is always adequate but no more. They try to sit in places that are to the side of the centre of attention. They do not draw attention to themselves by doing bad work, or making a noise or being disobedient. They are the silent majority.

All children develop different forms of social skills which relate to teachers and the running of schools. They know where and when to do what they want to do so that they do not attract the wrong kind of attention – unless they seek it out, for some children find trouble irresistible. It is as if two levels of society were operating at the same time: one to do with the public order of schools and the other with the private lives of the individuals within them.

The school is nearly always the centre of children's social life, since that is where the largest number of people congregate. It is also the place where children learn about and experiment with relationships with each other. Pleasing the teacher and guessing what will please him is paralleled by an active exploration of different forms of friendship. Children test each other and themselves. This is why they often change friends. They form new groups, or are in one group but wish to be in another. They suddenly decide to discard an individual, sometimes cruelly. This testing of relationships is a volatile and continuing activity, and is different from the dynamic of adult friendships and relationships. It is far more emotionally charged and genuinely experimental. Children are trying out different tones of voice: whether they can be facetious, or whether some will bear teasing. They are discovering which topics will generate the most interest and which tastes and habits can best be shared. They are exploring the fears of loneliness and watching the effects of loneliness in others. They are testing the power of the group over individuals and their power over each other. Even the relationships between the bullies and victims are experimental and show a shared fascination.

> Children's social knowledge includes all those aspects of experience that we think are the marks of adulthood, like loneliness. Children of 4, 5 and 6 not only understand

loneliness but can define it; they know how much it depends on other people's judgements and behaviour, but do not feel any the better for that knowledge.[26]

Just as young children learn how to make a relationship with adults so they are
actively engaged in exploring all the emotions of friendship and authority: fear and
gratitude, joy, anticipation and disappointment. Many of their assumptions about
themselves and other people are formed at this time.

Learning depends on self-confidence, and failure in friendship can undermine self-
esteem. The teacher's awareness of what is going on between children is the more
important for this reason. Teachers can not only prevent cruel or hurtful behaviour
but, more positively, demonstrate the significance of fairness, equal treatment and the
celebration of achievements. The art lies in making sure that every child has the opportunity to be praised without being patronized. Alienated children are not 'problem
children' but children who have problems.

Children's anxieties about school can be related to work or relationships. Both
causes for anxiety need to be eased to fulfil their potential for learning. This can be
done to some extent in the classroom. Children will naturally wish to form friendship
groups and sit together, and avoid sitting with others. One of the social skills that they
need to learn in the classroom is the ability to work together with anyone, whatever
the age or sex. Allowing children to remain in friendship groups can sometimes be
unhelpful as well as natural. Some children hold each other back, not because they
are so busy giggling or disrupting but because they lower each other's expectations.
The art of the teacher is to balance those occasions when children are with their friends
with occasions when children are expected to fulfil given tasks with others selected for
a purpose. One does not wish to force certain children to be together as if it were a
punishment any more than one would wish to see children refusing to accept particular
individuals as partners.

There is always a connection between the ability to develop relationships with other
people and the ability to do well academically, despite the mythology about the lonely
recluse 'swotting' in the attic. Children of 4 years old at play centres who have good-
quality care and friendly interactions are happier, less shy and socially more competent,
and show the same advantages when they are 8, an advantage that includes academic
success.[27]

If one pays close attention to the way children work together one sees how important
it is that they learn to make relationships with a number of others, and that they
become accustomed to the normal expectations of courtesy and professional intentions. The balance is to be kept between the groups formed by personal choice and
those formed by the nature of the task in hand and set up by the teacher.

A balance also needs to be struck between the individual and the group. This can
best be illustrated in the psychology of avoiding disruption. One of the most visible
difficulties in the classroom is that of the child who wilfully causes strife. In its most
extreme form this can result in a stubborn refusal to obey the teacher. The fuel for
this kind of behaviour is the audience provided by the rest of the class. One of the
main techniques of discouraging bad behaviour is by making the others feel embar-
rassed or annoyed by bad behaviour. Thus when the pupil tries to raise a laugh by
doing something naughty it is those who laugh who need to be dealt with as much
as the naughty pupil. Peer-group support can be as dangerous as it can be useful. In
the end very few children will go on behaving in an inappropriate manner if they are

not making an impression on their peers. Isolating the main culprit is the first stage in dealing with problems of discipline. Teachers survive because all the pupils accept the authority they stand for. Once that trust breaks down both individual respect and group cohesion are lost.

> Children's sense of authority in society is shown by the way that they respond to different kinds of adults. Some they take far more seriously than their peer group, others far less seriously. They take into account the age and social position of the 'authority' more than the type of command given them.[28]

The understanding of group and organizations depends, in the end, on individual understandings. Contracts are personal things and manifestations of both personal agreements and individual understanding. Children need to be encouraged to explore the nuances of social behaviour, and not merely to practise them. The ways in which people should behave to each other, and ways in which people can harass others, need to be discussed fully. The ways in which people behave in society also need exploration, and the analogy between school rules and more general authority should be analysed. Children are skilled at social relationships. They also need to be knowledgeable about them.

Chapter 10

The Development of Group Work

'Well, she teaches the whole group and then she tells you on your own ... if you don't understand it you can go to the teacher and talk about it.'

(girl, 10)

There is a strong case to be made for encouraging group work. Children work well together when they have an interesting task to fulfil, they teach and learn from each other and they manage to explore and define issues. Working in groups is one means of allowing oracy to develop, and creating conditions in which some central ideas are tackled. Some would say that children will be talking anyway, and group work is a way of channelling talk into a constructive direction.

The principles for developing group work are quite clear. But there are also pragmatic reasons. It has become virtually automatic to rearrange primary classrooms from rows of desks into groups of tables, with four or five children sitting around them. The pragmatic reasons for working in groups include the sharing of resources, so that the same materials can be used by each group in turn until all have had the same experience of the material.[1]

> One research study in the United States looked at three different approaches to raising standards in schools. One method was to reduce the class sizes significantly. A second method was to increase the numbers of teachers and ancillaries in the class. The third was to set up circumstances in which children were encouraged to help each other, and work together on tasks.
>
> Each approach cost about the same when staff time and preparation were taken into account. But the most effective was not a reduction in class size or additional teachers, but children helping each other.[2]

Another pragmatic reason is that grouping children into discrete units simplifies the planning and assessment of what children are doing. Teachers can introduce an idea and provide resources for children without having to do the same activity with each child separately, and once in their group children can tackle a task in collaboration with each other rather than relying on the teacher for continual instructions.

Having pragmatic reasons for doing certain things is not a bad thing. Teachers need all the support they can get in managing the complexities of the classroom. Having children working in groups can be a very useful way of organizing at a number of levels: organizing the curriculum; organizing the routines of discipline by giving instructions to one table at a time; and organizing the uses of material from paper and pencils to artefacts.

Unfortunately the pragmatic case for group work can actually impede its true development. In order to produce the greatest benefits, group work needs to be thought through very carefully, for there is a marked distinction between the appearance and the reality.

The appearance of primary classrooms is always distinctive, but, given the differences in the shape and size of the classroom, fairly uniform. Whilst there are exceptions – you can get more children into a small space if you sit them in rows – most primary classrooms will be planned around discrete areas.

This can most simply be demonstrated by the 'before' and 'after', the 'before' being the 'old' days of 'chalk and talk':

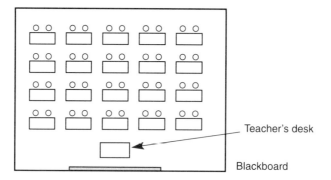

All the children face the teacher from behind their desks and are in the control of the teacher.

'After' is the creation of two things: groups and distinct areas:

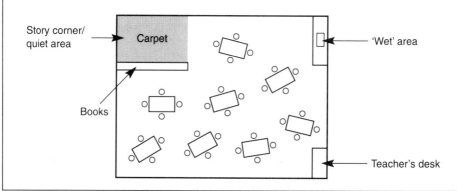

When a classroom is rearranged around the principle of developing work in groups, the greatest advantage is seen to be the possibility of collaborative work. If children learn by thinking through ideas and by discussing them, then every opportunity needs to be taken to encourage them to do so. If the children are sitting individually at their desks waiting for the next instruction of the teacher the kind of dialogue that takes place is limited to one child at a time. This can lead to practices which are very wasteful of time. There have been many teachers who are stuck behind their desks with queues of children forming up around them waiting to have their work marked, and when the children are 'getting on with work quietly' it could be that they are merely marking time.

> Children might be good teachers, but they find it difficult, like 'real' teachers, to mix instruction and friendship. Friendship makes great demands on children's social position; they find it far easier to accept the social relationship of helping others whom they do not know. Children who are helping friends find it much harder to focus upon the information.[3]

Reorganizing a classroom around groups does not in itself guarantee any fundamental change. When one looks closely at children working one can still see the same symptoms however the class is arranged. Even around a table children can work individually. Even if they are set a collaborative task, one or two children can remain isolated. Even when they are talking, children might be talking about anything other than the task in hand. The murmur of innumerable voices could be no more than idle chatter rather than the hum of a working atmosphere.[4]

Putting children into groups is not enough in itself. They need to learn how to use the opportunities that group work gives them. They need to be given tasks which demand collaboration. Think of the difference between the teacher who is constantly going round the class to mark the individual's work (rather than waiting for pupils to come to his desk) and the teacher who is making sure that a group of children understand a topic, are taking it further and are genuinely carrying out a detailed discussion of it.

> A number of studies of classrooms have looked closely at the amount of time children spend on different tasks as well as their achievements. This is termed 'time on task'. We have already noticed how easy it is to waste time, for children to sit idly, waiting for something to happen. But even time on task analyses only what children are seen to do, when they seem to be working.
> Children are good at disguises. Sitting over a piece of paper and working does not guarantee that learning is taking place. The quality of insights cannot be measured only by time.[5]

The distinction must therefore be made between groups as organizations, and collaborative working. One can arrange children in groups and yet not make them work. Once they are in groups distinct practicalities arise: there is more than one audience. One can put different children together; one can allow some to pursue their own special interests; and one can enable them to understand how differently people work with each other.

The standard size for group work is four or five. Having just three working together exposes one child to the danger of being isolated. Having more than five creates a group that is difficult to manage in terms of giving everyone a distinct task. The group then takes on a different function and almost insists on someone acting as the 'chair'. The ideal group is one in which each member has both an individual and a collective role, where each one can contribute and can do so individually.[6]

Not all work in groups, however, needs to depend on the same members. On the contrary, the membership of a group should not be static. There will be a number of occasions when groups will collaborate with each other and many chances to enable children to work with everyone else in the classroom. Besides, the organization of the room into distinct areas, like the quiet corner with a carpet for the sharing of stories, creates different group dynamics. Children need to be aware of the different levels of responsibility, when groups are to tidy up their own tables and when all the children are responsible for the tidiness and management of the classroom.

> There is one straightforward way in which one can insist on groups properly carrying out collaboration with each other, and that is to insist that there is no alternative source of information to the group itself.
>
> It is a grave temptation for the teacher to be constantly responsive, answering the individual needs expressed by upraised hands or work brought up for marking, and it is sometimes difficult for the teacher to send children away to find out for themselves. But when the teacher has enough courage – for that is what it is – to turn the children back to each other for information and for clarification, then real discussion takes place and standards are seen to rise. The emphasis is on the children learning.

Making flexible uses of groups rather than clinging to a rigid structure includes the recognition that there are many alternative methods of promoting collaborative work. We have already noted the importance of discussions with the whole class, and should not forget how much instruction depends on the teacher. This might as well be delivered to the whole class rather than repeated to group after group. There are also occasions when the teacher will insist on pairings; when, for example, one child has something to explain to another. And the whole class can be turned into one large seminar where, under the lead and direction of the teacher, everyone has a part to play.

But small groups, if they are well planned, have a distinct role. Small groups can learn for themselves and can be given a clear brief to pursue. Small groups can take part in extended discussions. Small groups can in fact be left to get on with work whilst attention is paid to others.

> In surveys of primary schools' practice it is interesting to note how often they come to the same conclusion: that teachers tend to group children as if they were forced to, as if putting them all together were enough. So there is a mismatch between the fact that children are put into gregarious settings, and the fact that they work in a solitary way.[7]

All this takes careful planning. There are three essential requirements in setting up group work:

1. That the teacher knows what concepts the children should learn. Behind every piece of knowledge is a reason for its being useful, for answering the question 'why?' A concept is more than a skill or cognitive ability. It is the crucial question that makes the task interesting. It can relate to science or maths. It is the crucial questions of character and right and wrong that underlie stories. Planning with a defined aim in mind clarifies what the teacher is trying to achieve.
2. That there should be enough substance in the set task, clearly enough explained, for the children to need to have time and discussion in order to fulfil the demand. The task should combine some things to do, to accumulate knowledge, which could include readings, with clear instructions about discussion: Can you agree why Mr A acted in this way? Was he right or wrong? Who was the kindest character? Scientific experiments can be genuine starting points for discussion: 'How can you measure the bounce of balls of different size and shape in a way that is fair and true?'

3. That there should be plenty of materials ready for the children to use. One of the clear signs of a well-planned classroom is that on the tables are all the materials – the equipment, the scissors, the paper or pens – that will be needed. The energy of the teacher can then be concentrated on the children learning rather than on organizing.

> Planning for lessons can take a variety of forms. Many teachers are encouraged to start with aims and objectives, and then work out general schemes of work, from which particular lessons will derive.
> Having a coherent vision that gives a unifying factor to all the work is important; besides, it gives an edge to lesson planning. But research on different teachers' preparations shows that the most successful forms of planning are very practical, rooted in the experience of the classroom rather than 'theoretical' and vague. Ironically, vague aims lead to narrow and pragmatic outcomes.

The teacher needs to plan well. But the difference between planning lessons for the whole class and planning lessons for groups is like that between lecturing and teaching. With groups the intention is to let them find out for themselves, to give them not every answer, but the opportunity to discover the answer. Part of the significance of children's collaborating is that they too should be able to make plans, to work out a strategy by which they will arrive at the answer or the finished product. The children will need to plan what they want to achieve, and how to achieve it, sharing the tasks and agreeing on the final presentation.

Whilst concentrating on the collaboration of children we should remind ourselves of the need for teachers to collaborate with each other too, not only to know what the children have been doing already so that there is no repetition, but to learn of the availability of other resources. It is too easy to be confined within the classroom. Groups of children can work in different places. It might be appropriate for them to work in the library or make use of resources elsewhere. But the boundaries of the classroom often lie in the imagination. Colleagues will have tried a range of approaches and know of a range of different resources. The sharing of all materials deserves to be encouraged.

> There was a time when new school buildings were built on the 'open-plan' principle. This meant that instead of having each classroom isolated within its own four walls, there would be areas that could be shared between classes, and far more flexibility in the use of space.
> Whilst cynics supposed that the principle for 'open-plan' schools was the saving of resources in the need for fewer walls, the essential idea was to allow for collaboration between two or three teachers. In the event, however, many teachers were frightened of the exposure to others, and felt safer in their own confined spaces. Cupboards, curtains and bookshelves were used creatively to close down the 'open' plans.[8]

There are three distinct stages to group work, and each one is important. First, in order to ensure constructive talk it is important that the children themselves experience planning. They must work out how they are going to carry out an experiment or how to find out the facts. They must delegate particular tasks to particular people so that everyone is involved in the collaboration.

Secondly, in the central stage of the work the children will need to be reminded of the importance of discussion; not merely sharing what they have learned but weighing its value and testing its significance.

> Success in group work depends on rewards in the shape of a teacher or someone else *outside* the group looking at the results. If a teacher is likely to select a child to present another one's work, then cooperation is more likely.[9]

The third important element in group work is the presentation of the outcome, whether this is in the form of a demonstration or written material. Groups make critical audiences for each other. They also give a sense of purpose to the outcome of the work. The constructive edge that can be given to children by wanting them to finish a task and do it well is through their sense of an audience. They are not just being given a task for its own sake, but being asked to present something new and as yet undiscovered to others. Presentations are themselves a form of learning and teaching. One need not necessarily have each group performing the same task in turns. Indeed, if one does, one should expect different outcomes, different enough to merit further discussion.

The presenting of work is important and deserves careful thought. The children need to find the best way of communicating with an audience, a way that is interesting and stimulating and, at best, can be carried out more than once. One does not wish children's achievements to be forgotten, or used only as a background decoration for a wall. The best displays, like the best presentations, continue to be used.

One of the alternative ways of presenting ideas is through drama. The reason for placing drama in this context is that one needs to remember that it depends on an audience. It is too easy to be caught up by the notion of school drama as some kind of group exercise. Improvisation, and the exploration of mime, or the attempts to think inside a character or mood, are all aimed ultimately at communicating with an audience. Sometimes this can be forgotten and the results of drama fail to achieve the intensity or interest that only the presence of an audience can provoke. If drama is seen as one form of communicating an idea to an audience it is given a sense of direction and purpose that makes it spare and to the point.

> In a reaction to formal theatrical traditions – children dressed in elaborate costumes doing their best to remember speeches – many educationists explored the psychological aspects of drama. They concentrated on the children's ability to feel their way into different roles, citing the need for empathy and strong feelings. At best children were enabled to understand their emotions better. At worst – and there were many examples of this, seen in many school halls – the children were allowed to create their own plays in an unstructured way, resulting, as often as not, in the simulation of rivalries between gangs and the subsequent fight. Conflict is, after all, the simplest material for drama.[10]

Drama is a way of engendering collaboration, planning carefully the best means of presenting ideas. In small groups everyone has the chance to join in. But physical education is another form of collaborative activity. One of its underlying purposes is to provide a means of learning how to work with others, whether in the form of dance or gymnastics or team games. There are many forms of collaboration, helping each other, trusting each other and working together. Nothing draws more attention to the necessity of making individual children work together. From the moment the children warm up in their own spaces, paying attention to the signals to start and stop, they need to be as aware of what others are doing as of what they are doing themselves.

The tasks that are most useful for small-group work, however, are those which afford opportunities not only to plan, construct and present findings, but those which demand a high degree of participation. Simulations and practical experiments are amongst the best examples. Simulations focus attention on the realities of many tasks; they are related to the world of work and remind pupils that what they are doing has an underlying purpose. Practical experiments can be pursued through the means of problem-solving, of constructing a solution to a particular task, not only on paper, but using materials.

> We know about 'invisible' children but it is a shock for us sometimes to realize just how invisible they are. When children were observed in the classroom to see whether they all escaped notice from the teachers it was clear that girls tended to be less noticed than boys. But that was not so significant. The least active child in the class had just seven contacts with the teacher in a fortnight – which showed a certain power in obscurity. The most active pupil had 123.[11]

Some of the most successful types of simulation are to do with the realities of work, whether that work is the entertainment industry or any other. We have already noted the technique of putting on a news magazine in the circumstances that would apply to a radio station – with set time limits and choices having to be made between different items of news. This kind of technique can also involve discussion, rather than action, about the choices that editors have to make about the news. If, for instance, there is room for only four items in a news bulletin, which two stories would children leave out in the following list and why?

1. A passenger aircraft crashes in Italy.
2. Two ferries collide in the Philippines.
3. A famous soccer star, like Pele, dies.
4. Ex-president Gorbachev takes up a teaching post in France.
5. President Saddam Hussein of Iraq orders all UN observers to leave the country within 24 hours.
6. The International Atomic Agency announces that Pakistan has staged an underground nuclear test.
7. The British government announces it is to stop funding the BBC World Service.
8. The European Commission announces it is to sell off all surplus beef and grain to Eastern Europe.

Each of these stories can be elaborated, but what children learn is to be aware of how the news is put together, the choices that lie behind the news, as well as different political perspectives.

Each of the news and entertainment media provides more than items to parody. They are all businesses and involve all kinds of planning, from layout to markets, from distribution to tone. Some of the businesses that children have experienced lend themselves readily to simulations. Are there strong reasons for the ways in which supermarkets are laid out? Where would a new supermarket best be built in a town? One can ask more interesting questions than what is the best route from A to B. The important factor is that there should not be just one right answer.

> Teachers' response – through praise and criticism – is very important. And so is the cooperative work of children. But many observers constantly report that little of this takes place in the classroom.
> There appears to be a gap between our knowledge of what is effective and what actually happens, between what we know and how we perform. Real effectiveness depends on the ability of the teacher to analyse what *actually* happens, especially in groups; easier said than done.[12]

Simulations often include a range of subjects and give a stimulus to background knowledge. Questions of transport policy would include aspects of history and geography as well as mathematical calculations. By presenting alternatives a group will need to work together to forge solutions. These forms of argument and consensus also underlie the making of constructional models to demonstrate solutions to set tasks. Can the group put together the design for a bridge that can be demonstrated not to collapse or to sway too much in high wind? Can they find out why bridges in different materials have been found wanting? Can they show different ways of using paper to make a construction strong enough to carry weight? Can they design a chair using paper?

Children like making models, even if they do not feel themselves to be very good at it. There are all kinds of models which need careful designing and not just making – of the movements of planets around the sun, of the display of materials in a shop, of a square in the town centre. Any idea is the starting point for children to think through and discuss their choice of solution to a real problem.

> Children are capable of working well together, but the more clues they are given as to how to do this the better. There are a number of ways in which they can be helped to work cooperatively.[13]
>
> 1.   Organizing ('You go next')
> 2.   Supporting ('Go on: try')
> 3.   Challenging ('You've got it wrong')
> 4.   Suggesting ('What about this?')
> 5.   Explaining ('It's because . . .')
> 6.   Commenting ('It looks the same')
> 7.   Finishing ('We've done it!')

When children work collaboratively they are learning extra skills. Group work can be applied to any topic and to any subject. It need not be seen as outside the normal curriculum since teachers can organize what they do in a variety of different ways. Whilst it was fashionable at one stage to think of the curriculum entirely in terms of discrete subjects, and equally fashionable at another stage to plan all lessons in terms of 'topics', the fact is that the curriculum will always be understood as a combination of discrete areas of knowledge and fundamental questions that connect different subjects. One needs a strong grasp of content to make proper judgements and must avoid the use of whatever topics happen to come into the teacher's head. The important point, once again, is the need to look for challenging questions.

> In one analysis of a number of primary schools the observers found that there were four different ways in which the curriculum was defined and delivered:
>
> 1.   Areas or subjects (e.g. maths).
> 2.   Organizational strategies (e.g. topics).
> 3.   Generic activities (e.g. writing).
> 4.   A combination of two or more.
>
> It was usual to assume that one technique was clearly superior to the others although the use of 'generic activities' was found to be particularly interesting as a means of organizing.[14]

There are, then, all kinds of reasons for putting children into groups. Sometimes one wants to stimulate children of particular abilities. Sometimes one groups children bearing gender factors in mind, so that girls have a chance to play a leading role on the computer or in technology, and so that boys have a wider range of experiences. One can group according to ages and interests and individual differences. But whatever the social aspects of group work, the main function is that group work should be demanding, should make sure that children not only talk to each other, but pursue ideas, and stimulate each other by initial disagreement. The truth about group work is that when it is successful it stimulates the individual, rather than the group.

> In organizing groups it is worth remembering that two children cleverer than a third will tend to leave out the third, slower, learner, but that one 'clever' child working with two slower ones works well.[15]

Chapter 11

The Use of Children's Experience

'I draw pictures. That's what my mum wants me to do ... my dad wants me to play snooker.'

Children first come to school with their characters already largely formed. However influential the teacher, she is not working with completely malleable material. To make the best use of his influence she needs to recognize all the other experiences that surround each pupil, especially in the early formative years.

Research study after research study consistently proves two important facts about early childhood (from birth to the age of 5). One is that the infant mind is very active and observant. And the other is that what happens to a child then has a strong influence on the subsequent years, including that child's academic attainment. Teachers need to recognize this – not in order to feel that there is nothing more that can be done, but in order to bring out the best of the previous experience.[1]

Whilst the importance of the early years is recognized, very little is done with this recognition. The education system, in all its weighty formality, receives children at the age of 5 or 6 almost as if nothing had happened previously. There are examples of attempts to help young children but they are nearly all based on trying to make up for what they lack – the 'deficit' model, based on the assumption that they lack almost everything. Few programmes to help young children treat *all* children as important, rather than only those who live in deprived conditions. Few programmes consider the part that parents play, and few programmes show an overall concern for the child from birth, let alone a continuing concern for the emotional and social development as well as the academic.

One example of an attempt to help young children is the Head Start programme in the United States. Great claims have been made for its success, and great doubts expressed about whether it really makes a difference.

Another example of an early-'intervention' programme is 'High Scope', also in the United States. Again, great claims are made for the ability of the programme to change lives.

> What makes both programmes interesting is that it appears that helping very young children as in these examples doesn't directly affect their intelligence; the methods work when they help children's social competence; they work by fostering academic intelligence indirectly, through teaching children about relationships.[2]

Children come to school with many underlying attitudes already formed, with confidence or fear, self-reliance or inhibition, with a desire to learn or suspicion, with the ability to make relationships and communicate or with sullenness and inactivity. Recognizing the past that has created them helps the teacher to make better use of all the other influences on the child that still surround him. The question is: how do we use this previous and continuing experience?

First we need to recognize all the sources or influences. These include:

- parents;
- friends and relatives;
- personal experience and observation;
- the mass media.

These sources do not always influence the individual child in the obvious ways. For example, a child might overhear a remark that his parents make to each other and misunderstand it because it was taken out of context. He might dwell on it for months. Or there could be a scene on television that lingers in the mind for years. Or one of his friends might give him exciting information that turns out to be completely wrong.

> Children can remember particular pictures on television for years. When in a large survey children were asked if they could recall anything that had frightened them, all of them remembered at least one thing, sometimes going back years; they all cited some kind of horror they had seen. Do all children who watch television therefore share some experience which disturbs them?[3]

Children cannot avoid making use of all sources of information and being influenced by them. They learn after all by witnessing, by contextual guesses, by making relationships with what they see. These different kinds of information are varied and complicated and very difficult to pin down.

There is, however, one obvious central influence: the parents. Some teachers like to explain all kinds of mischief by citing the parents. It is true that with disturbed children there is nearly always a root cause that lies in the home. But teachers are also tempted to blame too many things on the parents. Parents not only give insight into their children but can actively help the teachers. Parents need to be:

- allies;
- helpers;
- supporters.

No teacher can do a complete job without enlisting the help of parents. But this is still a new insight into the place of parents in education. It is as if parents had, from the point of view of schools, been newly invented. The reasons for this are many. The greater sense of accountability in schools with responsibilities to the 'client' group, and the growing awareness of the importance of the early years are two changes that overcome some of the older prejudices. But the older attitudes were in place because teachers considered themselves to be *in loco parentis* and professionals were not answerable to amateurs, however interested in their own children.[4]

Anecdotes about teachers' suspicion of parents abound, from notices on the school entrance – 'No parents beyond this point' – to statements by headteachers, like the one who sat at a large desk on which he rapped a ruler and intoned, 'All I ask of parents is that they should bring it to school clean and well-dressed. I shall do the rest.' But this was at a time when there was still a belief in asylums . . .[5]

At the level of the misunderstanding between teachers and parents lies a significant misapprehension about the role of the teacher. Parents and teachers have very different expectations. Parents want the schools to be disciplined, to teach morality, to instil social awareness into their children, yet they are suspicious of 'modern' methods of teaching. Teachers feel that parents do not understand the subtlety of what they are doing – teaching rather than lecturing – and they believe in the authority of each child making his or her own decision. Between the two it is easy to engender suspicion, especially if the parents have more and more control and the teachers feel misunderstood.

Some examples of parents' attitudes to school are expressed in interviews:[6]

'Let's face it: schools have relaxed discipline too much.'

'Not like when we were at school . . . I didn't understand it at first because they used to come home and say, "We've been playing." I used to think "Playing? playing? You should be doing something else; you know, reading and writing" but they didn't.'

'Well, we all try to have ambitions, don't we? . . . for our children. I want them to have a better education so they can get a better job than what I've done.'

But the parents are, in the end, allies and share the same concerns. The question is how well teachers can communicate what they are doing, how they are doing it, and what their sense of purpose is. Parents should be the most important source of understanding and it is good practice, in all senses of the word, to explain to parents what we are doing.

The fact that parents care can seem like a threat to some teachers. But teachers must show that part of their professionalism lies in understanding the kinds of demands parents make. Parents do not only say to their children, 'Go on'; they have definite ambitions for them. They want them to 'do well'. This is often expressed in pragmatic terms, but 'doing well' depends on the school. It depends on the acquisition of knowledge, and of qualifications. The uniting of a sense of purpose for each individual with the concern of the parents can create a mutual understanding that enhances the attitude of the child.

In contrast to parents, teachers in interviews tend to express rather different points of view about their ambitions for children:[7]

'Asking them to make decisions and to develop some degree of self-control and self-discipline.'

'Parents expect children to sit down and do sums and written work . . . they don't know what it is I do.'

'I've put a lot of emphasis on the right behaviour or the appropriate behaviour in certain conditions.'

Parents need to remain allies and understanders. They can help and support. The distinction between helping and supporting lies in the role that the parents can play

in the school and that which they can play at home. We have already noted how difficult it is for teachers to talk individually with each child. Having other people in the
classroom, properly supported and managed, is a potential source of great value; not
just listening to reading or making cakes, but having a role to play in talking and in
problem-solving and easing the distinction between the necessary authority of the
teacher and the pleasure of having access to an adult.

Parents have, however, an even more subtle part to play. Many like to help with
homework, and often the best schemes that use parents are those that, like many
reading programmes, give parents an almost formal role. Breaking the crude distinction between home and school involves cajoling parents into taking on a role that is
significant. Thus with all the schemes that involved parents with the teaching of
reading it was those that gave parents a formal part to play, that needed them not
just as sharers and listeners, that proved the most successful. This might be partly
because reading needs to be taught as well as learned, but also because children
perceive their parents as having a part to play in education.

> There have been many attempts to enlist parents' help in the teaching of reading. In
> reaction to the days when schools felt that they taught reading and any input from parents
> was a meddling intrusion ('If you say that my child mustn't read before coming to school
> so you can teach them properly, must I prevent my child being able to speak?'), the
> subtleties of children's reading progress are seen more and more to depend on the home.
>   But the interesting fact is that the more successful schemes are those that are most
> 'formal'; not just a casual sharing of a book, but a sense that the parent helps as well
> as sympathizes. Parents have a role in education.[8]

But the influence of parents is a more subtle matter. It is they who nurture instinctive
attitudes, who encourage or discourage curiosity and dialogue and who foster an
opinion of the school. They not only have had a formative influence on their children
through their relations with them before school but continue to influence their response
to learning.

If parents lose some of their influence as the years pass, this is replaced by that of
child's peer group. Attitude formation, through talk or overheard remarks, can come
about as much by the formation of groups who create an audience of encouragement
for all kinds of behaviour, good and bad, as by adult influence. In the psychology
of the classroom a teacher needs to be aware of the outside influence on children,
on their need for a variety of audiences, as fans or enemies or testing grounds.

> Most teachers will recognize three types of peer-group influence in the classroom. There
> are those pupils who constantly engage the teacher's attention, seeing how far they can
> go in sharing jokes; they are on the teacher's side but always a bit of a handful. There
> are those who remain quiet and unnoticed, the 'good' pupils who try to keep out of
> teacher's way. Then there are those who form gangs, not to tease the teacher but to annoy
> him, who wish to disrupt the teacher and the classroom. All three groups depend on
> mutual support, on an 'audience' for their vitality or destructiveness.[9]

Sometimes a great deal can be learned (and the children helped) just by listening
to their own experiences. This does not have to be forced on children ('You have two
minutes to tell me one thing you did over the weekend . . . No, John, you have already
told me one thing') but accepted from them when the need arises. What children
experience themselves has a very important bearing on their lives in school and this

must not be forgotten. Even in school, children spend as much time talking to each other, in the playground or at lunch, or in the pauses between lessons, as engaged in the work of the formal curriculum.

The sources of influence on children are not, however, dominated only by people and personal experience. The main media, in particular television, have a subtle and disorganized effect on the attitude and knowledge of children. Children happen to see items of news and they perceive their parents' reactions to them. In the absence of structured analysis of social events, children learn to interpret what they see in their own way. They do not like the news as much as they like other programmes, but they see it. The television is there in the background. The watching of television as a part of the living-room is a pervasive influence with children. These quotations are typical responses to the question, 'What do you do when you go home?':[10]

> 'Usually I go to the kitchen and get a biscuit, and I get the little kitten and put it on my bed and watch television ... sometimes it can be boring but sometimes it can be interesting.' (boy, 10)

> 'Well, I go and watch telly but then it's tea so I have to have tea and then after tea I go and watch telly again.' (girl, 8)

> 'Go and sit down and watch television ... but I think the telly's quite boring when the news comes on.' (girl, 9)

> 'There's lots of worrying things on the news. You can't really pick one out in particular, 'cos there's lots of things in the world.' (boy, 9)

Television presents a series of images of life in which the children, with all their ability to distinguish between fact and fantasy, see the real world.

Who explains to children the events that they see occur all over the world before they have even been taught geography? Who explains the reasons for events when they have not even begun history? Has anyone told children about how society functions? Yet they see the symbols of social unrest on television, they observe the quarrels of party politics, and the dogma of pressure groups. Long before children come to school they have on one level or another received a great deal of information, half-formed, half-interpreted and incomplete. They will have watched thousands of hours of television.

Although the difference between attentive and inattentive viewing is crucial, children not only have the capacity to analyse television but inadvertently store a great deal of information, especially visual. The visual impact of television tends to be stronger than the verbal impact for several reasons. Visual interpretations of events are more immediate and do not demand the same level of concentration. Children tend to resent programmes that demand analysis or 'hard work', which is why they prefer thrillers to documentaries. They associate the viewing of television with ease, as a way of passing the time. Thus the images they see inform their attitude at a level akin to those of the overheard remark.

> The kind of influence television can have can be illustrated by the way in which children view situation comedies or thrillers or Westerns. Children can evaluate the behaviour of different characters and can sympathize with some. But they view their heroes, or those they sympathize with, not as the characters who behave in a normal manner, but those who win, and those who are more entertaining. When one thinks of the formats and

formulae of television entertainment, where the hero has the faster gun, or is the best fighter, this is not surprising.

But what secondary messages do children receive?[11]

Children are not ignorant viewers but little is done to help them discriminate between the value or meaning of all they see. One must again make the distinction between their capacity to perform and the actual performance. Young children have to think in order to be able to make sense of their world. This doesn't stop even if they are casually watching television. They have to try to make their own sense of what they see. The ability to make genuine causal inferences develops between the ages of 3 and 4, for instance seeing the connection between a hammer and a broken cup, or a wet cup and water.[12] What peculiar connections, then, are they making of the imagery of television which gives information that is fast, varied and far away from the domestic scene? The time when it was assumed that children were pampered by ignorance, remaining in the innocence of not knowing, are long over. Piaget once tried to suggest that it took children a long time to understand the laws of conservation (e.g. putting the same amount of water into a tall or a wide cup and realizing that whatever it looks like it is the same amount of water); every year published evidence shows that infant as young as 14 months can understand them. These abilities are being applied all the time.[13]

It is not just children's intellectual abilities at a young age that are being discovered but more importantly their social abilities, their capacity to understand how people behave with each other. It is this extra dimension that they bring to school, more significant than the formal curriculum. Young children understand that other people can believe things that are false; a sophisticated notion.[14] They also understand the distinction between appearance and reality. They also know when others hold unusual or idiosyncratic beliefs about matters of taste and value. The only question left unknown is whether children develop these subtle social skills by the time they are 3 or when they are 4.

Television offers a variety of programmes and experiences and there are different ways of responding; not all programmes demand an equal amount of attention. The ways in which families watch television vary a great deal.

- Some families use television as background noise, as entertainment.
- Some families use television as a time keeper, punctuating their activities and breaking up the occasional conversation.
- Some families use television as a starting point for conversation.
- Some families use television as a means of avoiding other people.

What is clear in all the viewing habits is that it is rare to find people intent on watching and discussing a particular programme. Television tends to remain in the background.[15]

Children acquire a lot of information which is beyond our control, in terms of both content and the style in which they perceive it. One result is that children make distinctions between the kind of knowledge they acquire at home and the knowledge bound up in their formal school curriculum. They also make a distinction between styles of learning: relaxed at home and harder work at school. These differences can cause problems, since school seems to have a purpose that is all its own and ultimately irrelevant to the outside world. Too great a difference between work and play takes some of the pleasure out of both.

Teachers often realize (with trepidation) the significance of television in children's lives. They feel that they *ought* to pay more attention to general-interest programmes, or that they *should* use programmes to enhance language; but there tends to be a difference between intention and practice. Yet teachers *know* that children's experience of songs and stories is heavily dependent on television.[16]

> The most important role for parents in helping children learn begins very early and continues throughout their progress through school. It is not cajoling them or having high expectations or making great demands. It is not dependent on understanding or helping with the curriculum. The most important role for the parent is in talking to the children, in creating an experience of dialogue and shared ideas. It is the quality of the language that is essential.[17]

The most important rule about the use of television (and other sources of knowledge) is that the most effective way that children learn is by combining learning from television with other means of learning. By itself television does not have any profound intellectual effect. Combined with reading and significant input from teachers it can be very useful. Ignoring it altogether not only results in a waste of a resource but can undermine the work of the school by separating it and by letting the habit of passive attention contrast with and influence the demands of the school. In the many studies of television viewing it is shown that the heaviest viewers, who look at the screen for four hours or more every evening, find it most difficult to concentrate in the way a school demands.

The answer to this other side of life is not to try to prevent it happening but to try to help the children change their habits. Viewing changes when it is carried out critically, when children learn *how* to look at their everyday experience, rather than merely absorb it. For young children do not just learn; they learn how to learn and can be helped in doing so; we can encourage children to think about what they learn and assimilate so that thinking becomes habitual.[18]

> We often seem afraid in school to talk directly to the children about why they are learning things: what the purpose is and how we can derive more pleasure from learning. There are occasions when a slow learner who cannot grasp a concept is told why it matters, so that the dialogue moves in a different direction. That can be a breakthrough.
> It has been shown that children's awareness of their own learning can make a significant difference to their achievement.[19]

The real significance of children's previous and other experiences lies not in the isolating of cognitive ability but in all the other needs that make up an individual: cultural, psychological and natural. It is a telling fact that the most profound long-term effects on educational progress lie in the social basis of children's learning; on the relationships that they make and on their self-esteem. We need to remind ourselves of all these other motivations, so that the best can be brought out of children. Every child brings to the classroom personal views, personal interests and personal prejudices, as well as personal knowledge. The knowledge they have is drawn from the same bank that all people use; it is something that can be shared. It is knowledge based on a cultural inheritance that is unavoidable.

> The concept of 'innocence' in childhood is an interesting one and actually implies 'ignorance'. Every parent and teacher wants children to be optimistic and happy. Sometimes this leads them to try to prevent children knowing about concepts like death.

The trouble is that one cannot protect children from reality: they not only work out for themselves what is happening but are fed many reminders from many sources.

And yet we repeatedly meet teachers who say: 'But you mustn't talk about political issues in geography; children wouldn't understand them.' Children do; and they understand the difference between 'political' and 'party political' with the latter's set line of argument.[20]

The difficulties that children have in growing into an understanding of complex issues lie not in their ignorance but in the time it takes to acquire a point of view that is both subtle, fair and personal as well as being aware of other people's points of view. Every time *anyone* learns about a new issue, there are distinct stages that need to gone through.[21]

1. A single polarization of views; right and wrong.
2. Seeing there is a diversity of opinion.
3. Accepting diversity but as a temporary problem that will be overcome.
4. Seeing diversity as not a bad thing.
5. Seeing all knowledge as relative; as nothing more than individual points of view.
6. Seeing the need to come to a personal opinion.
7. Making a commitment to a point of view.
8. Experiencing the implications of this.
9. Understanding the context of this commitment.

It is the learning process that can be slow, not children's understanding.

Growing through personal prejudices to understanding is not an automatic process. The alternative to such growth is either decay into indifference or hardening into even more strongly held positions, with a 'habit' or 'set' of beliefs. Left without any challenge it is very easy for the mind to revert to the easiest of opinions or prejudices. What school can do is to encourage each individual to explore points of view as well as issues, to be willing to change, and to discover the pleasures of learning. And this cannot be done without understanding and addressing all the other experiences children have.

Chapter 12

Children's Experience of School

'Primary school should be fun and it is. Well, the fun is being with your friends around you and in the lessons you can actually see them around you.'

(girl, 10)

Teachers know how to prepare for their first day in school. They know what to anticipate and have their memories to shape what to expect. For children the first day of school can be a shock. They too will have inwardly speculated about what it will be like, but instead of memories they will have heard rumours. They will have had nothing to compare it with. It is worth examining what the first impressions are like for children, for some of these impressions remain.

School is the children's first impression of social order. In school the child discovers rules and regulations, social etiquette and social tensions, and a world more complex than the orderly relationships between adults and infants. Of course there are often many stages on the way to school: the crèche, the kindergarten, the playgroup and the nursery. Whilst these have some similarities in social organization, a school is different. Its ethos is that of work; it conveys distinct levels of demand.

Pupils' experience of school can often be disappointing, and they often look back on it, having left, not with a sense of what they are missing but with a sense of how much better it could have been. This sense of disillusionment grows as pupils grow older; motivation and positive attitudes steadily diminish. In one survey of 11- and 13-year-olds it was revealed that half of them were bored in some lessons. They also said that a quarter of their teachers were easily satisfied with their work. To this was added the observation that they felt they were praised only if they worked hard. They were not really judged by the results of their work.

Pupils value schools in which they are encouraged to gain independence, and where the curriculum had relevance to their future work.[1]

From the child's point of view the school contains two things: seriousness (often for reasons that are obscure); and the playfulness of being with friends. The school is a social centre and the testing ground for peer groups. It is the place that children look forward to (or dread) in order to be with their friends. The impression they receive is on more than one level: the order imposed by authority; the threat presented by older children; and the comfort and security provided by their own classmates.[2]

Children's experience of school depends largely on the way in which they understand it; on whether they feel attuned to and understand its purpose. The problem for many children is that the purpose of school remains obscure. Instead of being clearly presented to children the purpose of school is left for them to guess at. They consistently come to the conclusion that they are in school to prepare them for jobs. This leads them to assume that each successive stage of school is more important than the one before – the nearer employment, the more significant. It also explains some subsequent disillusionment. What do the many children who do not do well, including those who are unemployed, think of school, if there was only one serious purpose in it?[3]

> The way in which school is remembered by adults is often telling. These combine long hours in the classroom where there is a sense of security, the long hours of playing games with friends, and in contrast the moments of intense excitement and moments of terror. Intense moments and unthreatening hours. Perhaps the reason that people remember childhood so nostalgically is that they realize that the terror was restricted to moments rather than pervading larger areas of time.

It is very important for a school to share its sense of purpose with the children. The children will accept their own experience of school in such a way that it is easy for us as teachers to be unaware of any misunderstanding. After all, the children obey the rules, and believe in their necessity. They recognize the authority of the teacher and they acknowledge the need to do what is asked of them; not to misbehave, or to do the work cards. But the acceptance of what goes on is not the same as understanding it, and there are different perceptions of school between adults and children.[4] When children are asked about their experience of school they reveal their perception of school as a place where they must do whatever tasks the teachers set them, whatever the purpose. They accept that they must do certain subjects, some of which are more important than others, without knowing why. They are very aware, too, of all the routine work they do: 'working', 'problem-solving', 'work sheets', 'copying cards out'. When you ask a child what she's doing she will tend to say something laconic like working on 'topics', not out of a reluctance to explain but because, as the task set by the teacher, it defines its own purpose.

> It is very easy to take for granted that all the teachers say is understood by the children. There are certain misunderstandings that can last for years; this can last until the children reveal in their writing how well they listened with so little understanding: 'Our Father which chart in Heaven. Harold be thy name. Lead us not into Thames Station. Deliver us from Eagle . . . etc.'

Part of the security of school for children lies in its very boredom: the amount of time spent waiting, and the amount of time spent doing routine work. There is a difference between their experience of the result of the collective ('It's kind of like a family in the hall. We are all together in there' (boy, 10)) and being caught up in an individual task, passing time ('In the morning you get there, you're set your work, and you can go; 'Ah finish it by break' (girl, 11)).

Children's experience of school is both private and collective: their inner thoughts and day-dreams and the need to follow rules and procedures. The external and public experience of school is of rules and authority. For this reason children invariably think that school is there to serve the teachers rather than them. Clearly this is contrary to the purpose of schools; but children feel this strongly and consistently. They perceive all the teachers' effort as being for their own sake and their own convenience. This has a significant effect on children's overall views of teachers.[5]

> One clear indication of the tension between the formal system of school and the children's personal reaction to their own position is the change that comes over many of them at the age of 8.
>   This is when they learn the distinction between effort and achievement and begin to label each other and themselves as 'clever' or 'stupid'. This is when some of them (often girls) decide *not* to continue making an effort.

Children not only accept the authority of the professional role of teachers but expect it. They expect the teacher, within the professional role, to be human, to be able to share a joke, and to show an interest in children. And they expect the teacher to be able to 'explain'.[6]

Children invariably have both positive and negative experiences of teachers. They come across those who are liable to be too human, to lose their tempers or to show favouritism. They experience those who show no interest in children outside the classroom and are indifferent to incidents of bullying. They undergo those who do not bother to explain, or who set nothing more than routine work.[7]

> From the teacher's point of view the difference between those who are 'child-centred', i.e. imparting the necessary skills and abilities to children so that they can direct their own learning, and those who are 'curriculum-centred', i.e. imparting a body of knowledge, is great. For the children it is not easy to detect those who take on the difficult task of being responsible for the 'whole child'. The irony is that children respect teachers more for *knowing* than as people.

Underlying the individual differences of personality is the overall role of the teacher. Children expect teachers to be authoritative, to impose order and to make decisions. It is therefore very easy for teachers to accept this as the limit of their role, when it is only the basis of it. Relationships can be made differently in extra-curricular activities and the tone of communication can be very different given the time and the right setting. This reinforces the realization that once back in the formal setting of school 'normal' relations are again adhered to. But they are also enhanced. Very young children need relationships with adults. So do children in school.

The experiences that children would like are a balance of the formal and informal. Pure informality, the desire for close relationships, can lead to disaster, but recognizing personal interest and commitment makes a lasting impression on children's perceptions of school and its links to their inner lives.[8]

> Children's experience of books often suggests a rather peculiar view of the world. This is also true of the way that the classroom is presented to them, with their own work on display rather than examples of adult painting and literature, and with an air of studied innocence. It is as if teachers instinctively want to create an environment that is especially child-centred, and different from the outside world with special corners for special activities. Sometimes the world of the classroom contains more than one interpretation: 'news time' is 'real' but pink elephants are allowed into the books on mathematics.[9]

One of the ways in which children can experience a different side to teachers is in extra-curricular activities. Often these are of a sporting nature and organized by men. Generally only a small proportion of teachers are employed in these activities and they are rarely organized by the pupils themselves. Many children say that they would participate far more if they were asked to. Their favourite phrase seems to be 'I wasn't asked.' Those children who do participate tend to be those who believe in the ethos of the school. 'Dropping out' can extend to a variety of pleasures outside school as well as in.

If teachers are the people who are there to set tasks they are also the people responsible for all the torrents of words that pour over children. For every sentence that a child will form, he will hear hundreds, both of information and instruction. The school culture is one of listening, and children are expected to listen with attention, all the time. This type of listening is different both from taking part in a conversation and from hearing the radio and television. Schools can be noisy places but for many individuals in them there are vast silences.

> Teachers tend to assume that children can guess background meanings when giving instructions. Children need to learn how to interpret what teachers say. Often the talk is oblique. 'Do you remember the address?' means 'Please give it to me.' 'Could you open the door?' means 'Do it!'

Children also experience the demarcation between work and play for the first time when they enter school. They are introduced into a culture which restricts choices and opportunities, which takes away rather than gives a chance for decision-making on the solving of problems. The active involvement in play is often replaced by a greater passivity, responding to instructions and completing set tasks. Work therefore can easily be associated with the negative, on what is carried out reluctantly. The pleasures of curiosity and exploration are natural in young children, which is why we see them working hard, as it were, at their play.

> Children's growing awareness of the definitions of work and play derives from their experience. Work doesn't simply replace play. It surrounds it and can be part of it. But gradually children perceive how teachers define play:[10]
>
> * Play is seen as a prelude to work or a reward for work.
> * Play can interfere with work, but not vice versa.
> * Work is what is done for the teacher.
> * Teachers work rather than play.
> * Work is done in the mornings, play in the afternoon.
> * The teacher defines when work is completed and when children are allowed to play.

Young children do not only experience the distinctions between work and play. They also learn to define play in a definite way. 'Doing things' or 'having fun', for instance, are not defined as play. Play is associated with activities that involve pretending and fantasy, which centre around a theme and contain elements of drama or of rules. Children recognize the 'play' elements in their textbook not as a lightness of touch but as a concession to fantasy, not as a different style of learning but as pieces of deliberate make-believe.

Schools inadvertently impose some arbitrary definitions of the curriculum, as something that is to be taken as a set task and that is important for its own sake. In some schools children find themselves doing 'topics' from which they derive history, geography and other subjects. In others they will have their work defined by tasks;

are they working together on writing, constructing something or on trying to remember things? The variety of subject matter is considerable and even in the more centrally imposed curriculum dependent on the interests and personality of the teacher. It has to be. Otherwise the subject given out to the children is autonomous and arbitrary. The problem is that from the children's point of view some subjects at least will hold no particular interest.

> Many people talk about 'child-centred' models of education, but it is very hard to detect these in practice. Studies of schools which include children's experiences and observation of teaching methods always find that in reality most schools are 'teacher-centred'. From the children's point of view, schools exist for the sake of teachers rather than themselves. This is partly because teachers let children fill in all background meanings, like behaviour codes, except in the case of the curriculum when children are assumed to know nothing.[11]

The school continues to define and impose its work. There are outcomes in assessments and examinations. For many children the expectations seem too high; the fact is that many children do not understand them, but they do know what is expected of them. Their capacity is high but rarely fulfilled. Let us take two examples.

The first is history. Children from the age of 6 are capable of a mature historical sense; they apply their awareness of mutability to a grasp of facts. And yet they are often taught on the assumption that they know little, but have the ability to 'empathize'. This means that they are expected to demonstrate feats of the imagination without any facts on which to base them. They are offered a mixture of historiography, themes and obscurities that stands little chance of being interesting. Children do not find 'familiar' material easier than what is new to them. Nor do they rely entirely on their contextual knowledge. They can understand the facts, the story and the relevance of history and yet are rarely called upon to do so.[12]

> Motivation is a difficult concept, for it depends on so many factors. Many children are motivated *not* to learn; they wish to remain 'invisible', building their security on passivity, inscrutability, boredom and unresponsiveness.
>   Motivation also derives from the kind of interest and encouragement shown by parents.
>   Motivation can be pragmatic (doing well for the teacher's sake, or for an exam), as well as being an inner drive (learning for its own sake).
>   Given what have been called 'hygiene factors' (i.e. the basic conditions of security, warmth, respect and confidence), all children can develop motivation: and that does make a difference.[13]

The second example is science. What is told to children about science is often the over-simplified version of theories which they have difficulty in applying to what they know. Children therefore work out their own solutions to problems, making their own guesses at how, for example, electric circuits work. This is because they are often offered blurred representations of the truth rather than clear experiments and demonstrations, and generalizations in place of a thorough exploration of what is familiar. Thus children begin to think of science (or maths) as a series of impossible rules, a coded system to which they have no access. Once this happens they cease to apply their minds.[14]

The problem for children is that such a gap between their understanding and what is presented to them can be found for some in part of the curriculum and for others in the whole of it. School then is an essentially bewildering place and the only part of the experience that begins to make sense is that which takes place outside the classroom. When school becomes an alien culture, an alternative culture is set up in the peer group and a different set of values defined. That is when we encounter the extraordinary phenomenon of children not wanting to learn and even believing that this is fashionable.[15]

> As mentioned at the end of Chapter 8, some secondary school teachers were asked to increase the amount of praise they gave; not general praise, but privately – individual praise. They were also asked to restrict their reprimands to individuals privately. The result of this change in style of discipline was a 20 per cent improvement in academic achievement.[16]

The problem for children is that the language of school can appear to be little more than jargon, a kind of alien culture. As we have noted, this can come about because of the clash between the language of home and the expectations of school. But this happens to some degree to all pupils. The way they choose their favourite and least favourite subjects is instructive. They are influenced as much by chance experience and a particular teacher as they are by their particular interest and capacity. And there are some subjects they refuse to believe they are ever capable of understanding until, years later perhaps, they find that they are more gifted than they had realized. Sometimes children instinctively specialize, to have room to breathe in a subject, and to hide from demands.

> The 'hidden curriculum' is a term used to describe two phenomena in schools. The first is the informal learning that takes place as opposed to the subject matter being presented – expectations about behaviour, for example.
>   The second is the actual message that the school is giving as opposed to its intended message – for example, that all teachers are committed to motivating individual children but the same children know no one has any time for them. The problem with the notion of the 'hidden' curriculum is that when you take a close look at any school it is not really hidden. We all know that more complex things take place than the stated intention.[17]

In all these different experiences there are still the good moments and they are not only those outside the classroom, like talking to friends or playing in the playground. Each pupil will have favourite days (or days he or she dreads) depending on the timetable, days which encompass all the 'hard' lessons or a subject that 'puts one off the whole day'. For the experience of school varies a great deal for the children. The classroom might be 'safe' and there might be excitements to anticipate, but they are never fully secure, as long as some lessons are pervaded with the difficult, the demanding or embarrassing. Some children dread school much of the time and nothing prevents good work more successfully than fear.

> Certain observations made in one study of classrooms should give us pause for thought. The predominant feature in primary schools seemed to be writing practice. There was great emphasis on quantity and on simple punctuation. Most teacher–pupil exchanges were concerned with spelling.
>   No wonder children associate teachers with phrases like 'Do it again' and 'Carry on where you left off.'[18]

Children in all their curiosity begin to perceive schools as places which depend upon control, on order. Either this control can be imposed on the pupils or a system can be mutually agreed. In many cases children experience arbitrary controls, inflexible rules, and order through the threat of punishment.

This is not the same as agreed values and standards. Teachers do not always have time to create mutually agreed contracts, sharing what is expected as well as those things to which children can feel entitled. This sense of a school as an imposed order tends to lead children to think of society in the same way. A school is, in a way, a miniature version of society as a whole, and the first social system children experience. Imagine how they see the hierarchy, with the teachers controlling them, the head controlling teachers and the governors controlling the head. The whole system depends on accepting authority but the authority is always being tested.

> The experience of childhood is similar in essence all over the world although there are variations from culture to culture between expectations and the stage at which the child is deemed an adult. The experience of childhood and the concept of childhood have changed over the years.
>
> One writer argues that there is a great contrast between the Middle Ages and the present day, between a time when people were full of unbridled passions, including piety as well as violence, and a later time of calculation, moderation and self-control. He suggests that instincts are no longer given free rein but are acted out vicariously as on films. The result is that the concept of 'shame' (doing some things privately rather than openly) has created a barrier between adults and children so that the latter are kept from the knowledge of many things, ostensibly to preserve their innocence. One wonders whether this concept of childhood will again disappear.[19]

Children's experience of school is therefore a complicated one. It is something that a sensitive teacher needs to take into account, for the experience of school can easily be negative and lack purpose. This undermines the achievements of the pupil and the success of the teacher. How can one draw up a picture of the school as any child would experience it?

Schools consist of three obvious constituents: the staff; the children; and the environment. All three play a part, before one explores the more complex matters of ethos and expectation, atmosphere and success. Each part is felt personally by the child.

Let us look at the environment. Children react to their surroundings and are sensitive to them. They are never indifferent to them and even respond to the wind. They have their favourite places and the corners that they dread. The look of the school matters, both as a place of welcome and as a place in which children appreciate that everyone cares about the school. It is worthwhile to look at the school as if one had not seen anything like it before. What are the hidden messages? Is it bleak? Is it tatty? Is it a place where one would want to spend time? The questions can be answered; if we approach them with a fresh eye for detail the answers might be surprising. It is easy to slip into a tired environment like an old shoe. There is no money and investment. Nothing symbolizes more immediately what a school stands for than its appearance; and this includes the signs. 'NO' is how so many of them begin.

What children need

- Children like classrooms that are full of things to do.
- Children like work that has a sense of purpose.
- Children like producing work that has an audience and is not just for the teacher.
- Children like to use what they have learned.
- Children like being given tasks that are demanding and stimulating.
- Children like work that is relevant to them and their interests.
- What children like is what they need.

Children actually like to be in a place that looks 'normal', that has real furniture and real pictures. They like places which are private and therefore, in most schools, difficult to find, like a corner in the library or a space outside the headteacher's study. It is difficult to change the architecture of a school, and rare to have the privilege of working on the design of a new school. But we can nevertheless be sensitive to how the school presents itself to children.

> There are a number of procedures that teachers undertake that do not motivate children and a number which do. Those that do not succeed are:
>
> * low marks;
> * being told off in front of the whole class;
> * detentions;
> * lines.
>
> Those that succeed include:
>
> * talking about work;
> * private praise;
> * showing interest in work;
> * the involvement of parents;
> * rewards.

We can also be sensitive to the way in which children experience teachers. Firmness, fairness balanced by responsiveness – we know how important they are. But we also know that children need to learn to perceive these values and to see that professional integrity is part of a fully rounded person – with interests and excitements as well as a sense of duty. Some of the everyday weapons of superiority such as rudeness or sarcasm ('Come here, boy; so you think you're clever?') do not work as well as politeness.

For many children teachers remain distant and separate because they show little interest in the children. They can do their job, but once outside the classroom all contact seems to end. A school clearly consists of more than lessons. One of the factors that makes school both significant and difficult for some lies in the peer-group relations, including bullying. Here children want to feel that teachers are interested, concerned and responsive.

One of the ways to elicit the children's commitment to the school as a whole lies in the drawing up of contracts: clearly stated agreements about what is expected of each individual in a community. More is then learned about experience and from experience than 'facts'.

> A contract can take any number of forms. It can be the published statement of the school's intentions, shared with parents and others, or a code of behaviours to be followed.
> What makes a contract work is the *shared* drafting, and the sense of what it means to *everyone* involved. Anyone can produce a mission statement. But it has meaning only to those who helped draw it up. The commitment to a series of statements is strong in those who signed it – and such a statement is a potential reminder of expectations at all times.

Chapter 13

Individual Differences

I'm good but I'm not absolutely perfect. I think there are people in the class who are better than me.'

(girl,12)

A teacher needs to deal with as many different personalities as there are children in the classroom; and each one needs a subtly different kind of attention. At one level that might seem both obvious and easy. Each human being is unique and we are accustomed to meet (or observe) many people. But the individuals in our classroom depend on us and the relationship we have with them needs to take into account the fact of their individuality.

> It is sometimes easy to judge children according to what are called 'common-sense' categories of success or failure based simply on home background/parental attitudes, ability and conscientiousness. But beyond this each child has not only his or her own learning style but an individual style of motivation. Teachers can detect what interests individual children: a sense of personal responsibility, or independence, or different social relationships.[1]

It is impossible to do more than acknowledge the fact of individual difference, for whether we like it or not we characterize people as different types; we classify them according to their background, knowledge or personality. We make mental typologies, starting from good or bad, whether we like them or not, as an instinctive way of understanding others. The study of personality depends on making distinctions between opposite characteristics. There are measurements and personality tests of different 'types' between those who are 'extrovert' or 'introvert', between 'convergent' or 'divergent' thinkers.[2] The study of individual differences is really a search for common characteristics by which we can understand how people perform.

Given so many psychological tests, the question remains: what does a teacher need to know about the pupils in a class? Most of the knowledge that teachers possess is instinctive. They note the reactions of different children to different treatment; they assume certain prejudices towards different children. But they rarely have the chance to analyse the children in their class. Having a general prejudice or expectation is not enough.

What needs to be known?

> Talking about individual children, as teachers sometimes do with each other in the staff-room, can come about as a result of exasperation – 'Not him again!' And it can remain on the level of gossip or anecdote, exchanging views on a particular child and his family, or telling the often foolish things someone has done.
>
> Is it fair to observe that one rarely finds information being shared which might help another teacher in bringing out the best in a pupil?
>
> Is it fair to suggest that most of the stories shared are about negative rather than positive qualities?

The most common kind of knowledge that a teacher possesses about an individual child is of the home background. Up to a point this is inevitable. Difficulties or disorders in the classroom with particular children are inevitably traced to the experiences received at home. This kind of awareness might explain the behaviour of a child. But does it actually help the teacher in dealing with the problem?

> The Converger and the Diverger: The Converger likes physical science or classics, likes technical and mechanical things, and tends to hold conventional, safe attitudes. The Diverger likes open-ended tests, prefers the arts and biology and tends to hold unconventional attitudes. Are these the inhibited and the uninhibited? Do these relate to 'Sylbs and Sylfs'? – those who are syllabus based and those who are syllabus free?[3]

An awareness of emotional difficulties can make the teacher more sensitive to the child, but it does not by itself construct a plan or suggest a development. Nor does knowledge of personality. A pupil has a particular characteristic. He is aggressive. She is shy. The question is: what can one do about it? and to what extent does personality interfere with, or aid, learning?

There are two levels of psychology of which teachers need to be aware. One is unavoidable. The other is often ignored.

Psychology unavoidably enters the management of the classroom. Teachers must know how to treat individual children; and there is great skill and subtlety in knowing when to confront or when to ignore certain behaviour, when to cajole and when to praise. The fact that this might appear unsystematic and not easily explained takes nothing away from the insight which is demonstrated by the teacher. Once a teacher has learned to cope it is this side of teaching that develops in interest. *Why* do people behave as they do?

> Teachers are strongly influenced by what previous knowledge they possess about children. If they are told that a particular child is 'very bright' they will treat that child in such a way that she becomes so; and even if she is not really 'bright' the teacher will continue to believe she is.
>
> But this is true of one person's reactions; someone's faults will always be more interesting – what they say will appear more significant than it is.
>
> If a particular speaker is described as either 'warm' or 'cold' before giving a talk, the audience will react according to its expectation.
>
> The 'Pygmalion effect' means not only that people label each other, but that the labelling affects one person's perception and the other's performance.[4]

Teachers are often afraid of 'labelling' children, of imposing prejudice on a particular child. It is something difficult to avoid, even if we cannot summarize a view in a few choice words. The only true way of avoiding any kind of prior expectation or prejudice – any kind of stereotype, in fact – is by having such a knowledge of the individual that any short summary becomes impossible. The only antidote to prejudice is knowledge.

But what kind of knowledge? Knowledge of personality when so many tests try to simplify people into types? Knowledge of the individual as explored in psychoanalysis? The teacher hasn't time.

The kind of knowledge that helps teachers more than any other in their understanding of individual pupils is the knowledge of different styles of learning. It is the kind of knowledge that is constructive and can be shared. This is the knowledge that is often ignored.

> When one discusses with experienced teachers the development of their ideas over a number of years it is interesting to observe shifts of interest. At the start of their career they are often immersed in their subject, in the content of the curriculum. As they get older this kind of interest is often replaced by a more holistic view of learning, in puzzling out what makes the difference between one child's grasp of a concept and another one's failure to understand it. Teaching itself becomes more interesting.

Underlying different learning styles is the fact that young children are capable of very complex tasks. This fact needs constant reassertion as it is continually reinforced by research. And yet the combined weights of mythology and Piaget still stress the incapacity of young children as if they were not able to grasp complex concepts or social realities. Like adults they do not necessarily want to know, or take a close interest, but any learning that adults undertake can be managed by children.

Let us take the example of a typical secondary classroom task in which young children are presented with two conflicting hypotheses and asked to find a test that will examine them against each other empirically. Children of 6 might not be able to do so but they can explain the logic of such a test, sharing their awareness of the distinction between 'evidence' and a hypothetical belief. This implies insight into different types of endeavour, into the difference between false evidence and truth and a mastery of creating conditions to explore truth further.[5]

> Different pupils demonstrate different learning styles. One study grouped pupils under four types:
>
> - attention seekers;
> - intermittent workers;
> - solitary workers; and
> - quiet collaborators.
>
> The first two groups need the most attention from the teacher. It can be tempting, sometimes, to let the others just carry on by themselves so that the demands of attention seekers can be met.[6]

Young children can do so many things, and yet we know that many do not actually bother. This can be because we do not make demands on them. It can also come about because children often lack motivation. What they are presented with seems to lack purpose or is a matter of routine. They have no strong urge to tackle an issue.[7]

Motivation is not a simple matter of some children wanting to learn all the time and others having no such urge. Every child has some kind of motivation to learn something – even if this is not what we feel is appropriate. Motivation is a matter of self-belief as well as curiosity. It is dependent on other people's expectations as well as their own capacity.

Many teachers puzzle over why it is that some children lose their natural zest for learning. We have already acknowledged the young child's need to learn, and the curiosity children can bring with them to school. But changes tend to occur in their approach to work whilst they are at primary school; gradually they learn that they have more ability (or interest) in one subject than another or they begin to associate learning with drudgery.

> The stage at which children become more aware of both their own and other children's capacities, and when they either become more consciously competitive or back away from challenge, is around the age of 8. This is of course a subtle and often hidden change, and it does not affect all children in the same way. But they themselves tend to dissociate hard work and success and use labels to characterize themselves and each other. For some, learning has already lost the zest.[8]

Motivation to learn rests on self-belief. Everything is possible to those who do not question this. Any task can be tackled and any new subject understood. The relationship between self-confidence and academic achievement is a very close one. As children get older they have an increasingly accurate impression of their own abilities. This is not altogether a positive thing. Even if they are wrong to have such overwhelming confidence in their own abilities as compared to those of others, this kind of confidence can sustain them and bring out better performances than would be possible if they started by assuming that they cannot do anything.[9]

Self-confidence is highly affected by the way in which children compare themselves to others. It can be increased or diminished by the right or wrong conditions. If children observe others with low self-confidence gradually improving it gives a definite encouragement to their own work. On the other hand, if children merely observe other children with high self-confidence behaving confidently it diminishes them.[10]

Children are bound to compare their own characteristics to those of others and this includes not only personalities and interests but abilities. Perhaps competition is the wrong word for their mounting sense that some are better than others. They are, after all, recognizing the differences in status or fame between people all over the world. There is a mounting sense of contrast in rewards and a mounting sense that sheer hard work or desire is not enough to guarantee success. The sad fact of the matter is that children's ratings of their intellectual ability decline as they grow older.[11] They replace their judgement of themselves based on their effort and mastery of certain tasks with more objective information based on their comparison of themselves with others.[12]

> It is possible for teachers deliberately to raise expectations in their pupils by assuming their ability. We have noted that pre-formed labels create a kind of self-fulfilling prophecy. But it is also possible for teachers to convince themselves that their pupils can go far beyond some set criteria of the 'next' phase. No technique succeeds so well in teaching children a new concept than that of jumping to one that is more difficult and more demanding, and then returning to the concept that now looks comparatively easy. It does not matter if these explorations beyond the next stage are not fully successful. Often they will not be, first time.[13]

We have to decide whether children lose motivation because they have a more realistic, more objective, sense of themselves compared to others. On the one hand, children need the stimulation of the clever and curious to raise their own standards. Low expectations lead to poor results. On the other hand, children can be diminished by the easy success of others in their peer group. It is certain that children of 7 or so naturally and almost gleefully over-estimate their abilities; by 11 they have become self-analytical against objective measures. They tend to rate themselves lower when compared to their classmates rather than to children in general. This is the clue to what a teacher can do to improve the way children work.

Before we look at the motivation of peer groups let us remind ourselves that self-confidence and motivation are not some kind of universal commodity. Every individual child has self-confidence in one thing – even if it is not productive. Every child is motivated to learn at least one thing – even if it's something we would rather they did not. It is important to discover what interests each individual child; what kind of hobbies or what kind of subject. There will always be a territory which is no longer neutral; where a child feels with intensity and personal ownership. This discovery is a starting point even in the most unwilling learning. Once the achievement of carrying out a demanding task has been tasted, the pupil will want to try it again.

> Every child goes through a phase of collecting things – even lists. It can range from dolls to stamps, from facts about football stars to badges. This is in itself a starting point for the organization of memory, or categories, for a way of showing a sense of command over things, of demonstrating that not everything is random.
> The same capacity to spend hours on one thing can be used, given the motivation, on materials that are shared in the classroom.[14]

Children possess the capacity to learn. But they do not all learn in the same way. Understanding how they learn is a central insight for the teacher. This is a complex subject, all people being different and difficult to understand. But fortunately, as in so many contrasts of character, there are some fundamental distinctions to be made.

The first division is between those children who are *adapters* and those who are *innovators*. In approaching and solving a problem the *adapters* will try to understand the given term of reference and work out logically what the next step should be. The *innovator* will try to look at the problem in a new way, standing back from it and seeing whether there is a completely different solution, hoping for insight rather than working out a defined approach. Children who favour one approach over the other can be helped to learn faster by having materials adapted for them – *if* the teacher can diagnose the learning style. The teacher needs to know when to draw attention to the logical technique and when to the underlying significant points.[15]

At the heart of understanding different learning styles are two pairs of alternatives, like two dimensions. The first is the distinction between a *holistic* and an *analytical* approach, and the second between a *verbal* and an *imagistic* style.

- Do the children see the overall problem and then look at the details or do they piece each bit together bit by bit?
- Do the children think more easily in words or in images?[16]

All children fit somewhere on a two-dimensional grid made up from both:

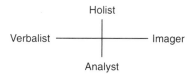

At the same time as there are those differences in learning there are also differences in children's intentions. The relationship is a close one. Some children show a difference between 'deep' or 'surface' learning; either trying to go to the root of the problem or hoping that the solution will be clear and obvious.[17] Learning style includes motivation. It depends on the amount as well as the type of effort. There is a big difference between the real grasp of the material and a more superficial acquaintance with it, often associated with learning.

> Think about all the opposites or alternatives that help one understand the differences between one child's learning and another.[18]
>
> • Learning styles v. cognitive styles
> • Learning styles v. strategies
> • Holistic v. Analytic
> • Holistic v. Serialistic
> • Field dependent v. Independent
> • Impulsive v. Reflective
> • Convergent v. Divergent
> • Levelling v. Sharpening
> • Verbalistic v. Imagistic

A teacher will always be sensitive to the individual differences of each pupil; but this includes recognition of general characteristics as well as the innumerable idiosyncrasies of personality. One can observe whether a child likes to be an independent learner, or likes to collaborate. One can see when children want to be dependent on other people, especially the teacher, and when they avoid such dependency. One can also see if their instinct is to participate in common activities or whether they remain motivated by an inner sense of competition.

> Some of the differences between children are also a matter of gender. There is a tendency for boys to be more active, to ask more questions, to receive more praise, to be more confident, to talk more. Girls tend to have less confidence, be less physically boisterous, be more willing to fit in, and be 'teacher's pet'. Even very young children show different behaviours: 4-year-olds separated from mothers show different attitudes, boys being aggressive, assertive and attention-seeking and girls being compliant, accepting and dependent.[19]

Some children learn just to meet and overcome the next, short-term problem. Others have more complex long-term goals. Some children work in a spontaneous way, never quite knowing how or why they are doing something. Others need to be far more systematic.

We can discover more about the individual characteristics of learning styles by fitting children into yet another (overlapping) matrix. Some children are far better at understanding concrete tasks; others prefer abstract thinking about the matter rather than doing it. Some children reflect when they observe, stand back from the task and think about it; others become actively involved, their observation being more like an experiment.[20] From these different approaches we begin to define:

- doers;
- brainstormers;
- theorists; and
- turners of theory into action.

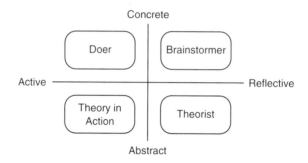

Some children are active, whilst others are passive. Some go deep; others remain on the surface.

There are some implied consequences of this:

e.g. Deep and active = someone who criticizes and tries to justify
Deep and passive = someone who tries to understand the overall argument
Surface and active = someone who merely describes
Surface and passive = someone who has a haphazard response to the problem
Deep or surface as necessary = these are the ones who get high marks.[21]

Observe the children in the class. Some will be impulsive and unsystematic. Some will try to work out a problem logically and carefully. Some will never want to make a decision. Some children reproduce what they are given, whilst others understand the implicit meanings. Uniting and dividing their different approaches is the question not only of *how* they learn but the intensity with which they do so. Do they really want to understand or do they think it enough to seem busy? Do they want to know the *reason* for things or accumulate facts? This is where styles of learning are related to motivation. Wanting to learn is clearly influenced by rewards; those things that are easier to learn seem more rewarding, provided this term 'easier' means the satisfaction that comes from achievement.

The difference between styles of learning can be encapsulated as essentially that between 'surface' and 'deep' approaches. 'Deep' learners search for meaning and explanation. 'Surface' learners try to memorize distinct parts.

There are also extreme forms of both approaches. 'Surface' learners can get so caught up in details that they fail to see any relationship between them. 'Deep' learners, on the other hand can, in their desire for meaning, jump to superficial conclusions.[22]

All pupils like some subjects more than others. They are normally aware that this depends on passing and ephemeral variables, like teachers. But it also has a lot to do with the relationship between the learning style and the way the subject is presented. There is a tendency for some subjects to be taught in a certain way; history as surface, as serial, for instance? Maths as something for the passive receiver? Science as deep and abstract? Any subject can be taught in a way that captures the ability and motivation of each pupil.

It is a difficult but constructive task to draw a distinction between styles or types of learning and the amount of effort and ability. It is too easy (and unrewarding) merely to divide pupils into 'clever' or 'stupid'. That might be an individual difference but not very rewarding to the teacher. There are the hard workers and those who are lazy. There are those who keep so quiet that one does not notice. The good teacher knows that each individual has a personal way of working that can be encouraged. That depends on the high expectations and on the knowledge of the teacher.

There are many different ways of categorizing types of learning, dividing people into one type or another. These are not labels if they are associated with something active, like learning, rather than something passive like personality. They are insights into ways in which children can be helped.

> Another typology of learning. Does this also fit?
> There are two different *motivations*:[23]
>
> * concerned with conclusions;
> * describing enough facts;
>
> and two different *means*:
>
> * detailed;
> * mentioning.
>
> So we have those who are:
>
> * conclusion orientated + detailed (e.g. summaries + evidence);
> * conclusion orientated + mentioning;
> * description + detached;
> * description + mentioning.

Underlying most of the distinctions to be made in terms of learning style is the one between those who are 'holistic' and those who are 'atomistic', between those who want to understand something new by having an overview and those who attend to every detail. The 'holistic' learner wants to be able to summarize the essential points and try to probe beneath the surface. The 'atomistic' learner will want to follow the details, the step-by-step logic of the arguments. Perhaps the one can be called a generalized thinker, wanting all materials to fit together and excluding those details that don't. The other is more methodical and does not always see the connection between things.

These distinctions matter, because understanding them enables the teacher to adapt materials to the learner. Everyone learns best when presented with materials that match his or her own style. For example, think of the subjects *you* are good at, and those you wish to avoid.

It is not only important to see the benefits of understanding individual learning styles. Ignoring them can cause severe problems. There are some children who will, for example, prefer to approach writing by drafting and re-drafting, by planning the whole structure and then adapting. Others will want to go through the logic of their piece bit by bit, agonizing over every sentence but not thereafter changing it.[24]

> There are many differences between children according to gender. The question is whether these are superficial or profound. Boys are observed to be more physical, playing

with trucks and climbing, whilst girls play at quieter games like housekeeping. We also know that associations of jobs with gender start very early: doctors are male, nurses are female in stereotypes, even if not in real life. We also know that boys demand more attention and girls can be more invisible, and the boys tend to be physical bullies and girls more adept at teasing. All these things need to be taken into account, but from the teachers' point of view there are factors that need to be understood to make sure there is equality of opportunity – in computing, science and games.

Teachers tend to *assume* girls are better at languages and boys at science. Boys tend to receive more attention, both positive and negative, from teachers, especially in secondary schools.[25]

There are also what could be called pathological forms of the same types of learning. Autistic learners can display an obsessive concern for details, without seeing the connection between one part and another. Holistic learners can have such a desire to see the underlying connections that they jump instantly to a conclusion and then try to make everything fit into that. Pupils can approach a whole subject in such a way that they cannot see what all its constituent parts amount to, or they can assume that all a subject consists of is a few generalized conclusions, obvious and dull.[26]

In most learning there is a tension between the two styles. Take memory as an example. Remembering consists of a conscious effort to store information, but also of chance associations. Things we like to remember stay more easily in the mind than things which we would prefer not to, whatever effort is made. When preparing for an examination it is impossible to remember every fact and figure that might come in useful. The only way to organize memory is by constructing an argument, a framework around which to cluster the facts. Once we have done that we can reduce all the relevant facts (and their place in the evidence that supports the argument) to, say, a sheet of A4 paper. We can then reduce that to one side of a small file card. That is what we then try to remember. But the irony is that we will have subconsciously absorbed many of the details we make no conscious effort to retain.

We have talked about different learners and their individual styles. But it is possible for everyone to go through various styles, sometimes depending on the subject and sometimes on the amount of experience. Thus one could characterize differences as a learning circle.[27]

The learning circle

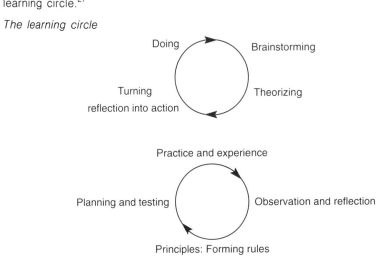

When children are asked what they like about some lessons rather than others they single out 'variety'. What they mean by this is not just the avoidance of routine but the chance to try out different styles of learning. They wish to explore other things, like problem-solving, rather than the repeated generalistic accumulation of a list of facts; they recognize the need to have evidence to support a generalization that, without the illumination of details, remains vague. Without being theoretical about it, children have a thirst for exploring different ways of learning.

Understanding individual learning styles is very useful and practical. It immediately influences children's motivation. When children see the purpose of what they are learning, they are partly perceiving the skills that underlie what they learn; they see they are learning how to do things and not just what to do. Nothing succeeds with individual children as much as their achieving some success, in their own way.

It is often pointed out that praise is very important. Children see through meaning-less praise. They know when there is a disparity between what they have done and the response of the teacher. They do not respect the acceptance of sub-standard work. They not only want their best efforts noticed, but want to understand the means by which they achieved them – and not just the effort. Finding something that a pupil can do well, and making him aware of the skills that he has employed, is a significant way of helping motivation.[28]

Children become well aware of their own abilities. Up to the age of eight they have the advantage of over-estimating their abilities, but as they get older they not only view their achievements more objectively but see them as accurate tests of their attainment. It is when their self-assessment is most accurate that their motivation becomes a positive factor. But, significantly, children rate their own achievements higher when they compare themselves to general tests – and to *all* other children. It is when they relate themselves to their immediate *classmates* that they rate their abilities more negatively. The individual needs to be helped in relation to the group.[29]

Chapter 14

Organizing the Classroom

'When we are making something we work in groups and our topic is working in pairs or threes.'

(boy, 10)

A classroom is a workshop unlike any other, and cannot be likened to an office or a factory. Some have tried to draw analogies with the work of industry – producing goods and serving clients – but such a model does not explain what goes on in the classroom. What makes the classroom a unique environment is the fact that there are two underlying tensions or excitements.

The *first* is that each classroom contains a number of children confined to a distinct space whose purpose is both to collaborate and to compete. They are not there just to create a product collaboratively. They are aware of themselves as the individual 'product' or purpose.

The *second* is the fact that there is a constant interplay between the teacher in his or her role and the collective and group dynamics of the children. The teacher imposes a will, and is responsible for organization, but this is for the children's sake, whether they like it or not!

The classroom is a complex place to organize. It can also *look* a complex place, with cupboards and pictures and desks and blackboards and computers and books and water and sand and carpets . . . There is, then, more than one aspect to the organization of a class; it consists of the people and the environment and how one can be used to support the other.

The classroom can look complex. But we have also seen classrooms in their simplest stage: a row of desks facing a blackboard. There are still some people who, given all the equipment they could want, hanker for this simplicity because they associate it with formality. Everyone knows from the layout what he or she is supposed to do, and who is in charge, who is doing the teaching and who is doing the learning. Such a layout does not prevent collaboration, at least in pairs, but it does not emphasize it.

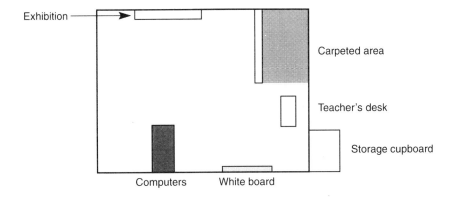

Exhibition

Carpeted area

Teacher's desk

Storage cupboard

Computers   White board

Figure 14.1

It has become routine in many schools to view the lines of children behind their desks as old-fashioned and uncreative. There are some schools where the classes are so small and the equipment so lacking that it is difficult to have any alternative arrangement. But the more normal classroom is set up in a very different way (Figure 14.1). It emphasizes the diverse possibilities in using space, creating corners for different functions, using the whole of the room in a way which is flexible and which can be adapted to different needs, to groups of different sizes, to places for particular kinds of work.

One of the pleasures in taking over a new classroom is the opportunity to re-create it according to how one thinks it should function. It is tempting to think solely of the way the classroom looks but it is important to think of how it will be used. There are many functions in a classroom; they include storage of equipment and materials, resources which pupils can use as well as places where they can carry out their tasks. It is impossible to fix on a particular formula, because each room will be so different and the availability of resources will vary. Are there computers available, for example?; where are the books kept – in a central library in addition to the classroom? The important point is to match the availability of materials to the needs of pupils. This is what makes the possibility of group work so significant.

> There was a time when it was fashionable to build new schools with large amounts of shared space, so that teachers were forced to collaborate. Either three groups of the same age would be put together or groups made out of different age phases so that the development of the curriculum could be better understood. Teachers did not always like having collaboration thrust upon them and hammered out their 'own' space.[1]

Each classroom has its own dynamics. But it also reverberates to a tension between the desire of the individual teacher to create a space of his own and the possibility of collaborating with others. There is a tendency with many teachers to avoid 'open-plan' schools where one classroom shares space with another (Figure 14.2). But in terms of classroom organization the need to collaborate only draws *more* attention to the meticulous details of where things should be kept so that everyone knows.

No teacher really likes being overheard by others. This is not just a matter of self-confidence but group dynamics. It is nevertheless something that teachers become accustomed to, and as they do so they realize it is not so much that their privacy is being invaded as that they are being given an opportunity to make use of a far wider

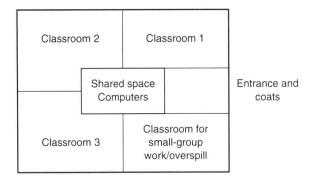

Figure 14.2

range of resources. Apart from anything else, collaboration draws attention to the need to manage not just people but time.

The organization of a classroom needs careful planning as it depends on a number of factors:

1. where to store things;
2. where to do things;
3. the use of time;
4. how to facilitate group work; and
5. rules and contracts.

Where to Store Things

There are two kinds of resource that every classroom needs: the materials from which pupils learn and the materials they use to learn.

Not all information comes from the teacher. Being well organized means making sure that children have access to books or other forms of stored information, and that they know not only where to look but how to use the material creatively. This means that children do not merely repeat what they have been told – by copying out a passage – but they learn things for themselves and realize that the habit they will develop during their lives – finding out the information they need – is an important one.

Having books which are attractive – not battered, never thrown on the ground, clearly labelled and properly stacked – not only enhances the look of the classroom but draws attention to the individual's responsibility. The use of books for information or of computers needs careful management, so that children all have a turn. This is one underlying reason for organizing children in groups.

> Every teacher will have experienced (once) not having enough pencils to go round. It is a sign that the pupils do not respect what they are using – things disappear ... The result is an excuse for anarchy ... 'Please, Miss, she's stolen my rubber ...' or the fights in the corner for the ruler. All equipment needs looking after and respecting all the time.

Seemingly small things can be symbolic of the management of a classroom. Making sure that all the equipment is in good order and clearly available seems almost too obvious to mention, but there are too many classrooms that exhibit a messiness of purpose and a lack of attention to detail. We need only to imagine the chaos that can result from one missing ruler to see the importance of organization. But a deeper purpose is served by respecting the tools of the classroom, the work that is done and the way in which it is done.

Where to Do Things

There are a number of different activities that take place in a classroom. At one point pupils will be silently and individually reading, at another they will be carrying out scientific or technological experiments in small groups, or they will be listening to the teacher or taking part in drama. If the proper storage of equipment is symbolic of management then the adaptability of the classroom to different kinds of use of space is symbolic of an adventurous and varied approach to teaching. Having a space which is comfortable for individual reading encourages it. Making sure that the computer can be used without continual interruption makes it the more attractive. The classroom needs to be able to demonstrate its use in a variety of ways.[2]

> Some children are not good at listening and, instead of seeking clarification from the teacher, respond to ambiguous messages by guessing what they are supposed to be doing. This leads to poor performance. However clear that teacher is, there will still be some children who find it difficult to listen precisely. They can be helped to learn to ask (and respond to) categorical questions through training, like 'Twenty Questions'.[3]

The Use of Time

It is easy to waste time in a classroom, waiting for the next instruction, or the next opportunity to avoid work. The teacher needs to be ambitious about making the maximum use of time available.

Managing time well means being flexible. The curriculum can be organized on a central basis with all subjects given their number of hours, as they are in a secondary school: so much for maths, so much for geography, Friday afternoon for art. But provided that the overall curriculum is covered – and this does deserve some element of timetabling – it is helpful to make use of a certain flexibility. The reason for this is that one can then allow sufficient time for certain kinds of work, so that one can vary the expectation and the speed of completion.

This does not mean that one allows vast tracts of time for any topic. It means that having sufficient time for some things, like a construction project or experiments or a presentation, is balanced by a sense of urgency in others. There are some tasks that pupils know they must finish quickly. Planning time means drawing prior attention to those parts of the curriculum which can be covered within narrow deadlines, and those to which you will give more time to but also with a clear end to aim for. It is better to come to the deadline and allow a little extra than to give too much time to an inappropriate task. Planning needs to be both meticulous and flexible, and there should always be work available for those who finish more quickly, provided that what they have done was up to the standard expected.

There are many tasks, especially focused around discussions in groups, that are given an extra edge if there is only a little time given to them. The sense of urgency when there is just five minutes for work at, say, three important priorities, or where each person stands on an issue, gives an excitement and sense of purpose that is the very reverse of filling in time until the bell.

How to Facilitate Group Work

Group work, as we know, depends on the extent to which pupils and teachers actually work together. It is not a matter of seating arrangements around a table. Group work means collaboration: the sharing of resources and the sharing of ideas.

Group work needs careful organization and planning. It consists of more than collections of children engaged in individual work. There should be co-operative enterprises where each pupil knows what task is expected and what can be contributed to the group. Group work is also the opportunity for intense discussion, for hammering out ideas. Group work can entail children working with each other, with a task or with the teacher. Group work demands forethought, planning and speculating, not merely rehearsing information.[4]

The temptation for the teacher to dominate every discussion is strong. But children also need to have a sense of autonomy over their own opinions. There are times when they must find out for themselves.

There is the acronym GOFO.

It stands for 'Go Off Find Out.'

It can mean, 'Don't bother me.'

It can, however, mean something more positive. Let the pupil know she is also responsible for her own learning.

She will know and properly experience this only if she communicates with other individuals.

This is the importance of the group.

The underlying point about working in groups is their use as a technique that enhances what each pupil is learning, through the means of argument and individual experience. There are many techniques that can be applied to any subject. Circular interviews are one example, where one asks specific questions on a topic for a minute before the next person takes over; No. 1 asks No. 4 and so on (Figure 14.3). Each has a chance to explore their own approach to a topic. Similarly, you can ask a group to find their own position on an issue by seeing where they stand on a line,

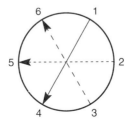

Figure 14.3

concerning a dilemma, e.g. 'We should be in school for shorter time, or for a longer time':

shorter _____ longer

and then discuss *why* different people have different views on the issue.

Rules and Contracts

There are two very different ways of planning the organization of learning. One is through 'control' strategies and the other is through 'independence' strategies.

Control strategies   = use of objectives
                            highly structured courses
Independence strategies = learning contracts
                            problem-based learning

Of course every teacher can and does make use of both. Knowing what the learning outcomes are and what competencies are expected helps clarify planning. One cannot rely entirely on patterning behaviour through a set of distinct steps of learning. Each individual needs his own strategy. At the same time, to lack clear objectives is to run into the danger of having goals so imprecise that nothing happens.

A learning contract draws attention to the individual and collective responsibilities of everyone in the class. There are some which make clear distinctions between 'I' and 'you' ('I, the teacher, will be responsible for . . . You, the pupil, will be responsible for . . .').

One does not need quite such clear distinctions. It is, I think, better to go for the collective 'we' (even if it is imposed by the expectation of the teacher).

A contract can be a simple matter of making sure that all subscribe to a set of class rules that make sure the classroom is well organized: Do's and Don'ts, i.e. DO tidy up, DON'T bully.

But it can be more sophisticated, either by adding individual responsibilities for certain things at certain times ('every Tuesday Mary will make sure things are packed away') or by exploring more subtle responsibilities like learning outcomes. The point about any of these is that they involve children in the sense or purpose of their own learning.

'Tied team tasks': One way of enhancing the group's performance and giving both interest and cohesion to their work is by getting them to make a presentation of their work – either of what they have discovered, or of what they think. This can be put on the wall so that other groups can assess each other against criteria such as (a) quality of argument, (b) clarity of presentation, and (c) originality.

A well-organized classroom therefore draws attention to the underlying purpose of learning; it is not organized for its own sake and just for the convenience of the teacher. It emphasizes the high expectation that should be shared by teacher and pupil. It also emphasizes the abilities of children not only to think and be sensitive to others, but to be responsible for themselves. A well-organized classroom is one which has definite 'outcomes', that creates and celebrates the achievements of pupils. The effective teacher begins by making sure that everyone knows where things are and how to use them, continues with the development of effective and individual responsibility, and ends with a classroom that almost seems to run itself. All the initial planning and the tidying up leave the teacher far more time to teach.

A well-organized classroom is a relaxed place where the tension of control and instruction is no longer a distraction. This implies that it is both 'formal' and 'informal'. Within the framework of clear expectations a teacher is free to vary techniques, using simulations and drama, supervising experiments and having time to talk to individuals.

There has been a lot of debate about the best technique of teaching and classroom organization – whether 'formality' or 'informality' works best. This is, however, a difficult debate to sustain. The more we experience teaching the less easy it is to understand what the terms mean. Every teacher will be formal, to the extent of expecting order and social courtesy, and expecting recognition of the role of the teacher. And every teacher will be 'informal' to the extent of showing individual attention and being responsible to the children's needs.

> Every now and then 'formality' becomes a political issue. A mythology is created in which the classroom teacher is characterized as being too informal – with a vision of chaos and indiscipline and an emphasis on children merely 'playing' and not being taught.
> The fear of politicians is that 'modern methods' mean that their memories of teachers as authoritarian are eroded and their desire to have a set curriculum 'delivered' challenged. Does 'formality' really mean the belief that whatever the teacher says, i.e. delivers, is what the children learn? Ah, if it were only so ...![5]

Children therefore appreciate teachers who are 'strict' and well-organized and who also can 'share a laugh'. It is only when the rules of the classroom are firm and understood that teachers can afford 'informality'. But even then children will always see a teacher in a formal way. The alternative is simply not a teacher.

> Given the number of children in classes, it is not surprising that there is little time for talk with individual children. Indeed, one survey showed that for less than 5 per cent of the time is a pupil in direct contact with the teacher. Two-thirds of the child's time is spent working alone on individual tasks set by the teacher.[6]

There are many different styles of organizing the classroom, and the style chosen affects how well children learn. There are always three possibilities in teaching: working with the class as a whole; working with groups; and working with individuals. Relying on just one technique never works. It is essential that all share information, that children help each other and that each individual's work is evaluated. Recognizing this demonstrates the different opportunities; every moment is an opportunity to teach. The teacher can demonstrate the use of vocabulary and ideas; the children can, in groups, extend each other's ideas; and there always needs to be the space for a demanding individual exchange (*'Why* do you think that?').

Teachers rarely think of their own 'styles' of teaching. It needs outside observers sometimes to articulate what we are doing – whether certain children gain far more attention than others or whether they keep interrupting rather than helping children in their work. One study of teachers pinpointed six different styles of classroom management.[7]

1. *Group instructors*. These worked with groups, having given them information. The

children worked on their own and made few demands on the teacher. (These teachers were mostly in their thirties.)

The children were better than average at listening and acquiring information but less good at reading and mathematics.

2. *Class enquirers*. These worked mostly with the whole class, spending a lot of time explaining and asking for questions. The children worked by themselves, avoiding personal contact. (These teachers were mostly over 40.)

The children were better at maths and languages, but less good at reading and low on originality.

3. *Infrequent changers*. These gave high levels of individual attention in the context of occasional changes in organization. The children were encouraged to sort out their own tasks and ask for attention. (These teachers were mostly over 30.)

The children were better at reading, quite good at maths, maps and languages but less good elsewhere.

4. *Individual monitors*. These worked with individuals rather than with groups or the class as a whole. They would briefly tell the children what to do rather than discussing work. The children were intermittent workers, mixing work with social chat. (These teachers were mostly in their twenties.)

The children were better at reading, graphs and drawing and worse at maths and maps and languages.

5. *Habitual changers*. These switched unpredictably from class teaching to individual work in response to the behaviour of the class. They believed mostly in topic work and shared small talk with the children. (These teachers were mostly women in their twenties.)

The children were better on study skills and mapping and worse on reading, maths and languages.

6. *Rotating changers*. These organized their classrooms so that different groups worked on different curriculum areas at the same time whilst the teacher gave the signal for children to change. Children were less disciplined and came in for criticism. (These teachers were mostly in their twenties.)

The children were worst in all curriculum areas.

One interesting result of this study of teachers is how badly two of the most common habits of classroom organization came out: groups and topics. The reason is not difficult to see. In both cases what appeared as organization was really a kind of routine, without any real thought given to its purpose. If children happen to be working together it does not mean that their ability to challenge each other is used; they can be ignored in their obscure corner. If a topic is taken up and children gather information, it does not mean that they are thinking or learning what needs to be learned.

Successful classroom management means that children have high standards, that they are self-confident and self-disciplined, unafraid to ask interesting questions and able to work collaboratively with each other. All the time the teacher is working to find a style that is a balance between two extremes: too much teaching and too little. Does a teacher want the children to be:

- passive with low motivation;
- driven purely by the teacher;

or to be:

- involved and taking initiatives;
- responsible and self-evaluative?

> There was one unusual and successful teacher who found her own method of working. All the children would be working on their own, in a position in which they could all see each other. Whilst working in silence there would be just one conversation going on, in which all were expected to join, never interrupting but keeping up the topic of conversation until another subject developed.

The achievement of this balance involves rethinking the classroom, allowing children to participate in some of the decisions and making them responsible for resources, so that they have a sense of 'ownership' of their learning. The teacher's time is effectively used when he can do all these tasks:

- have time with each child;
- review each child's work;
- assess, and identify problems;
- respond to opportunities;
- inspire the whole class;
- reflect on what is going on; and
- *enjoy* it.

To have time for this high-quality teaching means avoiding all the small distractions that divert attention from learning. It means being organized about materials, and having plenty for the children to do. Children can be responsible for servicing the materials: organizing paper, pencils, paints, watering plants, looking after the pets, keeping things tidy and by looking after the materials and treating them with respect. This means that the teacher can concentrate on the curriculum.

> All the sounds that a teacher does not want to hear:
>
> 'What do I do now?'
>
> 'Kevin's pulling my hair.'
>
> 'I've done a page. Is this enough?'
>
> 'There isn't a ruler on our table.'
>
> 'Aren't we supposed to be in the gym?'
>
> 'The computer won't work.'

Whatever the curriculum, however, there will be times when the children have finished their work and there is spare time. For this a well-organized teacher has 'extra' tasks that are stimulating, like 'Twenty Questions', looking for words in a dictionary, changing words in a sentence, describing one incident in different styles – from the personal to the purely objective.

One checklist of effectiveness that a teacher can use as a reminder is the following:

1. Be clear.
2. Be enthusiastic.
3. Use a variety of approaches.
4. Ask good questions.
5. Do not waste time.
6. Use indirect information so children find out.
7. Give children the opportunity to learn.
8. Make comments that help structure their work.

Chapter 15

The Classroom Environment

'It's good being in the same classroom all day, because you know where you are going and you get to know your classroom so you feel comfortable there.'

(girl, 10)

Classroom organization is essentially about people and how they carry out their roles. It is symbolized by the way in which the space is controlled and how the classroom looks. Inspectors who make many visits to different schools are very quick to detect differences in the first few minutes, according to the feel of how the children are working, the quality of the welcome and the displays on the wall. Sometimes it seems enough just to inspect what the classroom *looks* like to know the quality of the teaching and learning that take place there.

Children are very sensitive to places and to atmosphere. If you ask them to name a favourite or least favourite space they are very quick to cite both.[1] They are in no way indifferent to their environment and, even if no more articulate than architects about the effects of buildings, very sensitive to them. Nor are many children unaware of the social dimensions of the environment. They know the distinctions between areas that symbolize richness and estates that reveal immediately the sense of apathy and neglect. They are also aware of the symbolic nature of schools: which ones show a sense of concern and well-being and which seem to have sunk into neglect, under a weight of litter.

> The classroom is a complicated place where a lot of different things are going on at the same time. But it is all held together by the teacher. Teachers' use of non-verbal communication is concerned with control and management, and remains a central focus of children's attention.[2]

Coming into the school, children, like inspectors, are even more discriminating about the environment. They can detect the extent to which they or their parents are genuinely welcomed. They can see whether the work that is achieved is celebrated, and they can detect care and quality. One might wonder whether there are schools where children (leaving parents aside) are *not* welcome. But this is how it feels to many of them. Schools can be forbidding places.

Schools look unique. They are not easy places to make inviting. The lack of resources for carpets and curtains, the mass of equipment with little storage space, the need for many lavatories and places to hang up countless coats, all add together to give the staff of a school some interesting problems to overcome.

But let us start with the classroom. Whether open-plan or not, the classroom is a complete space that can be made one's own. There are some children who like the secondary school model of going from place to place, of visiting specialist rooms. That has the same advantage that a particular room gives an indication of what it is for. What children like is not the adventure of travelling but the security of arrival.

> The classroom environment consists of children's behaviour as well as wall displays. The indications of well-being are seen both in the way the children's work is used – how recent, and how well mounted – and in whether there are any children seeming to do nothing. These are the children who develop a dread of success, who want to be anonymous and who build their security on passivity, on boredom, and on having no mental life.

Like schools as a whole, classrooms can be very distinctive places, with children's work covering the walls, with miniature furniture and with a whole crowd of objects and things to do. Classrooms can also be a mess. Yet the opportunity of planning how the classroom should look and how it should be organized is the start of imposing some authority on what should be learned as well as the first stage in creating an environment in which children will want to learn. The eventual concern is for the functioning of the classroom, for clear organization, for adaptability to different needs, and for the best way of using groups and individuals. But the final result will not only be an abstract list of rules and expectations. It will demonstrate itself in how purposeful the classroom looks.

Children notice two essential ingredients in a classroom: order and excitement.

The *orderliness* of the classroom derives from planning where things should be. One does not have to leave the chairs where they are, whether they are in rows or in groups. One can earmark particular corners for different things so that children know exactly where to go at particular times. The classroom that is well ordered reveals itself in the tidiness: without litter or half-finished work, without pieces of paper on the floor and stray pens. Instead there will be places clearly labelled for the use of equipment. And even if carpeting a whole classroom is a luxury, it is always possible to create at least some corner where children can sit comfortably together, and where there is a more immediate, almost domestic contact between teacher and children.

The *excitement* of the classroom derives from two things: the displays and the equipment. Children can immediately sense when there is something worth looking at, not only because it is effective decoration but because it is interesting. The classroom with blank walls suggests a blankness of purpose. The classroom in which every bit of space is covered for its own sake is one which suggests an incoherence of purpose.

The classroom is a storage place for information, in the form of artefacts and pictures and computers perhaps, but mostly in books. The way that the books are kept and displayed reveals a great deal about the way in which children are learning and whether they respect their own learning.

The fundamental question about the classroom environment is whether it has to look so completely 'child-centred'. Do children really like nothing but their own work displayed? Is it their pictures or their furniture that makes the classroom so distinctive?

> It is often confirmed that rewards are more successful than punishments. One study of secondary schools showed that there were certain types of punishment or sanctions which were ineffective:
>
> - being told off in front of the class;
> - being given low marks;
> - being given lines;
> - detentions.
>
> All these almost 'standard' procedures did not improve the quality of work. Private praise, however, did. Pupils also thought that the most effective 'sanction' is the involvement of parents.[3]

Children actually have more sophisticated tastes than they are normally allowed. Very young children entering a reception class will naturally be concerned with all the things they can play with – all those things to do! They then settle down with their favourite task, leaving all the accumulated piles of alternatives for another day.

There the riches have a function. Children choose and are reminded of availability. But as they get older, children appreciate the quality of what they see and not just the quantity. They like their attention directed.

Although teachers and children collaborate on running the classroom, the teacher should remember that the class serves him as well as the children. There are some things that the teacher should display because of his own interest. Children like to see things that are adult. They appreciate real pictures, decent curtains and all the comforts that people would expect there to be in a house. No one would wish to make the classroom look exactly like a sitting-room, but the obvious distinction between school and other buildings in the environment can be overdone.

> It is good for children to notice that the teacher has interests of his own. One of the simplest yet most effective ways of demonstrating the pleasures of reading is for the teacher to read a book – not aloud to the children but to himself. There is then the realization that reading is not just a task undertaken at school, or something done only by children because they are learning to read, but by adults who have their own interests and pleasures.

The teacher should also contribute something of his own to the class: books he wants to use, a picture he wants to see, an artefact that has a personal interest, and plants because they give life to a room, whether something will be learned from them or not. A classroom is a place for the teacher, and not just the children, to feel at home in.

At the heart of the classroom environment is the display of children's work. There are few teachers who do not agree with the idea of display, but not everyone does it well. Success in display lies in two things:

- The work needs to be displayed neatly, with double mounting where possible, perhaps a hessian background, and with an eye to colour. This is also a matter of practice and a belief that paying attention to detail is important.
- The real success in wall display lies in using the children's pictures with purpose;

once they are up they should not be ignored or left to languish for months. They are part of a learning landscape where attention is directed not only to the achievements of individual children, but to the continuing learning that is taking place. This implies that the teacher needs to concentrate on a definite theme and that different kinds of artefacts can be combined, some demonstrating the teacher's input and some the children's. A display of children's face masks, for example, is not complete without examples of where they derived their inspiration.

The importance of wall displays is their use. They are a way of lightening up a classroom, but this can also be done in other ways.

> When a group of children were asked what they thought about wall displays some interesting attitudes emerged. They longed for 'real' pictures and 'real' posters to add to their own. They didn't remember exactly what was on the wall or where, after about a week, with one exception: they did know where their own work was displayed.[4]

Wall displays are an extra way of drawing children's attention to what they have done in a way that rehearses it. Children learn by associating and recognizing concepts; they also need to learn to seek out materials. The display of a particular theme makes children more observant and more analytical, provided the teacher draws attention to it.

Putting up displays takes time, as any exhibition does. It is sometimes tempting to leave things on a wall in the corner because there are other things being done. It is sometimes tempting to concentrate on putting things up just to cover space. But it is worth considering wall displays as a deliberate strategy – especially if the classroom environment is attractive enough in itself not to have to be disguised in a glazing of children's work.

> A sensible use of space in classrooms, carefully thought out to promote learning, can make a significant impact on pupils' learning. Careful scheduling of time and organization of equipment and material themselves bring out the ability of children to work. One way of organizing the learning environment is by having specific work areas, for language, maths and science, for creative and for visual and auditory skills.[5]

Sometimes the whole classroom should be directed to one theme. This places the attention not just on celebrating the children's work but on presenting and communicating it. The classroom then becomes a resource for other children to visit. When children know that their work has an audience greater than each other and the teacher they should take an even greater pride in what they do. They think of how to communicate ideas visually: how much information should be given? will the audience be stimulated?

A classroom is after all a resource that should be used by the whole school, and the whole school used by the class. For whilst the classroom is a self-contained unit which can be devoted to one exhibition, there are many other spaces that can be used for display, like corridors and halls. For parents and other visitors there are many significant areas in a school outside the classroom which deserve the presentation of children's work. When children realize that there is a larger audience for their work, that they can share with parents, they will also pay more attention to each other's work.

> One class had become engrossed (again) with dinosaurs. Despite visits to see huge skeletons, despite pictures and discussion, they found it difficult to envisage the huge size

> of some of them. It was then decided to transform the door of the classroom into the mouth of a dinosaur, so that everyone walking in did so past rows of teeth ... and, of course, straight into the stomach.

Environment means more, of course, than just the classroom. We talk about the importance of tidiness, as well as displays. This has a wider context and there is no reason why an analogy should not be drawn between the two. Caring for a classroom therefore has a deeper purpose than making it into the best context for learning. Children need to know, and deserve to know, more about the personal responsibilities for, as well as the universal dangers to, the environment. There is no place that is not affected by changes to climate or by pollution. The classroom needs to be clearly a clean and healthy place, in which everyone shares pride and responsibility.

The environment that lies outside the school is, however, more problematic, if just as important. There are few schools that do not have areas of grass as well as playgrounds, but how often are they really used and developed rather than neglected? Gardens are a very useful resource, for demonstrating and teaching about both the wilderness and cultivation. There could be areas left wild deliberately to experiment with how different plants grow when uncontrolled. There can be the deliberate cultivation of vegetables, and there can be the general enhancement of the surroundings of a school.[6]

The school gardens are a resource not for exploiting children – selling vegetables – but for teaching them something about biology and economics, about science as well as horticulture. The gardens also demonstrate the difference that people can make to the environment, the difference between pride and neglect. The classroom should not, therefore, be seen as an isolated phenomenon, but as a place that has a connection with the world outside.[7]

So far we have dealt with the classroom environment as with inanimate things. But the classroom environment also includes people. There is one resource more than any other that can help encourage and develop children's learning: all the other adults who come into the classroom.

Teachers like their own space but they do not have to remain isolated. Increasingly there are opportunities for other people to come into the classroom: ancillary staff and specialists. All these give individual children the chance to extend a particular skill or overcome a particular problem.

> There are many additional people in classrooms, from other teachers and support staff to parents. But some of the most effective visitors are those who come in because they are interesting in themselves: anyone who can talk with enthusiasm about their job, their past, their experiences or their hobby.
>
> In one study an attempt was made to see how children's work could be improved with additional resources: more teachers, or more visits, or more equipment. But the researchers began to discover that children gained most not from the systematic inputs but from those that came by chance, like the local mechanic talking about cars, or a deep-sea diver talking about his experiences.[8]

Among the greatest resources, however, are willing parents who come to the class, provided that two things happen:

- they feel they have a definite part to play; and
- there is a well-organized plan, where every adult knows what is expected.

There is a temptation to use the parent as an extra pair of hands – to deal with cooking or listening to individuals reading. If parents are restricted to this role they will tend to be marginalized in their eyes and the eyes of the children. But every parent brings with her additional skills and expertise. It is the responsibility of the teacher to create a clearly differentiated role for the other adult.[9]

The classroom environment is very different when the traditional dynamics of one teacher and many children is replaced by team teaching. One way of ensuring that teams work well together is by creating three separate roles for people in the class:

- an activity manager;
- an individual helper; and
- a mover.

The activity manager is concerned with the class as a whole while it is engaged in consolidating a task. The individual helper will concentrate on individual children and have clear tasks to do for short, intense periods. The mover makes certain that the others are not interrupted in their tasks, by dealing with interruptions and making sure the children have appropriate equipment.[10]

Other adults provide a resource by their very presence, by creating a link between the environment of the school and what lies beyond, and by giving the opportunity for individual conversations. They can also join in the making, and celebration, of displays.

Chapter 16

The Uses of Educational Technology

'They have a lab and it's properly laid out and they've got more expensive stuff there.

(boy, 10)

There was a time when a great investment of hope, if not of resources, was placed in educational technology. The teacher, bleakly struggling to interest hordes of children, was to be replaced by a host of machines: videos and computers, radios and record players, films and models. This vision of the future took one of three forms:

• teaching machines;
• resource centres;
• computer networks.

The argument for *teaching machines* was based on two premises. The first was that people learn through a series of short, specific behavioural steps. First one small fact, or one small skill, is learned and then another and another through a series of logical moves. Learning is divided into a series of segments that everyone, including children with special educational needs, can understand and develop.[1]

The second premise was that only machines would have the patience to keep repeating and repeating the same instruction and the same response. Thus the Plessey teaching machine demanded that pupils give simple 'yes' or 'no' answers to questions by pressing buttons, and that, like rats learning by trial and error where the reward lay, they would make inexorable progress. Each individual would be pushing the necessary buttons at her own pace.[2]

The argument for *resource centres* was based on making independent learning possible through the provision of all the necessary equipment. A school would become a series of workstations surrounding one central library and store in which all the necessary information, whether in books or films or computer programs, would be placed. The separate classrooms with their groups of children would be seen as subservient, and even unnecessary, compared to a well-stocked resource centre, with pupils finding out the solutions to problems for themselves rather than having to rely on the teacher. The supporting materials of the individual classroom would be replaced by a well-equipped and central powerhouse of knowledge.

The argument for *computer networks* was based on the idea that technological advances were so rapid, and the information available and necessary so dense, that the only way in which it would be possible to keep abreast of knowledge would be to have access to a range of machines on which information would be kept. There would be no need for schools, except for the social functions, since everyone would have their own computer at home, networked to experts, the very best, who would give the required answers. Such an idea, it was suggested, would mean that in the place of expensively built and maintained schools, there would be not only all the work-stations that would replace travelling but access to the best experts.[3]

> Many visions of the future, some educational, some bordering on science fiction, have been based on the possibility of real mastery over machines; and the mastery of machines over men. It seems odd to reflect that many of these strong and persuasive visions are already thirty years old – the idea of the disappearance of the school or the abolition of teaching. It is as if all the human functions of relationship and dialogue would eventually be replaced by a stronger and more controlling input of information to the learner.

All these ideas were – still are – attractive. They suggest independence of learning and access to the most carefully produced and most advanced products. They are ideas that will not simply fade away. Yet nothing of the kind has happened. It is instructive to understand why.

The reason is not simply a matter of expense, although few politicians can easily produce extra resources because of a good principle or a good idea. The reason why this vision of the future based on educational technology has failed is that it was based on false premises. The 'vision' left out the one vital ingredient in any independent learning: the teacher.

The teacher might not be enough all by himself, but nor is the existence of educational technology, however sophisticated and however interactive. All depends on how one makes use of the other.

One of the signs of a creative teacher lies in the preparation of materials to make the lessons more interesting. It is not only concepts and strategies that need thinking through, but actual examples. The teacher who gives an abstract outline of what he will be talking about is not going to have the immediate effect of a teacher who brings a box and places it in front whilst the children wonder what is in it. Materials not only demonstrate the idea, but are the starting point of ideas. The more equipment the teacher has the better, provided it is used creatively.

There is a wide range of materials available and some of it is very sophisticated. The teacher is constantly looking for materials that can be used; the teacher also needs to be aware that the children are accustomed to witnessing a great deal of educational technology outside school. This is especially true of television, where they can compare the quality and vitality (and expense) of commercial programmes with the quality of programmes seen in school.

> Children's views of the qualities that make up the effective teacher include firmness, humour, praise. But they also, significantly, include the ability to make things interesting by giving pupils things to do, to touch and talk about. Part of what the children define as 'explanation' is the ability to demonstrate.[4]

The teacher does not, however, have to rely on the intrinsic quality of the material he uses; it all depends on how it is used, whether it is of interest to the teacher and whether its use has been prepared. Educational technology is not just a matter of sophisticated equipment. It is any device which enhances and demonstrates an idea by giving a visual example or by increasing pupils' active skills.

Some of the most everyday objects can be classified as educational technology, from worksheets to blackboards. The use of even the simplest of devices needs thinking through. The difference between good and bad worksheets, for example, is enormous. The poor worksheet merely occupies the child, under the excuse that certain things are being 'reinforced': it is possible to prepare them without thought or exploration. The good worksheet asks open questions, demanding original thought or the discovery of new information. The central distinction that underlies technology is made: has it been thought through so that it is part of what is being taught, or is it merely a 'free-standing' device, occupying time?

> Teachers often express their wish to use the best resources for their pupils. They want to put their pupils' needs first, but their real constraint (as a survey shows) is not lack of money or equipment so much as organizational difficulties: lack of time and space for preparation and planning.[5]

One of the most everyday pieces of equipment is the board, be it black or white. It is interesting to note the political nostalgia that allies itself with 'chalk and talk', as if there were no better means of conveying information than writing it up on the blackboard. In fact the use of the board, in a time of photocopying and work arranged for individuals and groups, is not a simple matter. Is the board used to give instructions so that children at the start of the day know what they are expected to do? Is the board used to give particular messages? Is it to carry information, previously written up? Or is it to be used as a collective drafting device, in which a large number of people can take part?

The presentation of information on a board so that it can be copied down is probably the least satisfactory way of using it. What the board does do, apart from carrying messages in larger script than a notice-board, is promote collective discussions: brainstorming, Venn diagrams, extensions to vocabulary or ideas.

If primary school teachers are associated with blackboards, lecturers feel exposed without their overhead projectors. These have their advantages in the classroom too: they allow the teacher to prepare written material in a less painstaking way than writing with chalk, and they can also reproduce visual materials: pages from books or pictures.

All these are devices to convey secondary information. Some of the most stimulating teaching aids are artefacts themselves: items that are historically interesting and give the flavour of a particular time, items which demonstrate a particular religious belief or culture, and items which symbolize the ways in which different people live. These items can be found in almost any house; the habit of accumulation ensures that we collect things which we realize to be unusual. It is a strong stimulus for children to see the 'real' thing and be able to handle it. It also enables them to work at objects in a new way, realizing that everything has its own style and story to tell.

> One of the most successful ways of creating a stimulating and usable wall display is through the collection of objects centred round a theme. The children can then approach them as in a 'user friendly' museum: full of interesting things, but things you can touch.

An example of such a display is putting together items that symbolize the Second World War, or even a decade like the 1960s: tickets, newspapers, toy cars, photographs, etc.

The stimulus given to children's imagination by music, sculpture and painting is obvious. But it is one which depends on the extent to which the teacher actually draws attention to it. If left as a background, or something imprecise, such manifestations of art can be ignored as totally as objects gathering dust in a corner. Although there is a lot to be said for encouraging children to enjoy art without being forced to analyse it, they only learn to look and listen when they pay close attention. The teacher has a crucial role to play.

It is easy for children to ignore the sights and sounds that surround them. To some extent they have to learn to do this, or how else could they concentrate? But the medium which is the most ignored is also the one supposed to be most stimulating: television. Before we discuss the use of television in the classroom it is worth reiterating the facts about how children watch television at home, because they can transfer this habit to school.

Children's favourite programmes are those which make fewest demands on them. These programmes tend to be ostensibly aimed at adults: soap operas and thrillers. Children express a distaste for programmes that are designed to make them think, such as educational programmes. They do not like those programmes which depend on talk, like the news and documentaries.[6]

The unpopularity of certain programmes does not mean that they are not watched. The television tends to be on for hours. Most, if not all, children spend about three hours every day watching television. This implies that they are learning a great deal of information. But are they? It depends on how they watch.

When one studies the way that people watch television, by observing their behaviour on a camera in the television that records who watches when it is switched on, one notices two things. The first is that for a significant amount of time individuals are actually out of the room. This casts doubt on many of the 'ratings' which depend on recording when the television is switched on. The second is that even when watching their favourite programme, viewers pay scant attention. They do not look intently, searching for every detail. They rely on a minimum number of clues to understand what is happening; this is what makes visually frenetic action films so easy to watch.

This does not mean that children are not capable of paying close attention. On the contrary. If you ask a child to look at a programme on which he will be asked questions afterwards, he will demonstrate the ability to recall even small details. But viewing a programme as a prelude to being tested contrasts with the normal style of viewing. The 'normal' style is such that if asked questions about what they've seen children find it very difficult to recall very much. They know what they've seen. They will recognize something that they have seen before. They will become familiar with advertisements that are repeated. But they will not be analysing a wealth of new, carefully constructed information.

The greatest investment of hope in educational technology was in television. Here seemed to be the ultimate resource. Programmes could be specially made on a variety of topics, conveying pictures – say, of other countries, of wildlife, or experiments – that no other resource could match. And the programmes could be made by acknowledged experts in their subjects, able to talk with enthusiasm as well as erudition far beyond the scope of the generalist class teacher. In fact, educational television has proved a great disappointment. Why?

The main reason for the failure of television to make an obvious impact on education is that it does not actually 'teach'. It gives an opportunity to learn. This opportunity relies on a teacher to prepare, direct and follow up. Television is not a substitute teacher, nor is it an automatic conveyor of information. Whether designed as a replacement or an extension of the teacher, television is not enough in itself.

> The hope that television could transform people's learning is also manifested in other ways. The Open University was designed to help people learn at home, in their own time, without the need for specialist centres. In fact, the Open University depends centrally on written materials and personal support. Television is an 'extra'.
>
> Many countries with less well-developed education systems have hoped that the absence of teachers and schools could be offset by a sophisticated television system, conveying knowledge across vast tracts of land. But, again, there is a gap between the vision and the reality.[7]

Television remains, nevertheless, an extremely important resource for the teacher. But the teacher needs to control and explain what is seen. Even devices such as arrows, or pauses between shots, aid the understanding of the viewer.

There have been many attempts to find out the extent to which television can inform. There is, after all, a mass audience. Television is viewed as the ideal vehicle for mass communication, for conveying facts and for influencing people. And yet study after study has demonstrated how little the audience remember about programmes they have seen. The simplest facts, however often they are conveyed, seem to pass them by.

> It is disappointing to note how often an educational programme is put on without the surrounding work that is needed to make it worthwhile. The children are lined up: 'Go to the hall, sit down and wait for the programme or video.' They seem to watch with interest – they are at least quiet. They then line up and trail back to the classroom.
>
> If you ask a question then, they will be able to come up with some answers, if not very interesting ones. By the next day nearly all they have seen will be forgotten. It will have joined the mass of material that they look at every day at home, soon to be ignored.

An audience of standard television programmes tends to remember just a general outline; they have the 'feel' of what they have witnessed. They know the keynotes rather than the details; they will have a general picture rather than understanding. Emotional reactions go deeper than new ideas. Even the Open University has discovered that the most successful programmes are the most general introductory ones that give an outline, rather than programmes which try to convey specific facts.

Some of the best examples of the belief in the power of television to teach, and of its subsequent disappointment, are American educational programmes such as 'Sesame Street'.[8] Here all the sophisticated techniques of presentation were at the service of an educational goal: trying to stimulate children, and getting them to model their behaviour on what they saw. But the programmes, for all the sophistication and enthusiasm in their making, did not have, in themselves, any effect on their audience. Any success depended entirely on the additional help of parents.

> Sometimes when people learn from television it is not the obvious or the expected. There was one programme, for example, designed to teach its audience how to speak French. The audience were obviously committed to learning, or they would not have watched. After several weeks the audience were tested for what had been learned. It was

discovered that any advance in knowledge about the French language was slight or undetectable.

At the same time it was discovered that the audience had learned to be more afraid of learning French and more apprehensive about France.[9]

Even in the different conditions of the classroom, television programmes are not closely attended. Success in using them as an educational device depends entirely on the willingness of the teacher to embed the programmes within other work. This is where the video is invaluable. Not only can there be proper preparation beforehand, in terms of knowledge, but the programme can be stopped at any moment for discussion. It might seem a pity to break the flow of a story, but it is only when this is done that children really learn. Discussion before, during and after the programme not only stimulates the children to think, but enables them to look closely at what they see. The programme is no longer just a series of entertaining images.

Even embedding objective devices within the programme causes children to watch in a different way. Pauses, or pointers, the juxtaposition of the story with someone's commentary, all make a difference. Even half a second's pause between each new shot significantly helps improve children's recall of what they have seen.[10]

Many teachers believe that television programmes can enhance learning, of facts of language. But not all make use of their possibilities. This depends always on the combination of the programme with a teacher. A story read or a story seen on television might be interesting, but the story is only really understood and recalled in detail when it has been prepared and followed up by the teacher.[11]

The television programmes that teachers can use do not have to be specifically educational. General-interest programmes make very useful starting points for discussion. The reason for this is that it depends on the teacher to make comments, rather than on a talking head embedded in the programme. At the same time a teacher can help the children to look more closely and more critically at the programmes, learning how to analyse style, rather than letting themselves be distracted by it.

Through their considerable experience of watching television, children are sophisticated in their knowledge of all the techniques of editing. They know what the stereotypes mean: the difference between head-shots, understanding the angles of the camera and what the angle implies, and the difference between what is real and what has been made to look real. This is more complex than it seems to those who take it for granted. It has to be learned.

At the same time that children learn about the ways in which films and videos are made, with a sophistication that demonstrates the power of the human mind to interpret clues, they are relatively unsophisticated about the information itself. They see *how* things are conveyed, but not always *what*. They need to understand the stylistic conventions, but no one helps them understand what they are seeing. Thus they watch, or overhear, the news, even if reluctantly, with all its drama and terror, its sensations and images, and they have to make sense of it in their own way.

The media themselves need mediation. This is because they do no more than present information and the individual learner needs a teacher to help him understand it. Children need to analyse the way that information is conveyed, not merely become accustomed to it. They need to understand the information, not merely accept it.

The great advantage that teachers now have (which is why I do not even mention the use of films) is the video. This gives important control over the selection of material and the way it is presented. Videos also have the advantage of being able to record any material. Added to control over the material is the scope for a far greater, and freer, choice. Those programmes presented as a normal part of a television station's output are also usable in school. The use of this material has the advantage not only of the school's not needing to hire it, but also of referring children back to think about what they watch habitually.

All kinds of educational technology have their uses, as well as their limitations. Photographs give graphic detail but cannot be used for large groups. Slides and filmstrips are a useful way of presenting visual information but cannot always be easily acquired in the form that one would like. Sound recordings can be very useful and stimulating, but they are not easily made with quality. Tape and slide combinations are a very effective form of presentation, but need careful preparation.

In many of these media the emphasis is on the producer, or the person who believes in them and makes them. There is less emphasis on their effects on the learner. Each producer of a television show will believe that if only people watched his show, the world would be changed. But educational media are like lecturers as opposed to teachers: what about the audience, the learner? The have their own individual and strong needs; and these are not the same as the producer's.[12]

How, then, can one help learners react to, and interact with, the media they watch or play with?

Computers are one way in which it is possible to manipulate information rather than be manipulated by it. Computers have replaced television as the greatest hope of educational technology. In some countries there has been a real investment of time and material in information technology as well as a concern to keep up with the latest models. The technological implications of these advances are great; but have they made that much impact on schools? All surveys of the use of computers in schools come to the conclusion that, despite the investment, they have made a minimal impact.[13] But could they have done more?

Computers are used in schools in two quite different ways:

1.   as tools which one needs to learn how to use for their own sake;
2.   as a means of access to computer programes.

For a long time schools concentrated on the first, in the belief that children needed to know how to use computers for social and vocational reasons. This is a limited view of their use, but if that was the only aim, one could argue that children could learn equally well from computer games. But as a means to an end, as access to software and individually tailored programs, computers are another matter.

Children are naturally gifted in computer literacy. Their ability to learn how to manipulate the machinery often puts adults to comparative shame. Children do not share the fear and the suspicions that afflict some teachers who lack confidence. They do not find it at all difficult to use keyboards, to search for the relevant parts and even to use the 'megabyte' vocabulary. But it all depends to what end this skill is developed.

Computers can be very time-consuming, and time can be absorbed as simply and as mindlessly as in watching television. Children can be addicted to computer games, and there are many examples of obsessions with popular ones. This is computer literacy taken to a pathological degree. There must be alternatives to the display of such an ability.

At the lowest level of its use as a teaching machine, a computer can offer simple, rather mechanical, exercises rather than anything more challenging. But there are two important extra dimensions to a computer other than access to information. The first is its interactive nature, and the second is word-processing.

Interactive video uses the ability of computers to offer alternatives, to respond to the choices of the pupil. Once that power of idea is unleashed the possibility of a computer helping individuals to learn particular things is greatly enhanced. It is through interactive video that one can imagine the possibility of a network of computers, of having access to a range of knowledge that is not only a list of facts transferred on to the computer screen.

One way in which computers have made a definite impact on pupil learning is through word-processing. The ability to draft and re-draft, to look at all the different aspects of a text from style to presentation, is offered by a word processor without some of the attendant difficulties of writing out something again and again. The concentration is on the thought that goes into drafting the finished text, not the mechanical labour of doing so. The word processor is an open-ended writing tool that helps develop thinking.

Interactive video depends on the quality of the programmes available. Like word-processing it can only work with individuals or possibly a small group. So the teaching needs to be carefully prepared to allow creative learning to take place; and what happens to the other children meanwhile?

The more one studies information technology, the more one returns to the basic truth: the most gifted and adaptable, imaginative and resourceful piece of educational technology is the teacher himself.

Chapter 17

The Use of Books

'And after that we normally sit down and read. It's ever so quiet and peaceful.'

(boy, 10)

Books are one of the most significant of all the links between home and school. They provide private pleasure and one of the most important means of learning. Educational technology might be associated with hardware, with the many technical resources that are available to support learning, but the most efficient, and the most helpful to the teacher, remains the book.

It is interesting to reflect how often prophecies have been made which suggest that books will soon no longer be used, that there are other far more practical electronic means of communication. First the television was supposed to replace books, and then computers were. The book was associated with old-fashioned methods of learning, with having to memorize swathes of cold print, of having to concentrate. It is as if any medium which demanded an individual response was assumed to be automatically subsumed in the new visual and oral systems: telephones and televisions, computers and clocks.

All these prophecies have been proved wrong. Television might have taken up much of people's leisure time, but it has not prevented the increasing publication of, and interest in, books. Technology might offer the teacher a new dimension in description, but the most basic tool remains the book. For this there are several reasons.

- The first reason is that the book offers a connection between the inner world of the individual and the shared structure of the outer world.
- The second reason is that the book is under the command of, rather than dominating, the reader. The reader chooses the time and the pace.
- The third reason is that the written word explores dimensions of thought that no other system can approach – even if visual means can give evidence. How do we explain 'thought' except in a word?

- The fourth reason is that the book is not only private but shared, not only depending on the individual response but a source for discussion.

The book remains the primary resource for the teacher. But this is where the difficulties as well as the opportunities begin. The book can be used or misused, a chance for liberation or associated with pain and failure. For the book serves many functions.

> The most famous predictor of the demise of the book was Marshall McLuhan.[1] He suggested that the technique of printing had changed the way that people think, and that television and other electronic media would change thinking yet again: 'The medium is the message.'
>
> Three quotations summarize the argument and the contradictions:
>
> 1. 'Printing, a ditto device ... the printed book added much to the new cult of individualism. The private, fixed point of view became possible and literacy conferred the power of detachment, non-involvement.'
> 2. 'Until writing was invented, man lived in acoustic space: boundless, directionless, horizonless, in the dark of the mind, in the world of emotion, by primordial intuition, by terror.'
> 3. 'We now live in a global village, a simultaneous happening.'

First, children need to learn how to *use* books.

Some children have the great benefit of knowing all about books from home. Seeing books read and enjoyed does more than teach them about the mechanics of reading. They see the use of books for pleasure, a use that should be continued by the teacher as part of the everyday routines of the school. For many children, however, the use of books at home and at school can be a contrast. This is either because there are so few books at home, if any at all, or because the way that books are approached at home is with so much more pleasure.

The art of learning to read is to cross over the gap between reading as a skill, to be learned for its own sake, and the pleasure that derives from using that skill. Similarly, the use of books depends on convincing children that reading books, whether for a story or for information, is not a chore that has to be done because the teacher demands it but something worth doing to satisfy curiosity.

> Many of the books that children come across in the classroom treat information as if it had to be adapted to a different kind of world that might appeal to children: simplified and fantasized. Even maths books contain elements of deliberate imprecision, using elements that are supposed to appeal especially to children – like asking them to sort out plastic shapes into sets of yellow dogs, orange pigs or purple elephants.
>
> No wonder children comment on them: 'I've never seen people with red or blue faces.'[2]

The books that are available in the classroom should be presented as attractively as possible. This is not always easy. They can quickly become battered and torn. It is important that books should be respected and attractively displayed. This means making sure that children know what books are available, have access to them, and enjoy using them. It is easy to collect books on a particular subject and let them languish on a shelf, rarely being approached by anyone in the class. Explaining what is available is in itself an important task.

The teacher should always be aware that she is teaching children how to use books, techniques of reading that include scanning and searching for information as well as reading the book through. Children need to be challenged by books, by being shown books that are not necessarily at their level, but which contain information they need. It is tempting to restrict the choice of books to those that look attractively packaged; but not all books published for children (the market for school books is large) are as good as they could be. The teacher also needs to use books at her own level and share the resource.

> Children find it easy to be restricted in their reading by arbitrary school rules. This can be through the grading of reading schemes when only books of a predetermined level are available, or through the expectation of teachers. Two children were reading a page: 'The yellow cat saw the brown dog.' They were then asked to read the next page: 'The brown dog saw the yellow cat.' They did, but then they said: 'We can't really read that yet. That's tomorrow's page.'[3]

Whilst some homes demonstrate the pleasure of books, it should be every teacher that does so. This means being seen to read books and to have read them. It means sharing passages with the children, not only because the passage is relevant to the topic but because the teacher has found something genuinely interesting. The books in the classroom should not be restricted just to those provided for the children's use – illustrated story-books and simplified books on topics – but books for the teacher. The gap between the ethos of the classroom and the ethos of the adult world can be overcome by the teacher's own library.

The provision of the teacher's own books is not only a demonstration but a resource. To make the best use of the books the teacher needs to develop the technique of reading to the children. This deserves practice. It is not enough to make sure that the children are listening quietly and paying attention, so that there are no interruptions. Nothing is worse than the 'Sit down and pay attention!' when half-way through a sentence. Whatever is read deserves reading well, and this can only come from practice: putting a genuine relish into the words and being able to communicate the words through gesture, and through being able to glance at the children. The story teller, after all, has direct access to the attention of children. The story reader needs to get as close as possible to the same rapport.

> Sometimes the gap between school books and children's own interests is wide – not because the school books are too demanding but because they try too hard to be at children's own level. This implies an odd mixture of fact and fantasy.[4]
>   One group of children had been reading a book about a fantasy island with strange creatures on it and were asked to draw a picture as a result. Meanwhile they carried out a conversation:
>
>   'I can roll my eyes round.'
>   'When I do that I go cross-eyed.'
>   'If you press the skin it goes white.'
>   'You can paint it white.'
>   'What happens if you turn your eyelids up?'
>   'If you close your eyelids you get a lovely picture in your mind.'
>   'You've got one blue eye and one green eye.'
>   'I know. I've got one which is hazel.'

A book will be either read quietly by one person or read by one person to others. There is no place for any other use of books, like reading round the class, which is a sure way of reducing a text to boredom. The only time when two people should be reading the same text is when one of them is learning to read, or learning to understand what a particular text means. Apart from that the book will need to be used with an audience in mind: the single person reading it, or sharing the one text aloud with others.

Some books can look and be dull. This is one of the problems with reading schemes. Produced cheaply in large quantities, they reduce reading to a task rather than a pleasure. They can actually impede the progress made by children. From the busy teacher's point of view it seems attractive to have books that seem to help teach the children to read and monitor their progress. But teaching reading consists of more than that. One aim is to make sure the children turn to books for pleasure, that there is a genuine discovery of something new.

> 'When I was in the Infants we had the Ladybird books; by the second year I'd finished every single Infant book they had so I had to go to the Lower Juniors. I finished all the books there so I had to get them from the Upper Juniors. In the Upper Juniors I nearly ran out of books. Because there was such a restricted thing and I found I was going ahead of everybody else.' (boy, 11)
>
> 'I get fed up with reading because I've read the book so many times, the same one. It's a little thin story-book, not a library book. I've read it about three or four times so I won't forget it. So I learn the words again.' (girl, 10)

There are many illustrated books that are produced for young children that are easy to read, and easy to learn to read from, whilst still retaining the pleasure of a good story. It is a very demanding task to write a story in language which is simple but not stilted, that appeals to young children but still contains the flavour of real language as it is used every day. But the focus on such stories is on their quality, not on the mechanics of reading; it means that reading has a purpose.

There should always be room and space in a classroom for the reading of stories, setting the foundation for a habit that should last a lifetime. Children need stories for their mixture of personal response and the reflection of a shared world; stories help them make sense of the world. This attempt to enlighten and understand should be true of all stories from the simplest to the most sophisticated.

Even the stories that appear simple, and rely on illustration, can be made into the subjects of discrimination. Children need to learn early the ability to discriminate. They have their favourite books, and they prefer some to others. They can be encouraged to say not only why they like a particular story (rather than be asked 'What do you think of it?' to which the reply is 'good' or 'all right') but something about the story, whether about its subject matter (is it realistic?), its style (are certain phrases repeated?) or its illustrations (are they full of detail yet easy to understand?).

> Not all stories written for young children succeed in combining simplified language with reality. Many of them tend to ask children to collude in an adult construction of 'child-like' playfulness, and use short words which are not easy to decode. A typical example[5] is:
>
> 'Meeow, I like fish',
> said Mr Whiskers.
> 'I can have
> the big yellow fish with green spots.'
> 'No, No, No, Mr Whiskers',
> laughed Mother.

Each book can be responded to at a number of levels. Whilst some are far more demanding than others, a lot depends on how the child interprets the story. It is worth encouraging children to mix stories of different levels of technical demand rather than try to confine them to the 'appropriate' reading age. They should learn that there is a purpose behind different levels of demand and a pleasure that can be derived from a wide variety of texts.

> When one thinks of all the fantasy of children's stories – animals that behave like people and trees that move and talk – it is not surprising that children can be puzzled, whilst accepting this anthropomorphism with equanimity. But how can one explain that an elephant, with such big paws and feet, can carry out all the usual manipulative functions that a human being would do with his hands?
>
> Children have to learn to accept it. Two children are overheard; one says to the other: 'Don't be silly. Father Christmas lives up a chimney, not in a house.'

It is of course possible to ensure that 'real' books all have the same reading age. There are published tables of well-known books that are as sophisticated as any reading scheme in terms of level of demand. But the more closely one looks at the text the more problematical the concept of comparative difficulty becomes. The two extremes – one of big words and simple pictures and the other of densely written, long and closely printed text – are obvious. But in between it is surprising to find what difficulties individual children might have, sometimes with the simplest words:

> 'Once I was trying to read a word and I couldn't find out what the word was and I went to Miss. It was 'the' and because I couldn't read it I was ever so frightened because she kept going on and on and on. (boy, 9)

As we know from the teaching of reading, the ability to decode text is a complex matter, depending on the ability to make physiological and psychological connections. Formal support is helpful, even when we know it is the learner who has to work out how to read. But reading also depends on context: knowing language and knowing about books. This is why there must continue to be a place for extending reading and for continuing to have pleasure in it. It is not always crucially important for children to read ever more difficult material; they can take pleasure sometimes in less demanding texts. They can discriminate between levels of demand. And they can recognize how illustrations work with the text. It does not matter *what* they read. It matters *how* they read.

> There are some authors who are very popular with children and very unpopular with adults. Enid Blyton is the most famous English example. Her texts manage to balance simple security with just enough excitement and are written with unselfconscious simplicity, relying on stereotyped views of foreigners, professors and dogs . . . In a typical scene the 'Famous Five' or 'Secret Seven' go down a dark cave, but one of them remembered to bring a torch and soon they come across steps, so they are safe really. It does children no harm to be voracious readers of books we realize are not demanding.[6]

The taste for reading turns into a habit. Children need to be encouraged to fill with reading every moment when they would otherwise be doing nothing. When they first come into the classroom in the morning they can read a book. The aim for the teacher is to enable children to associate books with pleasure, and to develop a voracious appetite for reading, to make reading so habitual that (as many adults do) they read anything which is available. Once that habit is established then children will want to read texts which are more demanding.

One way of exciting children's interest in books is by looking at the whole process of making them, from meeting authors to looking at production methods. Understanding the author's point of view, his motivation and the way he approaches writing helps children appreciate better their own reading as well as writing skills. It shows there are practical things to learn about style, and that every text is full of choices that have been made, that every sentence is a struggle to find the right words.

Books are also a stimulating insight into the world of industry, with its concern with a product and with marketing. How was the book put together? Why are some books more attractive than others? Why do they range so much in price? How are they distributed? How many similar books are competing for the same market? How do we make choices? The answers to all these questions give children a critical insight into decision-making at a number of levels and with a product that has an immediate and familiar interest.

What one is trying to achieve is to extend children's critical awareness. There are many different styles of reading. No one reads a magazine in the same way as a novel, a newspaper with the same intensity as an academic paper. The critical point is to help children realize and understand the differences, in attitude to audience and in style. Any newspaper is an example of a range of decisions: about which story to carry, and how to illustrate it, which story to give the most prominence to, and which to shorten, if not discard, so that each page has the right balance. Children learn, through parody or emulation, about all aspects of newspapers, including the particular language that is used.

> A class can become involved with the production of a book or a newspaper, from the manufacturing of the paper itself, if the equipment is available, to the finished product. This is an enterprise in which children can take on different roles, from writing and illustrating, to editing and organizing the production. It means careful planning and an enthusiasm for and pride in the finished product. The class newspaper is a useful first start in giving as many chances as possible to put together stories and make choices between them. But the class newspaper works best when it is fairly regular, like a real newspaper, rather than an idea which folds after the first edition.

Every reader is aware of style. This is not an erudite matter. Style informs people's choices, which magazine they read and which books they prefer or avoid. But readers are shy of expressing their reasons for their preferences; they do not feel they have the necessary vocabulary. This is just as true of children as of adults. The use of a book lies in responding to it, and children can be helped to develop a critical frame of reference against which they can reflect on their responses. The easiest kind of text to analyse in terms of style is often the least demanding – or the kind that is written to cause an immediate effect. The editorial sections of popular magazines are prime examples of text written without any care about cliché or stereotype, about non-sequiturs or mixed metaphors. They are therefore the easiest to use in demonstrating differences in 'style'. Thus what can be a complicated analysis can also be carried out simply; and what is an immediate response made articulate.

> Books create a strong 'dialogue' with the reader. They are active instruments of learning. This relationship with the text can be enhanced by tutorials – one to one discussions about

> what children are reading. This has the benefit of creating a real dialogue: not answers to set 'closed' questions, but personal judgements.[7]

This does not imply that the classroom should be deluged in comics, newspapers and magazines. Indeed, there is a danger in using secondary texts of this sort as an easy way out, in seeming to appeal to the lowest common denominator of taste. It is essential that when these texts are looked at in the classroom, compared and contrasted, they are examined seriously, in the kind of way that gives children the deeper thirst for literature of a more satisfying quality. The crucial insight for children is to realize the different levels of reading, and to be capable of reading complex texts in a different way from glancing at the headlines of a newspaper. Comparisons are crucial; the aim is not merely to reproduce material, but understand it.

The taste we wish to encourage in children is, first, for the habitual pleasure of reading and then for the development into the excitement of reading, especially novels. They might read anything but one wishes to see them develop their preferences. This is why contrasts are so important, and why the ability to write a page, like a parody, of a 'real' novel encourages more sophisticated demands. The reading of stories and then novels should be an integral part of classroom learning rather than something carried out in contrast to it.

> One of the mythologies of learning is that whatever the teacher says is what the pupils learn. A similar mythology affects literature; thus what a book contains is understood by all in the same way. Of course the moment literature becomes a study then it is clear from all the critics' quarrels that there are any number of interpretations. Even students studying literature come out with strange idiosyncratic understandings of texts.
>
> Differences of interpretation are to be encouraged as a form of dialogue and understanding. It does matter what the text says and it does matter that each reader can demonstrate his understanding.[8]

Children do, however, associate classrooms with certain kinds of books – with maths schemes and with topic books. In both cases it is easy to use books at a low level, with repetitive exercises or the copying out of information. There are not many occasions when children have the chance to apply their critical skills to information books. This is a pity. There are many contrasts between the ways in which information is presented, in the choice of fact and the choice of illustration. When children are asked to gather information from books it is important that they learn to discriminate:

- Are there contradictions between one text and another?
- Which are the most significant facts?
- Is there one diagram that best sums it up?
- Do the illustrations really help the text?
- Can they remember where they found the information?

Exploring books as a source of information needs to be encouraged; it is, after all, not only a useful resource for the teacher but another style of working that children will continue to develop throughout their lives. In order for it to be successful the children need to know exactly what they are looking for and why. Using work cards with explicit questions can help. Having an audience to whom to present the material can give an extra sense of purpose. But all the time the emphasis is on active judgement, and not passive reception. It is when the text receives little response – another boring magazine or a mass of facts – that the reading becomes linked with inactivity, with passing time.

Reading a book is usually an individual activity. There are only so many occasions on which one would wish to share a text. But there is one way in which the personal response can be linked to others and that is in acting as a critic and recommender of books to others. The comments that are made on books should have a purpose: to encourage others to read them, and to enable others to discriminate. Children are natural critics.

Chapter 18

The Uses of Assessment

'Lately I got quite low, right, because the fourth year words I get are quite hard . . . Spelling is difficult. I've had a cry but on my own.'

(boy, 10)

Teaching depends on assessment. It is possible to give a wonderful lecture or a brilliant broadcast from which people might learn, but sustained teaching relies on the ability to analyse how pupils are learning and to diagnose what they need. At the end of a lesson or a day one evaluates what took place, and concentrates on what concepts the children have learned, what knowledge they have acquired and the skills they have displayed. Preparation relies on that critical insight into individual children's attainments.

In one form or another it is impossible not to assess. Everyone has an opinion of other people. Some are judged to be intelligent, and others less so, some friendly and therefore preferable and others deemed inadequate or stupid. Children themselves are as quick as any one in making judgements, and have some very clear views about themselves.[1] We therefore need to start from the premise that assessment is inevitable. The question is how we can use it in a constructive way, how we can replace subjective prejudices with objective judgement, and how we can use assessment to help rather than hinder.

> Every interview panel and every person who makes appointments relies on assessments, and for hundreds of years these have been made against a series of clear criteria. The interview panel for the post of Kapellmeister in Leipzig in the early eighteenth century were especially assiduous in having very clear guidelines on which they would make their judgements, balancing previous experience with qualifications, ability to compose music with ability to run the choir. They were unanimous in offering the post to the best possible candidate.
>
> Unfortunately he turned it down, so they had to offer the post to the runner-up: J. S. Bach.

Assessment in education tends to be associated more with competition than with diagnosis, with personal success or failure against others rather than with the recording of achievement and the means of help. For this reason assessment has become a political issue, used as a deliberate way of making distinctions between people on the grounds that equality of opportunity leads directly to inequality, or that it is important to earmark and reward an elite who have capacity and to diminish those who do not. Assessment is associated in many minds with an examination system in which people are either successes or failures, or, even if successes, graded according to their individual rank: 'What marks did *you* get?'; 'How many exams did *you* pass?'; 'What class of awards?'

From the teacher's point of view achieving the greatest success in public examinations for her pupils is part of the good she is trying to do them, but it is not the central motivating force, nor the most significant. The traditional problem with examinations is that they are seen as a competition in which only a proportion can excel, and only a proportion pass. It is a way of dividing people into different grades of success and failure. Examinations are not seen as a way of recording the achievements of each individual. Thus the sense that many people achieve nothing is as much part of the examination system as the success achieved by some.

> *There is a close relationship between the social uses of personal assessment and educational achievements. This is the example of academic snobbery: What school did you go to? What college? What subjects did you take? Either 'Ah' or 'Oh', approval or displeasure.
> 'I did Greek and Latin.' 'Ah.'
> 'I did technology.' 'Oh.'

In the face of the misuse of assessment it is worthwhile constantly to remind ourselves that assessment is inevitable and that it has its positive uses. We can do little without it. One concern for the teacher is to differentiate between pupils, to provide appropriate material for each one, to make sure that the needs of all are catered for, whether pupils are gifted in particular subjects, or whether they have learning problems. Each one needs sustenance and individual help, and each one depends on the teacher's recognition of this and the diagnosis of what to do about it.

There are a variety of instruments that should be available to help the teacher, but in the end it is the teacher's own judgement that counts. This assessment must be based on as much analysis as possible. Some of the tests themselves depend on the teacher's first assessment. Does he suspect that underlying particular learning difficulties are other ones? Can the child see everything that is put on the board? Can the child hear every question that is being asked? Children are quick to assess themselves but are not good at self-diagnosis. They become accustomed to, and unwittingly disguise, the fact that they cannot properly see or hear. It is amazing how much prowess is put into adapting to, and disguising, physical limitations.

There is a great distinction between assessments based on impressions and assessments using a battery of standardized tests. True assessment and diagnosis lie somewhere between.

> Before the age of about 8 children are aware of and believe in their own abilities and are not afraid to experiment and try. There are exceptions, of course, when, for instance, the task of reading is imposed on them and they find that they cannot perform as expected. The starting point for understanding mathematical principles or any new 'language' of skills can cause fear and embarrassment. But these are private matters.
> After the age of 8 children are more aware of two things:

> - The first is the difference between effort and success. Some children find things easy and others don't succeed however hard they try.
> - The second is that they observe this discrepancy between effort and achievement in others as well as themselves; they are aware of competition.
>
> Unless the teacher is careful some children who find things easy will cease to bother and others who find things difficult will cease to try.[2]

Assessment means being sensitive to the way in which one can rely on prejudice, having a view of particular children which then is justified after the event, or labelling children in such a way that they can only fulfil pre-judged expectations. It also means being sensitive to the limitations of some tests. Much depends on the way in which tests are expressed and the way that children approach them. Fear of being tested is in itself a distorting factor.

Children do expect their work to be judged. This is both a positive and negative fact. It is positive because they want to test their achievements against the opinion of the teacher. They respect what the teacher says about their work, and they long for praise. The negative aspect derives from the same respect and the same wish to please the teacher. It means that they can spend more intellectual and emotional energy trying to guess what will please the teacher than in carrying out the task. It can also mean that the dominating motivation is simply to provide whatever the teacher wants. Work is then produced against the requirements of the test.

Children are not the only ones to work according to the test. If examination or test results are the most important indicators of success in the teachers' minds then there is a strong temptation to teach just those things that will be tested.

> A reminder: at the start of the new school year teachers observed their new classes, working out what they needed, how they would behave, and how they needed to be treated. At the end of the day the teachers were able to give a clear account of every individual in the class: which would be bright, which difficult, which would work hard. It was impressive to see how much knowledge had been acquired.
>   But at the end of the whole year, the teachers were again asked for their assessment of the children, and they gave almost exactly the same answers.[3]

Some material lends itself easily to being tested. Remembering facts, whether in a subject or general knowledge, is far more amenable to examination than skills, whether of expression in art and writing or of practice. Preparing material so that it can be tested can have an inhibiting and narrowing effect.

There are many different forms and purposes of assessment: formative, diagnostic, summative and evaluative. The first two are essentially to help the child's development. The latter two are more concerned with testing what kind of help and support the child is getting.

Formative assessment is concerned with recognizing and delineating the achievements of a pupil so that the teacher knows what she should learn next. It is the starting point for further planning.

Diagnostic assessment is concerned with finding out any learning difficulties the pupil might have, and what particular characteristics the pupil brings to the work, so that a teacher knows not only what she should learn next but how she can be helped.

Summative assessment is concerned with recording the overall achievements of a pupil judged against expectations, comparing the achievement of one against another.

Evaluative assessment is concerned with learning something about the achievements of a class, or a school as a whole, so that there is some indication of the success or failure of a particular part of the curriculum.

Formative and diagnostic assessment are both characterized by their positive concern for helping the teacher find out what the pupil needs to know and how to go about it. They are the everyday tools of the teacher, the creative aspects of assessment.

Summative and evaluative assessment are the instruments by which pupils, teachers and schools are judged. They are what the general public associates with assessment. To call them, in contrast, negative would not be accurate. The problem is that they are often used negatively. The headline that attracts the average journalist will be one that seems like a scandal: 'Standards are falling.' On the one hand all kinds of assessment, evaluative as well as diagnostic, can be used positively. The more we know about children learning and the difference that teachers make the better. On the other hand assessment can be used to highlight the differences between pupils and schools, to put down and dispirit as well as to cajole and support.

> There are two contrasting requirements of assessment.
> When the National Curriculum was introduced in England and Wales it was initially as a result of a drive to find things to test. The initial political impulse was to have simple national tests to compare successes and failures, to highlight the competitive aspect of education. From this impulse, by a series of accidents, grew a most cumbersome system which was to include not only batteries of national tests in a range of subjects, but the opportunity for teachers to compare work from each other's classrooms, all taking a great deal of time.
> As the system is simplified it has reverted again to the initial political idea; instead of being concerned with all aspects of assessment, formative as well as evaluative, the national tests are reduced to simple league tables of results, to compare one school with another.[4]

The debate about assessment centres essentially around the contrast between a record of achievement and a result of a test. This distinction can be put in terms of whether assessment is *criterion-referenced* or *norm-referenced*.

- *Criterion-referenced* assessment is a system based on the quality of work produced by an individual pupil without regard to how it compares with others' work. The criteria are the set of achievements one would expect of a pupil, but whatever is achieved is recognized.
- *Norm-referenced* assessment is based on the principle of comparing pupils with each other, putting them in rank order, so that the grade a pupil receives depends on how he compares with others. He might have done well, but if all others in the class have done better he is bottom.

Different exam systems use different methods. There is a general desire to aspire to criterion-referenced assessment; higher education is based on this system so that in any given year either many or few can achieve the honour of a first-class degree. Theoretically 100 per cent of students could do so. The exam system that affects 16- and 18-year-olds is also theoretically able to vary the grades given out according to the standards of the year. But that is where the problem begins. In the minds of most people examinations are inevitably norm-related. No one would believe that a large number of students could get first-class degrees. Above-average successes at Advanced level would provoke thoughts that standards had gone down rather than up.

The problem is that people's minds are imbued from an early age with the idea that all assessment is norm-related. Children compare each other in the class. They rate their own work more highly against theoretical standards and lower when compared to that of people they know.[5] Everyone knows where he or she stands in relation to the rest of the class. Thereafter examinations are associated with competition. Only some can enter a particular university or gain a medical qualification, or be trained to do a particular job. We are back to the assessment of character at interview. Even in marking, the tendency is to go for a norm, in case people get suspicious about 'standards' of assessment.

> There can be two reasons for pupils doing well at their work: because they are good at it, or because the task is easy. The two relate, as far as teachers are concerned. They try to set tasks which are demanding but which *can* be carried out well. There are times, too, when it is useful to set easy activities. This adds to the variety but also encourages. But we must be careful that children do not balk at more challenging activities.[6]

Assessment by examination can be contrasted with records of achievement. Examinations denote failure as much as success. Many pupils never receive any certificate at all, but pass through the education system without anything palpable to show for it in terms of the currency of public life. Examinations can therefore be traumatic, since so much depends on them. Records of achievement, on the other hand, attempt to delineate the strengths and the particular characteristics of each individual, giving a profile of their learning, from the subjects they are best in, or weakest at, to the skills they have learned.

When a teacher diagnoses the learning processes of children he can be aided by having a clear idea of what criteria to use, criteria ranging from learning styles to particular abilities: the ability to construct an argument, or use evidence, the ability to be original or to be precise. Thus he becomes aware of the characteristics of his pupils beyond their knowledge of content.

This implies constant attention to the progress of pupils and the use of a variety of sources of information. Teachers often find that the more formal tests merely confirm what they have already observed. They would be concerned if they did not. Some of the sources of information will be formal, and others much less so. Sources of information include general impressions as well as written tests, pupils' self-assessment as well as rating scales, marking course work as well as checklists, assignments as well as practical tests.

Assessment does not have to be formal. This is the distinction between the word 'assessment', which embraces a variety of techniques, and 'testing', which is associated with something precise and narrow. Assessment includes many forms, beyond written tests. Assessment needs to be constructed around three different aspects:

- the way that the questions are presented, e.g. oral or written, through a practical or by a computer;
- the way in which they are responded to, e.g. through practical skills, orally, mentally or written;
- the way the pupils answer, e.g. choosing answers from multiple-choice questions, putting a response into a computer, writing an essay, giving a prepared oral answer, being interviewed.

Every task that is given to children needs to be assessed by the teacher; for the moment the teacher notices what a child has done she will have made some kind of assessment of it, and there should never be an occasion when a child produces work that is completely ignored. Some forms of assessment will be set up by the teacher to diagnose particular problems; reading tests and analysis of visual or aural difficulty are examples. Other forms will consist of seeing whether the pupil has succeeded in fulfilling a task by answering a problem – like building a model of a bridge.

One can sometimes make too clear a distinction between the assessment associated with mathematics – a tick or a cross – and that associated with written work where the teacher's judgement is more subjective. Real diagnosis in mathematics goes beyond the right or wrong; it explores what concepts children understand and how they are thinking. Nor is assessment in writing purely subjective, influenced by presentation as much as style. There are clear criteria applicable to essays against which clear judgements can be made. But the more clearly assessment is thought about, the better the task that is given to the pupils.

Thinking about assessment is a starting point for the preparation of interesting material. These are two reasons for this. The first is that the teacher always wants to diagnose any learning difficulties and will think of tasks that meet particular needs. The second is that thinking of interesting problems to solve ensures that the task being presented has a basis in reality, and challenges the pupil with material he recognizes. Finding the best route on a map, judging which is the most popular breakfast cereal and why, learning how to test how high different balls bounce, working out how many beans there would be in a tin, testing the best shape for a paper boat to enable it to carry a heavy weight – all these different problems give pupils a chance to experiment, to find out, to explore.

Different forms of assessment have their strengths and weaknesses. The most perfect forms of diagnosis – like marking – can be so time-consuming that the teacher can never do it as well as he feels he ought to. The tests that are easiest to administer – right or wrong answers in mathematics – do not necessarily tell us anything. Tests which are composed of *discrete* questions – 'When was the Battle of Waterloo?' 'What is a watershed?' – can sample from a wide range of knowledge. But they make it difficult to assess the integration of knowledge and skills.

Tests of discrete questions:

• Can be easy to administer.

But can be artificial.

• Can be relatively objective.

But can yield results that are difficult to interpret in such a way that the pupil can be helped.

• Can be marked easily.

But cannot assess the answer to open questions like 'Why?'.

Tests which are made up of integrated tasks:

• Can be realistic.

But can also be very time-consuming.

• Can explore the way that knowledge is underpinned by skills and understanding.

But can be very difficult to mark.

Marking is itself a task that needs to be learned. Marking written work by children is time-consuming and is nevertheless often ignored by the pupils. All they want to know is: Did the teacher like it? and What mark did I get? At that level they will have learned nothing. In order to make something worthwhile the teacher needs to concentrate on two things:

• The first is to concentrate on one particular feature of the work. If, for example, the pupil has presented work which is full of spelling mistakes, a series of hieroglyphics down the page and into the text – 'Sp!' – will not necessarily help the child to learn, unless the teacher has set up self-correcting techniques when the pupil keeps writing until it is perfect (which works only with short pieces). It is better to pick out the most common fault, comment on it and make sure that the right answer is learned.
• The second is to make certain that the pupil looks closely at the work and the comments by asking a follow-up question which the pupil is expected to answer. This entails noting what the question is so that the teacher does not forget it. It is too easy to ask a question which remains rhetorical since one forgets one has asked it.

There are many things that we need to know about pupils, both general and particular. What they know is only one aspect; we need to know their skills and interests, their particular strengths and weaknesses. A record of achievement can be a cumbersome thing to do really well, including information from parents and the pupils themselves. Meanwhile parents as well as the teacher will wish to know exactly how the pupil is performing. This is where *checklists* can be helpful. They remind us of the skills that we expect children to attain. They can be filled in simply – by putting a tick in a box or shading in a criterion. They can be applied to a variety of subjects, and used right from the start of infant school.

The kinds of questions a checklist would ask can vary enormously. In language one would first wish to know whether the pupil can write his or her name, whether he shows interest in books, enjoys listening to a story, all the way to whether she can read complicated texts, and take part in debates. In maths one would first wish to know whether a pupil knows numbers, is able to measure, all the way to complex algebra. In science one would first wish to know whether a pupil is willing to guess, describe parts of the body, talk about natural things, all the way to being able to carry out an exact experiment. In art one would at first wish to know whether a pupil knows the names of colours and shapes, all the way to appreciating the aesthetics of paintings. One would also wish to record the pupils' social abilities as they develop them, from their self-help skills and motor skills right up to their abilities to maintain good working relationships with a variety of other people.

Checklists can be especially useful when assessment needs to be based on observation. As pupils produce more and more material the teacher accumulates a rich source on which to understand development. The work that pupils produce in the normal course of events is probably a truer guide to their achievement than a series of tests. Tests, even in the form of written examinations, can bring out information that is misleading for two reasons. One is that the conditions of an examination and the time-scale can cause panic in some who take them, and these will never do themselves justice. The other is that examinations can be culturally biased – depending on particular forms of knowledge and particular ways of expressing them.

> Some teachers find it hard to learn how to assess their pupils and their lessons. When making evaluations either of individuals or tasks it is far too easy to write things like:
>
> - 'That went well.'
> - 'The pupils enjoyed it.'
> - 'She really works hard.'
> - 'He's good at maths.'
>
> rather than trying to analyse the particular characteristics of the pupil or the lesson so that substantial help can be given.

Looking at pupils' course work is also especially useful when it can be shared with other teachers. The Task Group on Assessment and Testing recommended that teachers should meet on a regular basis to compare the work of the pupils in their classes, in order to contrast it with the national test results, and in order to make sure that their standards were as high as other teachers'. In the event resources were not forthcoming to enable this to happen but it remains a good idea and one worth doing within the school. After all, behind every assessment lies the assessor: and would everyone make the same judgement every time? Personal bias and personal mood can too easily affect assessment. This is natural, but it can only be overcome by recognizing the fact and sharing one's assessment with others.

> A reminder of the 'Pygmalion' effect. This is where a person, or an audience, is told something about another person before they have met him. If it is suggested that that person is 'cold'- or 'warm'-hearted, people will think of him as if he were one or the other and be biased for or against. They would believe him, or not, according to this pre-planted information. Similarly the child labelled 'clever' or 'stupid' before entering the teacher's class will be found to be so – for months, not days.[7]

It should always be remembered that there is a difference between assessment and evaluation. Many things are assessed but few are properly evaluated. Sometimes an obsession with assessment can even threaten quality, not just because of the time it takes – weighing a cow does not produce more milk – but because of the desire to create distinctions: the idea that there has to be bad, as well as good, in order to create a 'league table'.

Assessment can either be something threatening – performance indicators and examinations – or positive, involving praise. For a teacher it is important to remember that the positive aspects of assessment – making a diagnosis of what is needed and recognizing achievement – are a central part of teaching. No teacher should allow assessment to be dominated by tests that are imposed on him, but should show a more subtle and more creative use of all that real assessment entails.

Chapter 19

The Role of the Teacher

'If you had a teacher who was horrible you wouldn't want to get on and learn and if you've a nice teacher it's easier to learn.'

(girl, 10)

Teachers are closely observed by children, their personalities detected and their individual mannerisms analysed. But children also accept that, whatever their personalities, teachers have a professional role to play. Teachers possess a particular authority, and have their own place in the hierarchy of the school. One of the first things that teachers have to learn is to accept their role. One of the first things that children detect in a teacher is whether he has accepted it.

The difference a good teacher can make must never be underestimated. Sometimes it is difficult to detect exactly when and how the teacher has helped the individual pupil, and it is a characteristic of human nature not to wish to acknowledge it. Everyone has an instinctive sense that they have learned – 'I like learning but I resent being taught' – and that they are beholden to no one. But it is also the art of the good teacher, as opposed to lecturer, to draw attention not to his own performance but to the learning of the pupil. This partly explains why it is difficult to acknowledge the crucial role that teachers play.

> 'When I first came, when I looked at all the tutors, I wanted Miss L 'cos she looked, you know, the most unstrict. And when I looked at Mr P, he looked strict and I hoped I didn't have him – and when I turned out to have him I went "Oh no!" and then I found out he was a right softie.' (girl, 11)

There are two issues which underlie the role of the teacher, and which explain the difference that teachers make. The first issue is that of the teacher as *mentor*.

The idea of the mentor draws attention to the capacity in one person to bring out the best in another. The mentor can be a parent rather than a teacher, or role model as well as a role. The mentor is the person who has the authority to criticize as well as be constructive, to command as well as reflect. All depends on the relationship. We have already pointed out how crucial are the relationships that young children make; their academic development depends on their chances and abilities to share in extended dialogues. Relationships with teachers subsequently become one of the most important factors in children's learning, knowing that they have met someone who can take an interest in having a discussion, in bringing out and extending their ideas, in making them feel valued.

> There can be few people who do not remember from their own school experience at least one outstanding lesson that becomes symbolic of all the undetected mastery of the teacher: the lesson when a teacher became so enthused about a subject that he forgot what he was supposed to teach and began to explain something that mattered to him, or the lesson when, for the first time, some difficult subject was made understandable.

It is because of the authority of the teacher that mentoring is valued. It is not just a personal dialogue, as with a friend, but one which acknowledges a certain formality, and the desire, on the part of the pupil, to learn. This is an expectation that the teacher needs to make clear: that learning depends on the pupil and that it is a responsibility that the teacher fosters. The true mentor is the person to whom the pupil turns, the person who is seen as a source of interest as well as instruction.

The second issue is that of the teacher as *explainer*. When children describe what they like about the best teachers they often use the word 'explain'. The teacher makes a subject interesting; he sets up experiments, brings in interesting materials, and is not merely bound by routine. This means that the teacher becomes a source of knowledge.[1]

> Teachers face two problems in motivating their children, and the two problems are to some extent contradictory. One is the social ethos in many schools, especially secondary, which suggests to pupils that school work is a bad thing – that the norm is to do as little as possible, and that 'swots' are despised.
>
> The other is that when children do work hard they think of nothing but exams, as if no work is done for its own sake.
>
> These social positions, however, do clarify the solution: the importance of a relevant curriculum together with a clear sense of purpose that is shared with colleagues. Pupils, after all, need to know *why* they are at school and this is rarely explained to them.[2]

For many years a great deal of attention has been paid to the abilities of teachers to know and control their pupils and even more to their ability to develop social skills. Less attention, and sometimes too little, has been paid to content: the ability of teachers to know their subjects well and continue learning about them. A teacher is not expected to know everything. There are occasions when he will be learning alongside the pupils. But these are exceptional. The pupils like to feel that the teacher is able to answer questions that arise on a variety of subjects, that the teacher is an authority. This does not mean that the teacher has to worry in case he does not know; that can be readily acknowledged and the information sought out in books. But these are the exceptions that become valuable as a shared experience because the teacher is generally well-prepared and, above all, interested in the subject.

Children are quick to adapt to the teacher's style. They do not mind changing their methods of working or reorganizing the classroom. What they dislike is inconsistency and insecurity. They will put up with rather boring routines; but they do want to know where they stand in relation to the teacher. Children find temporary teachers more difficult because they cannot set up constant expectations, and they find them easier to resist. Children also want the teacher to retain the distance of the professional rather than become genuinely upset, or plead with them.[3]

The problem for many teachers at the beginning of their careers in particular is that they want to be loved, to be popular. This is a natural human desire, but it becomes a problem when it is explicit. The more a person wants to be loved the less easy it is to love him. The more a person seeks approval the less he gets. But it is sometimes difficult for teachers to resist the craving to be liked, and the tendency to pay more attention to the children who detect this and play up to it.

It is the pupil's role, and not the teacher's, to seek approval. Yet many teachers find themselves responding naturally to some children and therefore unintentionally ignoring others. Children detect in their teachers when they are responding to them, and when they are beginning to have power over them. In some ways the relationship between teachers and pupils can be seen as a kind of power struggle; who is to be in command? Children naturally seek the teacher's approval – for rewards and responsibilities. But they also know that there are teachers who do not have that inner security of accepting their own role, and treating all pupils alike.[4]

> 'If you're naughty she speaks deeply and when she looks happy she likes you. She always looks happy at me.' (boy, 10)
>
> 'I'm quite happy here because Mrs P likes me and she likes giving me responsibility. That's how I know she likes me and she doesn't shout at me a lot when I've done something wrong. She tells me off but that's not too bad.' (girl, 10)

When one studies how children behave in the class one can see how some of them, often the 'brightest', begin to acquire more and more of the teacher's attention. They know what the teacher wants and can reward the teacher for the time spent with them, confirming him in his own view as a competent (and liked) teacher. If some pupils have more power over the teacher than others this leaves a lot of 'invisible' children, who have not acquired the same art of teacher pleasing.[5]

The role of mentor and explainer depends on treating all children in the same way, in noticing all their needs, and in being consistent. The desire to be liked can be undermining because it leads a teacher to be over-responsive to certain pupils – to being 'controlled' by them. Other children see the unfairness of this and the abandoning of the role of 'teacher'. That is when the essential trust between teacher and pupils breaks down.

> One example of a teacher who is undermined by inconsistency – losing his temper and then revealing his desire to be approved – is summarized by an 11-year-old:
>
> 'Well, he screams at you; he doesn't just shout, "Don't do it," he screams at you and like afterwards, one of my friends got really upset 'cos he had a go at her about her work in front of the whole class, which I don't think's fair, and he kept me back 'cos I sit next to her and we're friends and he started, like, being more friendly, and saying, "I'm your friend." I don't think that's right – you go crawling back to a child after you've started at them just to become their friend.'

If some teachers inadvertently seek approval from their pupils, more seek it from their peers. Every teacher wants to be seen as able and to be praised, to be part of a community that acknowledges his work, and his success, whatever the circumstances. Teachers seek reference points for the support they feel they need, and they either find a group from which they gain approval, or leave teaching. Teaching can be a very lonely job despite the strong tradition of personal relationships: the one-to-one inter-action. Teachers need to replace the sought-out approval of pupils with the sharing of concerns with colleagues, and yet this is not always easy to do. The staffroom can be a lonely place when it does not provide professional relationships – and an intelligent conversation about teaching.[6]

It follows that the approval of the headteacher is an important factor in the teacher's security in his role; but this is not just a matter of liking or disliking personalities. Headteachers will always tend to have a special relationship with those teachers they have appointed. But the head's support for teachers comes about by setting up many professional dialogues, by encouraging as many discussions as possible about the curriculum, and about school policies.

> As teachers become used to their profession, their focus of attention changes from the teacher's own acts and planning, to pupils' acts or thinking. Gradually teachers accumulate knowledge of what kinds of teaching work best. They also become less interested in large quantities of fact and instead concentrate on a few principles or ways of reasoning.
>
> But on the other hand, as teachers become more refined, they can also get caught up in familiar routines. Just as they can become more effective, so they can become less so.[7]

As teachers get older they become more and more aware of staffroom relationships. They realize how important adult support and mutual interest becomes. This can be undermined by the strong tradition of isolationism, of each teacher 'doing his own thing'. In the end teachers need to extend their experience by sharing it with others. Instead of the shyness of being observed and the desire to be 'safe' in the classroom, teachers need to learn how to discuss what they are doing in a professional way, not merely sharing anecdotes about individuals but developing their ideas about the curriculum and the materials they use. Teachers can often enjoy their work without enjoying the conditions in which they do it; as they get older, teachers care more about their working conditions, not for their own sake but for the effect they have on their own standards of performance. Teachers learn that they need a framework of support outside the classroom.[8]

> There are many styles of teaching, but there seems to be one which is a certain disaster. This is the one where children are 'free' to 'discover' things for themselves, without any structure or 'scaffolding' for their work. Children, themselves, should not be expected to plan and manage their learning. That is the teachers' role.[9]

Some teachers in their first years try not to acknowledge their need for support, as if it were a sign of weakness. But apart from the pleasure of teaching, professional dialogue is one of the great excitements of the job. Teachers rate certain things about a school highly; and the two most important factors are sensitive and supportive leadership and well-motivated staff. They see those two qualities as far outweighing pupils' academic abilities or pupils' or parents' involvement in decision-making. What they mean by support and motivation is the ability to share in conversations and policy-making on professional issues, like the curriculum, special educational needs, and health education.[10]

When teachers have become experienced professionals there are four general rules that they have learned from their experience of teaching:

1. Their attention and interest changes from a concern with their own acts and planning towards a concern with the pupils' acts and thinking.
2. They accumulate knowledge about the way that different pieces of teaching work, so that they are able to choose which works best from a wide repertoire.
3. They change from trying to transmit large quantities of facts to concentration on essential concepts, a few principles of ways of reasoning.
4. On the other hand, when teachers have taught a long time their work can slide into a routine and as a consequence interest them less, so that they become less effective.

All these factors are helped or hindered by the amount of discussion teachers have about the issues of teaching. These are not just theoretical matters. They are not matters that the young teacher, first struggling to cope, finds important. But they are matters that become important to the teacher when he has accumulated experience and knowledge. It is then that issues about pupils' learning, methodology and concepts become so interesting, and the discussion of these issues with those who have daily experience of them is the mark of the professional teacher.

The question in the development of the new teacher is how quickly he will demonstrate this kind of curiosity. Of course the first concern is coping – surviving in the classroom. The second concern is having enough knowledge. But once these are learned they need to be refined. The first stages of teaching might centre on classroom organization and discipline; but the later stages are far more concerned with how pupils think and learn.

> Teachers' attitudes to pupils vary not only between individual children but, in terms of their general expectations, between teachers. Some, for instance, have a strong belief in the abilities of children; others think that children are not capable of doing much. Some teachers believe that they are nurturing the whole child; others, that they are giving children tools to work with – particular skills. Teachers can be placed between these variables:[11]

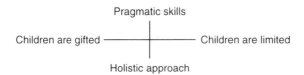

The problem is that some teachers never go beyond the first stage. They continue to 'survive', to occupy children with set routines. And the problem is that children put up with this. Some children are active attention-seekers. If all children were so active, some teachers could not survive. The children who do not make demands are, in a secret kind of way, a relief to the teacher: they can quietly remain obscure and let the teacher cope with the routine.

The great danger for every teacher is to rely purely on routine, and to mistake routine for good classroom management. This can come about when teachers do not have sustained conversations with others about their practice. The differences between good and bad teachers are very clear. With children in the early years, the good teacher demonstrates lively and purposeful involvement in the children's learning; the poor teacher merely lets the children remain occupied so that their activities are brief, unelaborated and desultory. With older children, the good teacher creates an atmosphere of excitement and sustained concentration and makes demands of each individual. The poor teacher engages children in routine, undemanding tasks.[12]

> When children are asked what phrase the teacher uses most their answers are surprising. They do not say 'Right', as they acknowledge that as a signal. Nor do they say that teachers say 'Well done', 'Stop!' or 'Naughty boy!'
> The phrase that children say that teachers use most of all is 'Do it again.' This is followed by the second most characteristic phrase, 'Carry on where you left off.'

It is worth pointing out some of the worse aspects of classroom practice in order to highlight what is effective. In sustained observation of teachers in many classrooms there were great variations in what was expected and obtained. The worst classrooms had some (or all) of the following characteristics:

- The predominant activity was writing practice.
- There was great emphasis on quantity and simple punctuation.
- Most teacher–pupil exchanges were to do with spelling.
- Uniform tasks were set whatever the ability of the pupils.
- Many tasks were far too easy for the pupils – like more and more simple addition.
- Teachers provided instant solutions to a constant stream of problems.
- Groups were used as convenient seating arrangements rather than specifically used for teaching.
- Children would queue up for considerable lengths of time to enquire what to do next.

To point out faults is easier than to put them right. But one of the difficulties for teachers is that children, as it were, connive with these routines. They might wish for something better, but if that is all the teacher wants, what can they do? They look happy and busy because that is what the teacher wants. They seek to please teachers by doing whatever the teacher expects. Children learn quickly the level of expectation – and the lower the expectation the easier it is for both teacher and pupil. Children soon work out what does please teachers: neat work, good spelling, following the right procedures; these are what attract the teacher's praise.

What is lacking in a routine classroom is the diagnosis of individual pupils' needs and the knowledge of how to match these needs with appropriate material. Thus the more able children tend to be given lots of practice in the same *routine* tasks – they do more, but not at a higher level. The low attainers, conversely, tended to be given lots of *new* material.

Part of the role of the teacher is to set up a framework of accepted ritual in which children feel secure. This is the structure within which real demands are made. The teacher needs to consider:

- Has every child a demanding task that he has not done before, and has understood?
- What is the underlying concept in this material?
- Is every child concentrating and sustaining interest in what he is doing?

The effective teacher is someone who is constantly analysing the processes of learning, by diagnosing what the children have worked on, and by considering their work in relation to the work of others – in the same school, or elsewhere. In the past teachers have tended to be characterized as either 'child-centred' or 'teacher-structured'. The 'child-centred' teachers have the virtue of being idealists but rely on feelings and intuitions rather than on analysis. The 'teacher-structured' tend to put emphasis on the need to 'deliver' the basic curriculum. In fact every teacher needs to combine an ideal concern for every pupil with the ability to analyse pupils' learning. This is, after all, where teaching becomes stimulating and challenging.[13]

The teacher needs other people to help him reflect on the practice of teaching. The teacher is, after all, himself a learner, and part of teaching is the reflection and evaluation of lessons, or what the pupils have really learned. It is not a question of saying, 'Well, they enjoyed it, and they behaved well.' The kind of insight a teacher requires is of a more penetrating kind.

> The difference between coping with routine and making real demands is often pointed out. It is also not difficult to analyse poor practice. The problem is that there is an ideal that we should expect from every teacher – an ideal not always sustainable. We need to realize that at best teaching is a very demanding job and we need some understanding about why some teachers use routines just to keep going. The reason for this is often the sheer number of children in a class. How much easier it would be with 10 or 15 children!

The role of the teacher includes reflecting on the practice of teaching and diagnosing the learning of pupils as well as inspiring and interesting them. It also includes the duty of passing on information, often at the service of an agreed curriculum. Sometimes the roles and duties come into tension as between the 'child-centred' or 'curriculum delivery' models of teaching. This contrast in style is illustrated by contrasting the ways in which French and British teachers are expected to behave.[14]

The French primary teacher's goal is passing on a body of knowledge. The British teacher views his role as imparting the necessary skills and attitudes which allow children to direct their own learning.

The French teacher accepts a traditional style of teaching and sees this as no problem. The Briton sees a tension between traditional and progressive teaching styles and is sensitive to the conflicting demands of governors, parents, headteachers and inspectors.

> Teachers need constant renewal. This is not just a matter of being up to date, or adapting to new demands. It is a need for fresh stimulus, for new insights, for the chance to reflect on what is happening. In-service courses are therefore crucial.
> But we sometimes forget that, for a teacher, to become a learner once again can be traumatic. Teachers find it a threatening experience, at first, to be on a course, and have difficulty in accepting doubts and uncertainty.[15]

The French teacher enjoys more support from other professionals such as psychologists and remedial teachers. The British one takes on far more responsibility for the whole child. When in difficulty, the French teacher calls in the parents. The British teacher tries to avoid doing so.

The French teacher is accustomed to the demands of a national curriculum and accepts the need to meet attainment targets; the desire to avoid having children repeating a year leads to didactic teaching methods. The British teacher is used to autonomy, with individual notions of pedagogy.

Of course some of these differences change, especially according to the changing views of a national curriculum. But they do highlight the alternative views one can take about the teacher's role. This is not a standard or a static concept. There are choices in style and attitudes that teachers make, according to their personal and shared beliefs.

> Some of the 'dilemmas', the points of conflict and choice, in the role of the teacher can be shown in the possible contrasts of view that can be found between French and British teachers:[16]
>
> | France | Britain |
> |---|---|
> | The child as student. | The whole child. |
> | The teacher in control. | The child in control. |
> | Public knowledge. | Personal knowledge. |
> | Knowledge as content. | Knowledge as process. |
> | Knowledge as given. | Knowledge as problematic. |
> | Extrinsic motivation. | Intrinsic motivation. |
> | Learning as serial. | Learning as holistic. |
> | Learning as social. | Learning as individual. |
> | Child as client. | Child as person. |
> | Children share characteristics. | Each child unique. |
> | Childhood continuous. | Childhood unique. |
> | Common culture. | Sub-group cultures. |
> | Equal allocation of resources. | Differential allocation. |

The teacher's view of his own role has a direct bearing on what children learn, for the higher the expectations the teacher has, the more likely children are to do well. Children fulfil what is demanded of them, and when teachers have high expectations they give children a far wider range of activities. Children also respond to different kinds of expectation. Teachers who are themselves interested in creative things tend to have a preference for pupil-centred learning.[17]

> Some interesting differences have been identified between teachers according to age and gender.
>   Older teachers, especially men, and especially teachers who feel their strength lies in maths and science, tend to prefer traditional instrumental teaching styles.
>   Younger teachers, especially women, and especially teachers who feel their strength lies in the arts, tend to prefer pupil-orientated approaches to learning.
>   Sometimes we take these stereotypes or characteristics for granted; they are no surprise. But should we?

But what characterizes success in teachers most of all is the *expectation* of success. If teachers are unwilling to accept low standards, and if they will not allow pupils to come to school without motivation, they will find that this affects their pupils and affects their own planning.[18]

Children detect teachers' expectations. They sometimes feel more rewarded for success, and sometimes more rewarded for sheer effort. Once they see the difference, by the age of 8, they need to feel rewarded for both. They also need to be led by the teacher into understanding the need to accumulate information and the need to develop their skills, for it is impossible to do one well without the other. Teachers have tended to make too much of *either* the process of learning *or* the content and have therefore not always helped children understand the ways in which topics and subjects are linked. And sometimes the assertion that it is the 'child not the curriculum' that counts has led to unfocused work and topics that merely reflect the teacher's own interests.[19]

The fact is that teachers by their own efforts can make a major difference to pupils' learning, and to assume that schools cannot do much to change children does them a great disservice. No one pretends that the children who enter school are all the same; by then crucial influences will already have had their effect. But it is too easy for teachers to be misled into thinking that there is little they can do, in one way or another. For there are many strategies that they can make use of and if concentrating on one approach doesn't work, there are a range of others that could: clarifying expectations; linking the work to everyday circumstances; concentrating on one theme or a particular skill, or discovering the pupils' own interests or strengths.

Teachers already define their approaches in different ways. When they deliver the curriculum there are four ways in which they structure it:

- through subjects (like maths or history);
- through strategies (e.g. a topic);
- through generic activities (like writing); or
- through a combination of these.

However the teacher defines his approach to the curriculum he needs to be aware of two of the difficulties he faces: the first is that of coping when he is a class teacher with responsibility for the whole curriculum; the second is that of overcoming the domination of maths and English.[20]

For teachers, however, there are many points of tension or potential tension in their role, and each of these needs to be thought through.

- There is the tension between subject specialism and subject integration: how can we make sure everything is covered?
- There is the tension between the need to listen and the need to tell: how can we find time to encourage each child to think through problems?
- There is the tension between lack of time and the need for teachers to talk to each other: how do we build in time for reflection as well as preparation?
- There is the tension between the expectations of teachers and of parents: how do we communicate what we are doing in professional terms that they understand?
- There is the tension between experiences that have meaning for teachers and those that have meaning for children: how can we enable children to understand why they are doing what they do?
- There is the tension between needs and resources: how do we achieve quality when we so often work in conditions that are undermining?
- There is a tension between explanation and performance: how do we communicate what we are doing without taking time away from its execution?
- Finally, there is the tension between the teacher as an individual and the teacher as a professional.

We have drawn attention throughout to the professionalism of teachers. But one feature of a profession is that it is work which has its own rewards beyond that of earning money. There are far easier ways of making a living than doing a good job as a teacher. The effective teacher cannot perform really well if under stress, or feeling beleaguered. One of the most important questions underlying the role of the teacher is how to gain that pleasure in teaching which communicates enthusiasm to the children.

In the past the teacher might have been content with the general recognition by the community of the significance of his status: this is no longer so. The teacher now needs to explain and define what he is doing.

In the past the teacher might have been content within the confines of the classroom: this can no longer be so. The teacher needs to make sure that what he is doing is consistent with other classrooms and an overall school curriculum.

In the past the teacher might have been content with a small group of familiar colleagues: this will no longer be so. For the way to survive the pressures on the teacher's role is to heighten shared professional understanding, to be able to find a language which conveys in a clear way what it is that teachers are trying to achieve.

One day the role of the teacher will be recognized for what it really is.

Chapter 20

The Teacher and Other People

'Parents are looking for advancement through education . . . they're looking for good jobs. I think they're disappointed in the kind of education they see. They think it is too informal: they don't really understand.'

(primary teacher)

The traditional picture of the teacher as alone and isolated in his classroom, with the door firmly closed, is fast disappearing. The teacher no longer has complete control over the curriculum and must therefore collaborate with others and conform to and develop the policies of the whole school. The teacher is also becoming more accountable, to governors and parents, as well as inspectors. For some this development seems threatening: more inspection, more questioning and more appraisal. But it need not be at all threatening; on the contrary, the greater stress on collaboration is one of the most fruitful developments for the teacher.

All teachers have an initial fear of being looked at whilst working. They are each in dialogue with their class, and create their own atmosphere in their own way. But once they have accustomed themselves to working with others, great advantages result. The first is the pleasure of thinking about the practice of teaching. A greater interest in the strategies of learning comes about partly as a result of dialogue with others. Finding the time for it is difficult; but if teachers are planning together, and sharing their strategies on the curriculum, it is time that is well spent and more stimulating than planning in isolation. The second advantage is the practical one that the more help one has in the classroom, the more attention can be paid to individual children and the greater the chance one has of diagnosing all their needs.

> If is often said that resources in themselves are not the greatest issue, although it often seems to the teacher that they are. The question is *how* resources are used. The greatest resource is people. The question then is how they collaborate, and whether they all have clear roles to play.
>
> There are some schools where 'extra' staff were either not used properly or seen as threatening the existing order: and these people virtually 'sink without trace'.[1]

When a teacher is first learning the art of teaching, of organizing the classroom, of diagnosing children, of playing the role of professional teacher, there is nothing so helpful, or so necessary, as being observed by a mentor, and having the lesson analysed. The important point is that the discussion about the lesson needs to be constructive; the observer is showing what could be done rather than merely listing the faults. The new teacher is willing to learn and able to accept criticism. There needs to be discussion, not just a few notes. It is as if the observer were able to play back the lesson as on a video so that not only mistakes but alternative actions are seen and discussed.

There are so many small points that arise from observation, ranging from the position in the classroom in which the teacher places himself to the language he uses.

- 'Why did you stand there, where you couldn't see them all?'
- 'Why, when you went "Sh", did you let them go on talking?'
- 'Why did you ask them all a general question, so that they all talked at once?'
- 'Why did you not ask them to put their hands up in answering a question?'
- 'Why didn't you explain exactly what they were supposed to be doing and then check they all understood?'

Up to this point one concentrates on the everyday craft of classroom teaching: the rituals of discipline and authority. The questions might sound like criticism but they all beg for an alternative strategy, one that the teacher needs to be aware of and learn for himself.

But classroom observation and diagnosis go beyond the essential strategies of discipline. They demand more constructive questions.

- How could you have made the introduction more exciting?'
- 'What other stimuli could you have used?'
- 'What other questions could you have asked?'

Every moment is an opportunity to teach. Thus, at the end of the lesson, as an alternative to 'Stop what you are doing and tidy up', one can suggest the way in which every child learns exactly what to do, and listens carefully while the teacher elaborates it: 'And those who have cleared their table tidy up anything that has fallen on the floor, and then read your books.' But one can also suggest more than classroom routines: One child was doing some interesting work, so why not share it and ask a question or two about it? Why not remind them of a question you asked them earlier?

There is a delicate diplomacy in observing lessons and offering advice. There must be trust, in the mentor as a professional who knows what he's talking about, and in the teacher who can take advice. This means a strongly professional focus. But the diplomatic difficulty is the balance of praise and criticism. Too much encouragement and the teacher can be complacent; too much criticism and he can lose heart. Just like pupils, in fact.

Students have to undergo many such observations; but teachers can go on benefiting from them when they are used as starting points for a discussion about which strategies work best with which children. The problem for teachers is that they link being observed with being assessed.

The traditional class teacher was alone in the classroom and was never formally assessed. Clearly there were informal views of his performance by children, by parents, by the head and other teachers. No one was unaware of how well or badly the teacher was doing. The evidence was all anecdotal; and, besides, there was little that could be done with the information. Nowadays there is an increasing tendency, all over the world, to 'appraise' teachers. This can be, again, a power for improvement and not merely a threat.

That teachers feel threatened by appraisal is not surprising. One of the motivating factors by politicians who set up teacher evaluation is to weed out bad teaching, to punish teachers who are not doing well and cajole them (or force them) into doing better. There is an underlying feeling that standards can be improved only through a series of sanctions, fines and punishments. But this is not the real purpose of appraisal.

> Early models of teacher appraisal, as practised in some parts of the United States, were crude and simple. A teacher was expected to meet the expectations of a checklist. Was he fulfilling the criteria and meeting targets set down by a centrally controlled curriculum? It was all done on a pass or fail basis and the teacher *had* to pass.
>
> The outcome of this system, ironically, was that teachers began to make sure that they fulfilled the criteria and passed. They did this by the sensible expedient of lowering the standards they had to meet in order to ensure they passed. They did not dare be more ambitious but instead worked out some general norms to which all had to conform.
>
> The result was a lowering of standards – quite the opposite of what was intended.[2]

The purpose of teacher evaluation is to help and support good teaching. There is no teacher who is so perfect that improvement is impossible – not even us. A successful system of teacher evaluation depends on this intention to improve: to share a professional insight into what makes an effective teacher and, if there are faults, to find the means of rectifying them. There are three essential elements in teacher appraisal:

1. Teachers need to be involved in every aspect of the process from the beginning, designing the evaluation methods and discussing the criteria.
2. There needs to be an emphasis on formative and collaborative, rather than summative and authoritarian, evaluation.
3. The criteria on which the appraisal is based must not be just those which are easily observed and checked. Simple checklists tend to limit themselves to such an extent that the subtle art of teaching, with its long-term strategies, is hardly taken into account.

We have already noted in a previous chapter how many more adults there are in any one classroom than there used to be.[3] Such extras can include:

- welfare assistants and ancillary helpers, like those concerned with children who have severe learning difficulties;
- peripatetic teachers, like those concerned with specialisms such as music;
- support services, such as speech therapists;
- remedial teachers, who, instead of withdrawing children, bring their skills into the main body of the school;
- nursery nurses.

These are the 'official' extras that a school might have, if it is lucky. They are an invaluable resource. But they bring to the teacher an extra management responsibility. The teacher needs to make sure that their skills are constructively used, with individuals and with groups. The class teacher becomes a manager of activities, keeping an eye on all that goes on; the others in the classroom either have clear tasks – for instance, with the diagnosing of reading difficulties – or can support the main activity by seeing which children need extra help. The most successful use of others in the classroom comes from the teacher's ability to share and explain what he is doing; this is another opportunity to plan the curriculum.

The greatest resource for finding extra help in the classroom lies, however, in the parents. One of the additional professional skills a teacher needs is in making the best use of parents. Parents are crucial in:

- helping in the classroom;
- helping at home; and
- supporting their children through their own attitudes to the school.

Over the past few years there has been a marked shift in attitude towards parents. It is as if parents had been rediscovered after many years, and their crucial role at last acknowledged. There used to be a strong tradition of mistrust between parents and teachers. This was because the schools were seen as compensating for the deficiencies of parents. School walls were as high as those of asylums and once inside the school the children were seen as belonging to that school: 'No parents beyond this point' was a typical notice at the entrance. Any work that a parent might have done with her children was seen as interference, as if helping a child read would get in the way of the methodology of the school.

> The considerable rise of parents as a centre of attention – sitting on governing bodies, belonging to parent–teacher associations, coming into the school – has meant a different relationship with teachers, not always a comfortable one. The awe in which teachers were once held is no longer there.
>
> The change can be shown by the parallel change in the role of the social worker. There was a time when the social worker was the formidable agent of the state, telling deprived parents what they should do. But now the social workers see themselves as working with the deprived against the state, to gain access to its resources, and to plead for their clients' rights.
>
> One of the reasons for this changed relationship with parents is the sense of parental rights: that teachers are accountable to *them*, rather than the other way round.[4]

Many parents were in awe of the school. They did not understand what went on there, feeling that there were secrets that they would never understand. This can still sometimes be the case:

'It confuses Clare when I try to help, so I don't help at all because I'm confusing her.' (mother of primary school child)

There have been many reasons, including political ones, for the rising recognition of parents, and the changed stance of teachers and schools in welcoming them. But the most significant reason lies in the fact that parents make the crucial difference to the success or failure of their children. We have already pointed out the importance of early relationships long before children enter school, but the expectations and support of parents continue to make a significant difference whilst children are at school. The parent's influence does not suddenly cease when the child is received into the school.[5]

There are two different definitions of parent involvement. One is the broadly *educational*: parents' attitudes and their interest in their children's achievements as well as their wanting to know. The other is *participatory*: parents' active help in the school, or in intervention programmes, as well as their rights as 'consumers'. In both cases there are delicate balances to be struck between the rights and demands of the home and the school. It is a subtle relationship as well as a significant one.[6]

The parents' style of communicating is the key to the child's learning style, but parents' expectations of their children and the school are also influenced by the teacher and the way that the teacher explains what he is doing. The problem is that many parents, whilst instinctively understanding the importance of the home in a child's education, believe that its influence is as nothing compared to that of the formal processes of education in the school. Once parents acknowledge their own importance and their own responsibilities, they begin to have a different, and more supportive, attitude to the school. The suspicion of both sides needs to be replaced by far more elaborate communication.[7]

> Parents' view of schools tend to centre on specific aims. They put priorities on reading, maths and writing, on developing children's abilities, on discipline and on passing exams. Only then do they mention being happy. Teachers tend to put social values first: the ability to get on with others as a more important matter than the curriculum.[8]

Many studies have shown that the attitudes of parents to education are a crucial element in their children's education and their interest in the children a most important factor. Children's achievements depend much more on the parents' attitudes than on their social standing. Also, something can be done about them. Many parents lack confidence and think they must leave it all to the teacher; teachers can give parents the courage to take initiatives. It is when parents can relate to teachers that they respect and support what they are doing.[9]

> We have already noted the most used words of teachers and the words that children think are most used, like 'Do it again!'
> Parents also have a subconscious mechanism that makes them repeat the experiences that have happened to them. Their favourite phrase is: 'Come on!'
> They are ambitious for their children without always knowing how to help. They cajole; they want the best possible successes in life for their children: 'Please', they imply to the children, 'for my peace of mind, will you "Come on"'!'[10]

From the teacher's point of view, therefore, there are a number of reasons for taking parents seriously. They are a double resource: a help in the classroom and an extra teacher at home. And they have a double effectiveness if they can motivate and encourage their children and support and understand the work of the teacher. Of course this, like most important maxims, is more easily said than done. Helping foster parents' attitudes – a belief in themselves and in the importance of their child's education together with a knowledge of how important intelligent relationships are, and what they can do to create them – deserves more time and resources than it is likely to get in the near future. There is no doubt that one day the evidence about the significance of early childhood will be listened to by those who have control of education systems, just as there is no doubting the unwillingness of politicians to listen to any evidence, preferring instead anecdotes that support their own opinions. But the economic argument itself will one day prevail; if once the connection between early influences (not economic background) and crime is made, to take one example, then politicians will not be able to resist taking concerted action.

Meanwhile, what can teachers do without all the support they could use? Simply being welcoming is not enough. One important line of communication is for the school to have all its policies agreed amongst all the teachers and written in such a way that parents (as well as governors!) can understand them. But, again, publishing them is not enough. What parents need to know is the way that teachers put these policies into action: how they analyse and diagnose children's learning; how and why they plan their work; and how and why they organize their classrooms and the management of time – all those factors, indeed, that reveal the teacher as an intelligent professional, with a core of knowledge that is as complex and as practical as a doctor's. Just as it helps to articulate the practice of another teacher, to observe and analyse it, so it helps to explain just what it is that he is aiming to achieve, and why.

> Several studies on the 'professionalism' of teachers have questioned whether teachers will ever be seen as professional in the same way as doctors. Parents tend to see teachers as nice and unskilled. Perhaps they do not find teachers frightening enough!
>
> On the other hand each profession – like teaching – has its own jargon that others do not really comprehend. The problem is that there are professions that hide behind their jargon, to keep their knowledge to themselves. Teachers cannot afford to do this. Their professionalism depends on being understood. Only by being communicated will the intellectual significance of what they do be acknowledged. In Arabic Africa the saying 'knowledge is power' has a particular significance. It means that if you know anything you use it in order to wield power over others – by using it or selling it. To the bewilderment of many, the teacher's responsibility is to give away knowledge – freely.[11]

Parents can do more, however, than encourage. They can also teach. There have been many experiments to see whether reading standards can be raised through the involvement of parents. Every one has shown a marked improvement. At the simplest level the parent is encouraged to read with the child on a regular basis. At more formal levels the parent shares in the diagnosis of what a child needs – difficulties with hidden 'e's or particular digraphs (like 'th') – and shares some of the responsibility. The more formal the involvement, the more successful it has been, for many reasons; not only because of the extra help the child receives, but because of the parent's strengthened relationship with both child and teacher.[12]

> In some recent advice to mentors – those teachers engaged in helping new entrants to the profession – an analogy was drawn with learning to swim. The conclusions were centred on how *not* to be an expert swimmer:[13]
>
> * concentrate on theory;
> * learn with someone who has forgotten what it is like to be a beginner;
> * learn with someone who has nothing left to learn;
> * go into the deep end or just the shallow end;
> * learn with someone who tries to refine your stroke as you learn to stay afloat;
> * learn with two teachers who have conflicting opinions.

Given the success of all these programmes, it is surprising how much opposition there has been to implementing them. This is for two reasons. The first is the suspicion that teachers have traditionally felt for parents, as if their involvement were interference, and as if they should not participate in or threaten in any way the job of the teacher. The second is that parental involvement is felt to take up extra time, as if the teacher had enough to do without this 'extra'. The truth is that this is not extra work but extra help; the parent can do what the teacher has for years tried to do single-handed: hear the individual child read. The job of the teacher is actually more threatened by parental distance than by anything else.

> Changing the attitudes of teachers to parents has been a slow process. Teachers have held stereotypical views of parents, as if the only ones that they have met are the 'problems'. Teachers have been known to find parents indifferent, incompetent, hostile and full of misconceptions. They have tended to despise them, as representing a mass of the population less educated than teachers themselves.
>
> Those parents who were exceptions were considered a greater threat: parent-governors, often well-educated themselves, determined and empowered to interfere. This is part of the inheritance that needs to be changed.[14]

The involvement of parents in the teaching of reading is not only an alternative way of organizing individual attention. Children who received extra help in school from other teachers were found not to improve their reading nearly as much as those who received help from their parents. Parents add something extra. Those programmes where parents have been visited at home, in order to discuss matters such as child development and learning skills, have also shown themselves to be markedly effective in improving children's school results. Even a few minutes of organized parental input brings about great improvements.

Underlying all the initiatives and involvement, however, lies a problem in understanding. Parents and teachers have different attitudes to the work of the school and different expectations. Parents express, for example, a great interest in literacy centred on books and on print-related activities. That is why reading programmes are so successful. On the other hand teachers place more emphasis, at the beginning, on pre-reading and pre-writing skills, feeling that parental involvement in pre-school literacy could, first, put children under too much pressure, and second, lead to the use of 'wrong' methods from which the children might not recover. What parents do not understand is what teachers actually mean by pre-reading skills. They would welcome being told far more about teachers' methodology. When they are not told they naturally revert to their own memories.[15]

> Like others, parents seek the advice they want to hear, and they subconsciously repeat what has happened to them when they were children, just as they look at a school and judge it by their own memories. This means that they think they know what happens and this assumption becomes a barrier to further knowledge.
>
> Parents are, however, ambitious in their own way for their own children, and all hold great hopes for what a school can do for them.[16]

To help create greater cooperation with parents we need to know something about the different points of view towards education, and where the barriers are. There is no doubt that parents are ambitious for their children and look to the school to help them fulfil their ambitions:

> 'Well, we all try to have ambitions, don't we? . . . for our children. I want them to have a better education, so they can get a better job than what I've done.'

Parents universally want their children to do better than they did; by passing exams and gaining qualifications. (cf. the phrase 'Come on!') They see the school's central role as concentrating on the same aim.

> 'I hope she doesn't end up in a factory. I should hate to see her end up in a factory.

I want more for my children really than what we had. I'd like them to have a better chance than we had.'

Such ambitions naturally put pressure on teachers. It explains the parents' emphasis on literacy. Certain private schools make use of these parents' wishes by catering for them explicitly. The problem is that for many teachers such forms of ambition are not what they see as the first priority. They do not express themselves in the same way. Instead, they emphasize the importance of social skills:

'I think you have to take the social side first. They've got to be able to integrate with others and build up their own self-confidence before they can really start on the academic side.'

Teachers tend to emphasize what many call 'the autonomy of the individual'. Parents sense this and therefore express a certain frustration that more is not being done on the 'basics' of maths and reading and writing. That, at least, is the impression they have.

'The three Rs, basic things – all I'm interested in. She's got plenty of time to learn about geography and history.'

It is partly a matter of parents' memories, and partly a sense that these central skills are measurable. They can see whether their own children are doing better or worse than others; whether they are 'up to standard'.

'I don't care what he is being taught as long as he can add the figures up.'

'Learning to read, and maths . . . that's what I call education.'

Parents' views of education tend to be very conservative. They are suspicious of what they call 'new' methods and long for old-fashioned methods of discipline. It is from the school that they expect their children to be taught good manners – the other interpretation of 'social' education. Parents remember how they felt at school in terms of discipline and do not see the same emphasis.

'Let's face it: schools have relaxed discipline too much.'

'There's not enough punishment.'

'Teachers are much more relaxed nowadays . . . but too relaxed.'

They also remember clearly how they learned maths and other subjects and have difficulty in understanding new methods.

'She came home with maths the other night and, even my husband, we were completely dumbfounded . . . some of the maths seems such a complicated way to get into what to us is a simple adding and subtracting.'

'Things were much more straightforward when we were at school.'

The confusion and bewilderment that parents sometimes feel is not healthy for the school. Instead of mutual understanding and respect, a certain antipathy can be set up. It is, after all, not only the parents who feel they do not understand. Teachers feel they are misunderstood.

'Parents expect children to sit down and do sums and written work . . . parents are ignorant.'

'Parents don't know what it is I do.'

'The parents would probably prefer that I was stricter with him and sat him down on a chair at a table and that he did more "work" of the sort that you can actually see the result in a book.'

Such feelings of misunderstanding are tragic for a school. No child learns in isolation. The effect of the parents on the child's education is crucial. But these feelings need to be understood to be overcome. There are various means that schools can use. These deserve reinforcing: consistent policies on matters such as the curriculum and discipline; clear and professional explanations to parents; and formal involvement of parents, whenever possible, in the life and teaching of the school.

> Teachers are not always helped by the way that children talk, or do not communicate, about what they have been doing in school. It is as it there were two separate worlds that children generally wish to keep separate. 'What did you do at school today?' 'I don't know'; 'Nothing'; 'We played with some bricks.' If one judged solely on the children's impressions one would have a very different idea of the school.
>
> Keeping the two worlds private can lead to children not wanting to talk to their parents about school. One child new to a school gave away nothing. His parents said they were going to write to his godmother and asked the child to say what he did at school. 'All right,' he said, 'I'll tell you as long as you don't listen.'

There is one way in which parents are formally part of the school and that is through their governing bodies and through the meetings of parents and staff. In some communities in Europe it has been taken for granted for years that everyone who has an interest in the school, including the caretaker and the ancillary staff, should have some part in the process of decision-making so that they feel it is 'their' school. But there have been many cases when the headteacher has sought for as little 'interference' as possible from anyone outside the school – governors and parents alike.

Once again there is a whole education to be undergone in creating around a school a community that supports and helps. This should go beyond having a parent–teacher association dedicated to raising money through various events. It should entail a formal programme of communication and assistance. From the point of view of the effective teacher there are two requirements, two ways in which he participates. First, in using parents as much as possible in his teaching, both at school and in the home, he brings additional resources to bear, and adds to the child's as well as parents' motivation. Secondly, through greater participation in the school's programme, he is actively engaged in helping to form policy, rather than having it thrust upon him. Schools themselves become more effective when all staff are deeply involved with each other.

Chapter 21

The Effective School

'In Germany we had a thousand in the school. It was like "Coronation Street". We knew the teachers only to speak to. We really didn't know them well. Just by name. Here you sort of know them personally, what they're really like.'

(boy, 10)

We know that some teachers are better than others and we know why. We also know that the success of a teacher depends to an extent on the school he or she is in. We are also beginning to understand what makes some schools more effective than others.

There was once a powerful mythology that schools made little difference, that no amount of extra help or resources, no amount of effort or concern, could make any difference to the achievements of pupils. One day, no doubt, this myth will be seen to be as primitive as believing that babies are brought by storks, but, as in the latter case, there are reasons why it has been perpetuated.

The first reason is that in the egotism of each human being is the instinct that they have made themselves, that they owe nothing to anybody, that any ability they have is innate. That people speak different languages according to their environment, have tastes according to their upbringing – all this is as nothing compared to the instinct for personal identity, free of gratitude.

> The influence of schools on pupils has been demonstrated by comparing some schools with others. But the influence of the school goes deeper than academic outcomes. It can make a profound difference to the attitudes that pupils have to other people's rights and freedoms, and the views they form about all aspects of a democratic society.

The second reason is the instinct to explain differences between people by pointing to their birth, as if whatever they inherited formed them. This belief in a quotient of intelligence serves both those who are fortunate and those who are not. Who can blame them if that is the way they are?

The third reason is the fear of change. If people could really be helped, if there really were answers to many social questions rather than 'That's the way things are', it would give a great deal of responsibility to people, especially those in power. 'The way things are' suggests an immutable force; that any change or alternative is difficult, if not impossible.

> It is an interesting aspect of our culture to observe that a great deal of emphasis is put on the autonomy of the individual, lauding the idiosyncratic, presumably at the expense of the 'masses' who merely follow others.
>   Some of the most famous catchphrases and songs highlight this praise of the individual as if it celebrated the human spirit:
>
>   'I'll do it my way.'
>
>   'Je ne regrette rien.'
>
>   'I'm doing my own thing.'
>
>   'Never apologize; never explain.'
>
> As alternatives to following some imposed creed – like an extreme political movement – such spirit is to be applauded, but it does not explain what has made that individual the person he or she is.

The fourth reason is pragmatic. If schools were accepted as making a difference, they would deserve many more resources. If the future were genuinely seen to depend on education, collectively and not just through parents' instincts for their own children, then education would be at the heart of all policy.

Teachers know that it is not so. But they also must know that the evidence that has been gathered shows clearly how much of the individual's future depends not just on the socio-economic status he begins with but also on the individual help he receives. Of course it is difficult to isolate particular events that make such a difference, given all the varied experiences of life. But that people are a result of their interaction with others, and that this depends on those they interact with, is clear.

All this needs reassertion not because it can be doubted but because it is being ignored. On the one hand, a great deal of political mileage is made out of the fact that some schools are more successful than others; on the other hand, the reasons for such differences are rarely explored. Differences do not depend on socio-economic status. Two large research studies, one in secondary schools and one in primary schools, have looked at all the factors that make some schools better than others, comparing schools that had similar intakes and similar starting points.[2]

Before we explore the differences between schools we should acknowledge the fact that individual teachers can feel isolated in the school, can feel they have no influence whatsoever. Many studies have drawn attention to the influence of the headteacher and the particular influence that he or she brings to the post. There are typologies of temperament for those who seek merely to please the outside world, those who merely seek to placate the staff, and for those who are like dictators. But the headteachers do not alone create a school: they inherit staff and traditions; they feel themselves helpless in the face of government policy, or the governors or the very staff they work with.

Four types of school categorized by teacher and pupil involvement:[3]

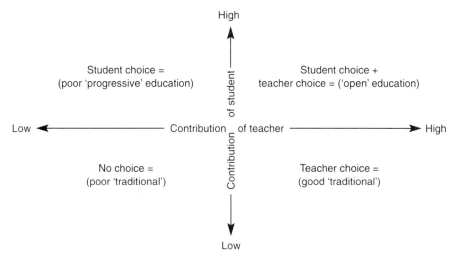

Still the fact remains that some schools work better than others. For the individual teacher the frustration might not be a particular headteacher but the fact that there are so many reasons for the school being as it is, as many reasons as there are people in it. It is bad enough if the head has rigid views or does not want to change, but if all one's colleagues seem to be in a trough of complacency, where should one begin? The answer lies in the very fact that there are so many people involved. A school is the product of all who are in it. One has only to begin to change a part of it, and the whole also begins to change. The way to do this, through looking at and sharing particular educational questions, will be explored later.

It should not be a surprise to the individual teacher that the influence of the school's ethos is so great. At the most obvious level, pleasure in the job, the pleasure that communicates itself to the pupils, derives from companionship, from having people to talk to, both in earnest and in humour. But knowing that all the teachers are going in the same direction, that their shared concern is for the children's best interests, and that they are not divided by rivalry, makes a crucial difference to the way the teacher develops.[4] It has been shown that teachers differ from each other to a great degree in two ways: the level of conceptual demand they make on their pupils; and their ability to enable pupils to attain the level they demand. This might seem a very clear distinction between the effective teacher and the ordinary one, but what is interesting is that these abilities are found to relate very strongly to the social context of the school. The school influences the individual teacher as well as the other way round.

Effective schools: seven elements[5]

Orderly and secure environment
Trust between pupils and staff
Awareness of the agenda of events affecting their lives (curriculum and beyond)
Personal involvement in learning (interactive teaching)
Understanding of the purposes of activities
Availability of opportunities and challenge
Sharing of the agenda by *all* children

A good teacher needs, as well as deserves, support. Any individual will be obviously or subtly influenced by those around him. In a school where no one seems to care and standards are lax, where children come to class out-of-sorts and bored, it is so much harder to sustain high standards. But when there is a shared vision of possibilities, when all seem to sense the excitement of achievement, the collective energy is such that every individual is affected by it.

The effectiveness of one school as against another is not a matter of competition in terms of results. Nor is it a matter of style. One can look at schools in salubrious suburbs, where their advantages in terms of parental support and financial backing are such that they achieve the kinds of examination results that lead to more parent support and more financial backing; but they might still be failing the children, by merely achieving the expected, the average for those circumstances. At the same time some schools can be struggling, against every political initiative, to do the best for their children, and succeeding, even if this success is not seen in terms of immediate examination standards.

Types of school[6]

Self-actualizing school: Free interchange of ideas
                           Self-development
                           Change supported by systems
                           In-service programmes
                           Advisory staff
                           Warm, informal interchange

Comfort school: Supportive but not 'synergetic'
                           Few 'formal' systems

Survival school: Phobia about change
                           Individuals remain covert about their own efforts

---

The styles of school can vary markedly. The one might give the appearance of great formality, from uniforms and the stiff flowers and paintings at the entrance, to the emphasis on certain standards of collective behaviour. The other might give the impression of being quite informal, with a casualness of attire and a welcome that denotes an open friendliness and equality. But differences of style at that level are comparatively superficial.

When people think of the primary school as depicted in the Plowden Report, with its optimism about human nature, they are thinking not so much about a philosophy as about a style. The notions that one could not be dogmatic about systems of knowledge, that knowledge was derived purely from personal experience, that one could impose nothing on children or that children learned merely from experience were a long way from the heart of learning. They were like clothes: something easily visible but on the surface. The fact that they were taken as essentials says more about the type-casting of educational ideas than the truth.[7]

Suppose one took an opposite 'style'; where instead of processes and procedures there were clearly accountable goals and products and where standards were assessed and measured against lists of competencies and criteria. Would this school, with its use of 'clients' and its performance indicators, be any closer to the heart of education? There are some arguments in which it seems that both antagonists have created each other, and themselves, as 'straw men'.

Each school is, however, different. This is not just a matter of style but of something else: ethos, perhaps. The differences depend on how the staff interact: not on the stand they take on particular issues, but on whether they do take a stand. The effective school depends on dialogue.

Some schools seem just to want to survive. They fear change. The teachers are covert about their own efforts. It is as if the threats posed by the outside world were so great that the only ambition is not to 'put a foot wrong' nor to be found to fail. To that end expectations are set low, and to that end children are set to fail, rather than the school be seen to do so. Held in a tangible vice of fear, some schools make sure that all they do is answer outside threats, guard themselves against inspection, make sure that they know whatever new policy is supposed to be implemented whilst not implementing it. In these schools teachers do not really talk to each other.[8]

Then there are those schools that have been called 'comfort' schools. In these schools the whole idea is to be supportive of all that goes on, however incoherent. There is a sense of complacency: not the same as contentment, but a system in which all feel that they are doing well enough, against some standard, at least well enough to stop any criticism, any questioning from parents. The main characteristic of these schools is their incoherence, the lack of dialogue, the lack of any focus for the collective energy of staff.

The school as an organization[9]

1. Order will always form and re-form but in a different way.
2. Structure is a description of the behaviour of people.
3. Organizations serve purposes; they do not have objectives.
4. The critical dimension in human organization is human behaviour, not technology.
5. Individuals always behave in terms of what they believe to be in their best interests. Altruism is best understood in terms of self-interest.
6. Organizational experience is always subjective.
7. Organizations are personal constructs, artefacts or fantasies, existing only in the imagination of individuals.
8. Organizational change occurs only as a consequence of changes in the individual's self-concept. It is the individual's view of himself that changes, not the organization.
9. Organizations function as expressions of collective value systems and are inherently in a state of conflict.
10. Activity is generated in terms of psychological exchanges between members.
11. Organizations distribute roles and status without respect to individuals.
12. Managers can only react to events; they cannot anticipate them.

The successful school, however, shows all the signs of teachers talking to each other. There is a link between an atmosphere of mutual respect and friendship and the more formal means of bringing about discussion. A self-motivating school exhibits not only warm and informal interchanges and the free exchange of ideas but a system that makes change possible by making the best possible use of in-service programmes and advice from outside the school. When there is a staff development programme in which all teachers have a place, when there is a clear idea what kind of developments a school wants to achieve, then it becomes clear what kind of external advice is worth seeking. Every school does need to be closely in touch with others, to avoid being isolated – whether out of fear or out of complacency.

There have been a number of studies of different schools, to explore what it is that makes some of them so much more effective than others. What is the atmosphere that one can detect as soon as one enters a school? Why are the children in one school working with so much more sense of purpose and achievement than those in another? The 'ethos' of the school has a lot to do with having positive views of children, with high expectancies of their abilities, and with their feeling part of the school, contributing to policies rather than only submitting to them. In an ineffective school children tend to be regarded as slow and unable to learn; the ineffectiveness is blamed on them. In an effective school there is an assumption that children are able and willing to learn.[10]

In one of the largest pieces of research into the differences between primary schools, there were twelve factors which the authors regarded as making a school effective and demonstrating a positive ethos.[11]

1. Purposeful leadership by the headteacher. Such headteachers were not 'controlling' everything by making sure that they could prevent things, were not suspicious of initiative, but in contrast were actively involved in all that went on, in a supportive way.
2. The involvement of the deputy head (or other senior teachers). Headteachers shared and delegated some of their responsibilities, and gave others a definite role.
3. Involvement of teachers. Teachers took part in policy-making, curriculum development and decisions.
4. Consistency of teachers in their enactment of policy; the school was seen to be 'fair'.
5. Careful structuring of pupils' work, giving them plenty to do, and encouraging them to be able to work independently.
6. Teaching that was intellectually challenging. The teachers used intelligent questions and statements and encouraged the pupils to solve problems and use their imaginations.
7. A work-centred environment. Instead of routine issues the teachers spent their time discussing the work; classrooms were busy without too much noise and too much moving about or the need to dwell constantly on disciplinary problems. Pupils enjoyed what they were doing and looked forward to starting new things.
8. Concentration on one or two curriculum areas in any one session. The focus was clear. This did not mean that the pupils were all doing the same work; the work was geared to their individual needs.
9. The greatest amount of communication between pupils and teachers. This meant a great deal of interaction between the teacher and the class as a whole; every moment was used as a teaching opportunity, so that all were involved in higher-order questions and answers.

10. Careful and meticulous records of pupils' work, including their personal and social development.
11. Close involvement of parents with the school. Parents were invited to come to the classroom as well as to attend formal sessions to discuss pupils' progress. Parents were encouraged to be involved in pupils' educational development.
12. An emphasis within the school on praise and encouragement rather than criticism and punishment. Classroom organization and management were firm but fair.

At the heart of all these points lies one essential: communication. In the place of the isolated teacher there needs to be intensive discussion and a role for all teachers in decision-making and the development of policy. The curriculum only becomes lively and useful when it is the matter of debate and when the resources that support its content are shared. To be part of an effective school, teachers need to be willing to talk to each other about educational matters; they need to be open-minded and have a sense of their own responsibilities. If they can make a difference to their pupils they cannot assume that there are no consequences to their actions. Instead they will debate not only 'what works' but what is worthwhile.

It can be difficult suddenly to raise the standard of staffroom debate. In the pauses between lessons teachers are not suddenly going to hold a seminar; and before and after school they will have plenty of marking and preparation to do. On the other hand, in-service days or staff meetings can be dominated not by debate but by individuals and by a heavy agenda. How does one generate the interest in issues in a school that will enable the right kind of dialogue to take place? How does it come about that instead of a passing remark about a child – 'He's at it again' – a more analytical, more thoughtful, point can be pursued?

Teachers do not always realize how many educational issues there are to be debated. Focusing attention on them begins to generate a more articulate awareness of where the teachers stand. Before an agreed curriculum policy can be implemented there needs to be an awareness of whether there are disagreements. Otherwise teachers will find themselves silently submitting to an imposed doctrine, one that they do not particularly like and in which they have no strong belief. It must be made apparent that each teacher will have his or her own point of view and style of working. This is why an awareness of differences is a positive starting point; for all are affected by some of the controversies, the matters for debate.

There are many controversies about teaching and teaching styles as well as about the content and meaning of the curriculum. Here are some examples:

'Discovery' or *'delivery'*. How do teachers see their role: as enabling children to learn by themselves, or by offering them subject matter? Some teachers assume that all they need to do is to give lectures: to tell the children what they should know. Others see their role as having a much wider impact, affecting the whole of the children's moral and social development. There are perhaps four different models of teaching.[12]

The first is of teaching as the process of transferring knowledge to the child (an empty vessel waiting to be filled).

The second is of teaching as a means of moulding children into a particular pattern through making them learn skills and behaviours.

The third is of teaching as the process of guiding children through subject matter, helping them explore it.

The fourth is of teaching as a means of helping children develop their intellectual and emotional abilities by providing the circumstances and the experience to assist them. This is the most 'child-centred' model, where the subject matter is subservient to the child's needs.

Teachers might not always reflect on their own teaching styles, but seeing different models or debating different choices – such as 'What does "formal" or "informal" actually mean?' – gives teachers a chance to communicate their own ideas in an open-minded way.

Individuals, groups and classes. What is the most successful way of organizing the class? How can groups best be used to foster cooperation and intensive learning? Children are often placed in groups as an automatic way of distributing resources, with as little thought about what groups are for as accepting that the desks are lined up in rows. Can one really make sure there is high-level debate without engaging the whole class? How much time can one build in for individuals? Is it possible to have some kind of tutorial system based on individual diagnosis?

Topics v. subjects. For years many teachers have based their teaching around particular themes or topics, such as 'change' or 'transport'. Every part of the curriculum is made to reflect this theme in one way or another, whether it be history or science, let alone maths and English. Even with a national curriculum schools tend to organize their work around agreed themes. Why? Is this a realistic way of working? What are the advantages? Can one make sure that important subjects are covered? What, for instance, happens to those aspects of history or geography that do not fit into the themes? How can one make sure that the whole of the curriculum is covered?

The class teacher v. the specialist. Should a teacher be expected to cover the whole of the curriculum; if so, what are the advantages for the child in doing so? Does the class teacher become a manager of other people in the classroom, some of whom bring extra help and some of whom bring specialist knowledge? If there are going to be specialists, and if teachers begin to take responsibility for distinct parts of the curriculum, perhaps serving as a consultant, how can that best be organized? How can one teacher transfer extra knowledge to his colleagues?

The school and the home. Where does the greatest responsibility lie and what should the relationship be? What role can a parent play both at home and in the school? What is the best means of communication with parents: well-organized, well-structured parents' evenings or more informal contacts? How can all parents be encouraged to develop their interest in and support for the school?

What is assessment for? For some people it is quite simple: exams demonstrate the success or failure of the individual against standard attainment targets, and through that demonstrate the success or failure of particular schools when compared to others. Assessment means knowledge. For others assessment is the starting point for change; it is there for the diagnosis of the learning abilities and styles of children, so that the teacher has a clearer idea of the complete work profile of the pupil. Assessment is not so much judgement as support.

All these controversies are matters that deserve debate, and the best people to take part in these debates are the teachers. They have the knowledge of the issues; they know what it is really like in the classroom. They also need to bring to their teaching the intellectual excitement that stems from thinking about their practice. Teachers also need to be able to talk to each other about the professional skills they are constantly developing.

To these controversies could be added many more; they draw attention to a focus on professional matters that experienced teachers need in order to sustain their interest in their task. A student teacher will have an interest in the debate as long as it is practical; but his mind is taken up with coping, or surviving. He will be concerned with knowledge, with keeping the children busy, with the skills of discipline. But as teachers gain in experience they begin to take for granted that they can run a well-ordered classroom. It is then that they reflect more on the children and their learning skills, on the concepts that are at the heart of learning, and on the means that bring the best out of children.

Changing a school so that it becomes more effective is not a simple task. Nor can a school be simply measured by examination results. No school will really change – begin to show how much progress the pupils are making – unless all the people in the school and in the community are working together. Teachers must have a sense of 'ownership' over what they are doing, or they will do it half-heartedly. Teachers see school management too often as something separate, even antagonistic. In this case they resist change, and try to preserve their individual autonomy. When a school does involve all the people in the dialogue that surrounds the making of a policy, then one does begin to see a positive ethos and positive results.

There is, of course, one more important group of people who deserve to be involved: the children. There are three kinds of issues in which the children also need to feel a sense of 'ownership'.

The first is the question of discipline. Rules are not just imposed. They need to be agreed. It is the children who will need to be responsible for their behaviour both within and outside the classroom. They must see why bullying and teasing are not acceptable, and why there are practical rules about running along the corridors.

The second is the question of assessment. Children can take part in self-assessment, so that they can share aims and use targets, review and record and help report their progress. Children like having clear learning objectives, and even very young children can see the difference between 'learning how to' and 'learning all about'. In involving children in assessment it is important to be precise; looking at particular areas to concentrate on, like good beginnings to stories, or measuring accurately to the nearest centimetre. The only difficulty children have is finding the technical language to talk about their work; but this they develop.

The third is the question of the curriculum. Too often children are doing work because it is imposed on them: 'writing' or 'English', rather than 'a story about ... that will help me learn'. The purpose behind the curriculum is too often hidden from the children. It can be a major help to many children to know why they are learning things, why those things are useful and why they will gain from learning.

Where the whole of the school community is engaged in talk, in open discussion, and in agreed policies, there is the basis for the effective school.

Conclusions

We all know that some schools are more effective than others. There is no pleasure in this differentiation and nothing to be gained from such a league table. For it means that we are failing some of our children. But then, when we think of the potential of education, that could be said of all of them.

We know why some schools are more effective than others. It all depends on the teachers and how they perform together. Knowing this is only a first stage in doing something about it; people find it so hard to change.

We also know that some teachers are more effective than others. Doing a really good job is challenging: hard work and rewarding. It is possible to coast; just to keep going. Somewhere between the miraculous, the counsel of perfect virtue, and the routine, we will find our way.

People can learn to become effective teachers. They cannot be *made* into them. They can be taught – but that is also to be involved, to create the art of learning.

It is the hope of this book to help thoughtful teachers become more effective. The wish is to support, to encourage and to stimulate. But it is for the individual reader to make the ideas his or her own. Tips for teaching are never successful when copied from other people. Methods imposed from outside make little difference.

All depends on the energies and creative abilities of individual teachers, to seek help, to share their professional wisdom and satisfy their curiosity about the art of teaching. If it does nothing else, may the book prove how complex and how important is the job of being a teacher.

References

This book has attempted to explain and analyse as lucidly as possible the complicated nature of being an effective teacher. It has sought not to draw attention to the complexities, but to clarify as much as possible.

This does not mean that the statements that are made are merely assertions based on the experiences of the author. Many teachers have been involved and much research has been carried out on children, teachers and schools.

These references are meant only to draw attention to the fact of so much research. Of course they are also there to enable readers to pursue ideas further. They are, however, *not* there to make the book weighty or to show off (which is sometimes a motivation behind some research).

Trying to outline what is true does involve a lot of engagement with other people's work.

INTRODUCTION: REFERENCES

1 Silcock, P. 'Can we teach effective teaching?' *Educational Review* **45** (1), 13–19, 1993.
2 Cullingford, C. *The Nature of Learning*. London: Cassell, 1990.
3 E.g. Hewison, J. and Tizard, J. 'Parental involvement and reading attainment.' *British Journal of Educational Psychology* **5**, 209–15, 1980.
   Dole, J., Valencia, S., Greer, F. and Wardop, J. 'Effects of two types of pre-reading instruction on the comprehension of narrative and expository text.' *Reading Research Quarterly* **26** (2), 142–59, 1991.
   Ball, E. and Blackman, B. 'Does phoneme awareness training in kindergarten make a difference in early word recognition and developmental spelling?' *Reading Research Quarterly* **26** (1), 49–66, 1991.
4 Rutter, M., Maughan, B., Mortimore, P. and Ouston, J. *Fifteen Thousand Hours: Secondary Schools and Their Effect on Children*. London: Open Books, 1979.
   Mortimore, P., Sammons, P., Stoll, L., Lewis, D. and Ecob, R. *School Matters: The Junior Years*. Wells: Open Books, 1988.
5 Freeman, P. '"Don't talk to me about lexical meta-analysis of criterion-referenced clustering

and lap-dissolve spatial transformations": a consideration of the role of practising teachers in educational research.' *British Educational Research Journal* **12** (2), 1986.

6   E.g. research on Nuffield Curriculum Development projects, carried out through (and evaluated by) the Schools Council.

7   Salzberger-Wittenberg, I., Gianna, H. and Osborne, E. *The Emotional Experience of Teaching and Learning*. London: Routledge, 1983.

8   Rowell, J., Moss, P. and Pope, S.: 'The Construction of Meaning from Text: Possible Effects on Different Reading Strategies', *Educational Psychology* **10** (1), 39–55, 1990.

CHAPTER 1: REFERENCES

1   Pye, J. *Invisible Children: Who Are the Real Losers at School?* Oxford: Oxford University Press, 1989.

2   Pollard, A. *The Social World of the Primary School*. London: Holt, Rinehart and Winston, 1985.

3   Kerr, J. (ed.) *Changing the Curriculum*. London: London University Press, 1968.

4   Kerry, T. and Eggleston, J. *Topic Work in the Primary School*. London: Routledge, 1985.

5   Bennett, N., Desforges, C., Cockburn, A. and Wilkinson, B. *The Quality of Pupil Learning Experiences*. London: Lawrence Erlbaum, 1984.

6   Bennett, N. and Desforges, C. *Recent Advances in Classroom Research*. Edinburgh: Scottish Academic Press, 1985.

7   Bruner, J. *Beyond the Information Given*. London: Allen and Unwin, 1974.

8   Elton: *Discipline in Schools*. Report of the Committee of Inquiry chaired by Lord Elton. London: HMSO, 1989.

9   Cullingford, C. *The Inner World of the School*. London: Cassell, 1991.

10 E.g. Cronk, K. *Teacher Pupil Conflicts in Secondary Schools*. London: Falmer Press, 1988. Anderson, L. and Burns, R. *Research in Classrooms: The Study of Teachers, Teaching and Instruction*. Oxford: Pergamon Press, 1989.

11 Bruner, J. *Toward a Theory of Instruction*. London: Belknapp Press, 1966.

12 Raven, J. 'School rejection and amelioration.' *Educational Research* **20**, 3–9, 1979.

13 Cockcroft, W. (Chairman) *Mathematics Counts*. London: HMSO, 1982.

14 Thomas, G. 'The new classroom teams.' *Education 3–13* **21** (2), 22–6, 1993; and *Effective Classroom Teamwork*. London: Routledge, 1993.

15 Ashcroft, K. 'The teacher and the ethos of the school', in Cullingford, C. (ed.) *The Primary Teacher*. London: Cassell, 1989, pp. 75–94.

16 Rutter, M., Maughan, B., Mortimore, P. and Ouston, J. *Fifteen Thousand Hours: Secondary Schools and Their Effect on Children*. London: Open Books, 1979.

17 Cf. Chapter 21.

18 Wilson, J. and Cowell, B. *Children and Discipline*. London: Cassell, 1990.

19 Rosenthal, R. and Jacobson, L. *Pygmalion in the Classroom*. New York: Holt, Rinehart and Winston, 1968.

20 Robinson, K. 'Classroom discipline: power, resistance and gender – a look at teacher perspectives.' *Gender and Education* **4** (3), 273–87, 1992.

21 John, P. 'A qualitative study of British student teachers' lesson planning perspectives.' *Journal of Education for Teaching* **17** (3), 301–20, 1991.

CHAPTER 2: REFERENCES

1   Bennett, N. *Teaching Styles and Pupil Progress*. London: Open Books, 1976.
    Galton, M., Simon, B. and Croll, P. *Inside the Primary Classroom*. London: Routledge and Kegan Paul, 1980.

2   Ashton, P. *et al. The Aims of Primary Education: A Study of Teachers' Opinions*. London: Macmillan Education, 1975.

3   Bettelheim, B. *A Good Enough Parent: The Guide to Bringing Up Your Child*. London: Thames and Hudson, 1987.
4   King, R. *All Things Bright and Beautiful? A Sociological Study of Infant Schools*. Chichester: John Wiley, 1978.
    Bennett, N., Desforges, C., Cockburn, A. and Wilkinson, B. *The Quality of Pupil Learning Experience*. London: Lawrence Erlbaum, 1984.
5   Thring, E. *Theory and Practice of Teaching*. New York: Macmillan, 1989.
6   Oliver, W. 'Teachers' educational beliefs versus their classroom practice.' *Journal of Educational Research* **47**, 47–55, 1953.
7   Plowden, B. (Chair). *Children and Their Primary Schools: A Report of the Central Advisory Council for Education*. London: HMSO, 1966.
    Blenkin, G. and Kelly, A. *The Primary Curriculum*. London: Harper and Row, 1981.
    Broadfoot, P., Osborn, M. *et al*. 'Teachers' conceptions of their professional responsibility: some international comparisons.' *Comparative Education,* **23** (3), 287–302, 1987.
8   Egan, K. *Teaching as Story-Telling*. London: Routledge, 1988.
9   Child, D. *Psychology and the Teacher*. London: Cassell, 1986.
10 Larsson, S. 'Learning from experience: teachers' conceptions of changes in their professional practice.' *Journal of Curriculum Studies* **19** (1), 35–43, 1987.
11 Croll, P. and Moses, D. 'Teaching methods and time on task in junior classrooms.' *Educational Research* **39** (2), 90–7, 1988.
    Blatchford, P., Burke, J., Farquhar, C., Plewis, I. and Tizard, B. 'A systematic observation study of children's behaviour in an infant school', in Woodhead, M. and McGrath, A. (eds) *Family, School and Society*. London: Hodder and Stoughton, 1988, pp. 96–111.
12 Barnes, D., Britton, F. and Rosen, H. *Language, the Learner and the School*. Harmondsworth: Penguin, 1969.
13 Rosenshine, B. and Furst, J. *Teacher Behaviour and Student Progress*. Slough: NFER, 1971.
14 Galton, M. and Williamson, J. *Group Work in the Primary Classroom*. London: Routledge, 1992.
15 Goodnow, J. and Burns, A. *Home and School: A Child's Eye View*. Hemel Hempstead: Allen and Unwin, 1985.
16 Richman, N., Stevenson, J. and Graham, P. J. *Pre-School to School: A Behavioural Study*. London: Academic Press, 1982.
17 Cullingford, C. *The Inner World of the School*. London: Cassell, 1991.
18 Sluckin, A. *Growing Up in the Playground*. London: Routledge and Kegan Paul, 1981.
19 Houghton, S., Wheldall, K., Jukes, R. and Sharpe, A. 'The effects of limited private reprimands and increased private praise on classroom behaviour in four British secondary school classes.' *British Journal of Educational Psychology* **60** (3), 255–65, 1990.
20 Cooper, P. 'Learning from pupils' perspectives.' *British Journal of Special Education* **20** (4), 129–33, 1993.
21 Laurence Sterne, quoted in E. Pound, *An ABC of Reading*. London: Faber, 1961.

CHAPTER 3: REFERENCES

1   White, R. with Brockington, D. *Tales out of School: Consumers' Views of British Education*. London: Routledge and Kegan Paul, 1983.
2   Marklund, S. *The Swedish Comprehensive School*. London: Longman, 1967.
3   Cullingford, C. '"I suppose learning your tables could help you get a job": children's views on the purpose of schools.' *Education 3–13* **14** (2), 41–6, 1986.
4   Blyth, A. J. 'Teaching young children about the past,' in Richards, C. *New Directions in Primary Education*. London: Falmer Press, 1982.
5   Compare the views of Gramsci, A. *Selections from Political Writings*. London: Lawrence and Wishart, 1977.
    Bowles, S. and Gintie, H. *Schooling in Capitalist America*. London: Routledge and Kegan Paul, 1978.

6   Lane, D. 'Violent histories: bullying and criminality', in Tattum, D. and Lane, D. (eds) *Bullying in Schools*. Stoke-on-Trent: Trentham Books, 1989, pp. 95–104.
    Besag, V. *Bullies and Victims in Schools: A Guide to Understanding and Management*. Milton Keynes: Open University Press, 1989.
7   Cullingford, C. *The Inner World of the School*. London: Cassell, 1991.
8   Burgess, H. 'The primary curriculum: the example of mathematics', in Cullingford, C. (ed.) *The Primary Teacher*. London: Cassell, 1989, pp. 16–36.
9   Davies, B. *Life in the Classroom and Playground*. London: Routledge and Kegan Paul, 1982.
10 Bennett, N., Desforges, C., Cockburn, A. and Wilkinson, B. *The Quality of Pupil Learning Experiences*. London: Lawrence Erlbaum, 1984.
11 Das Gupta, P. and Bryant, P. 'Young children's causal inferences.' *Child Development* **60** (5), 1138–46, 1989.
12 Eshel, Y. and Kurman, J. 'Academic self-concept, accuracy of perceived ability and academic attainment.' *British Journal of Educational Psychology* **61** (2), 187–96, 1991.
13 Underwood, G. *Attention and Memory*. Oxford: Pergamon Press, 1976.
14 Goodson, I. *School Subjects and Curriculum Change*. London: Croom Helm, 1982.

CHAPTER 4: REFERENCES

1   Chandler, M., Fritz, A. and Hala, S. 'Small-scale deceit: deception as a marker of two, three and four year olds' theories of mind.' *Child Development* **60** (6), 1263–77, 1989.
    Baillargeon, R. and de Vos, J. 'Object permanence in young infants: further evidence.' *Child Development* **62** (6), 1227–46, 1991.
    Papousek, H. 'Individual variability in learned responses in human infants', in Robinson, R. (ed.) *Brain and Early Behavior*. New York: Academic Press, 1969.
2   Pavlov, I. *Conditioned Reflexes: An Investigation of the Physiological Activity of the Cerebral Cortex*. London: Oxford University Press, 1927. Note the phrase 'Delivering the Curriculum'.
3   Piaget, J. *The Language and Thought of the Child*. London: Routledge and Kegan Paul, 1926.
4   Milgram, S. and Shotland, R. *Television and Anti-Social Behaviour: Field Experiments*. New York: Academic Press, 1973.
5   Compare the 'effects' of television. Cullingford, C. *Children and Television*. London: Cassell, 1990.
    Buckingham, D. *Children Talking Television: The Making of Television Literacy*. London: Falmer Press, 1993.
6   McLean, D. and Schuler, M. 'Conceptual development in infancy: the understanding of containment.' *Child Development* **60** (5), 1126–37, 1989.
7   Gibson, E. *Principles of Perceptual Learning and Development*. Englewood Cliffs, NJ: Prentice-Hall, 1969.
8   Gregory, R. *Eye and Brain: The Psychology of Seeing*. London: Weidenfeld and Nicolson, 1966.
9   Gibson, E. *op. cit.*
10 Clark, E. 'Some aspects of the conceptual basis for first language acquisition', in Schiefelbusch, R. and Lloyd, L. (eds) *Language Perspectives: Acquisition, Retardation and Intervention*. Baltimore: University Park Press, 1974, pp. 105–26.
11 Donaldson, M. *Children's Minds*. London: Fontana/Croom Helm, 1978.
12 Egan, K. *Primary Understanding: Education in Early Childhood*. New York: Routledge, 1988.
13 Stipek, D. and McIver, D. 'Developmental change in children's assessment of intellectual competence.' *Child Development* **60** (3), 521–38, 1989.
14 Dunn, J. *The Beginnings of Social Understanding*. Oxford: Basil Blackwell, 1988.

15 Dweck, C. 'Motivational processes affecting learning.' *American Psychologist*, 1040-8, October 1986.

16 Woodhead, M. 'The needs of children: is there value in the concept?' *Oxford Review of Education* 13 (2), 129-39, 1987.

17 See Egan, K. *Education and Psychology*. New York: Teachers College Press, 1983.

18 Gelman, S. and Markman, E. 'Young children's inductions from natural kinds: the role of categories and appearances.' *Child Development* 58 (6), 1532-41, 1987.

19 Sodian, B., Zaitchik, D. and Carey, S. 'Young children's differentation of hypothetical beliefs from evidence.' *Child Development* 62 (4), 753-66, 1991.

20 Fryer, M. and Collings, J. 'Teachers' views about creativity.' *British Journal of Educational Psychology* 61 (2), 207-19, 1991.
   Cortazzi, M. *Primary Teaching: How It Is*. London: Fulton, 1990.

21 Riding, R. and Cheema, I. 'Cognitive styles: an overview and integration.' *Educational Psychology* 11 (3 and 4), 193-216, 1991.

22 Cullingford, C. *The Nature of Learning*. London: Cassell, 1990.

23 Compare the many books on historiography.

24 Donaldson, M. *op. cit.*

25 Entwistle, N. and Ramsden, P. *Understanding Student Learning*. London: Croom Helm, 1982.

26 Witkin, H., Moore, C., Goodenough, D. and Cox, P. 'Field-dependent and field-independent cognitive styles and their educational implications.' *Review of Educational Research* 47, 1-64, 1977.

27 Galton, M. and Williamson, J. *Group Work in the Primary Classroom*. London: Routledge, 1992.

28 Hudson, L. *Frames of Mind*. London: Methuen, 1968.

29 Roehler, L. and Duffy, G. 'What makes one teacher a better explainer than another?' *Journal of Education for Teaching* 12 (3), 273-84, 1986.
   Cullingford, C. *The Inner World of the School*. London: Cassell, 1991.

30 Wells, G. *Language Development in the Pre-School Years: Languages at Home and School*. Cambridge: Cambridge University Press, 1985.

31 Chapman, J., Lambourne, R. and Silva, P. 'Some antecedents of academic self-concept: a longitudinal study.' *British Journal of Educational Psychology* 60 (2), 142-52, 1990.
   Blatchford, P. 'Academic self-assessment at 7 and 11 years: its accuracy and association with ethnic group and sex.' *British Journal of Educational Psychology* 62 (1), 35-44, 1992.

32 Pye, J. *Invisible Children: Who Are the Real Losers at School?* Oxford: Oxford University Press, 1989.

33 Lewis, D. *Mind Skills*. London: Souvenir Press, 1987.

34 Söter, A. 'Recent research of writing: implications for writing across the curriculum.' *Journal of Curriculum Studies* 19 (5), 425-38, 1987.

35 Jarvis, T. *Children and Primary Science*. London: Cassell, 1991.

CHAPTER 5: REFERENCES

1 Chomsky, C. *Language and Mind*. New York: Harcourt Brace, 1992.

2 Sokolov, Y. *Perception and the Conditioned Reflex*. Oxford: Pergamon, 1963.

3 Shvachkin, N. 'The development of phonemic speech perception in early childhood', in Ferguson, C. and Slobin, D. (eds) *Studies of Child Language Development*. New York: Holt, Rinehart and Winston, 1973.

4 Block, N. and Dworkin, G. (eds) *The IQ Controversy*. London: Quartet Books, 1977.

5 Wells, G. *Language Development in the Pre-School Years*. Cambridge: Cambridge University Press, 1983.
   Richman, N., Stevenson, J. and Graham, P. *Pre-School to School*. London: Academic Press, 1982.
   Heath, S.B. *Ways with Words: Language, Life and Work in Communities and Classrooms*. Cambridge: Cambridge University Press, 1983.

6   Miller, G. *The Science of Words*. New York: Scientific American Library, 1991.
7   Clark, F., 'What's in a word? On the child's acquisition of semantics in his first language', in Moore, T. (ed.) *Cognitive Development and the Acquisition of Language*. New York: Academic Press, 1973.
8   Whorf, B. *Language, Thought and Reality*. Boston: Massachusetts Institute of Technology Press, 1956.
9   Brown, R. *A First Language*. London: Allen and Unwin, 1973.
10   Nelson, K. *Structure and Strategy in Learning to Talk*. Monographs of the Society for Research: Child Development, No. 38, University of Chicago Press, 1973.
11   Ingram, D. 'Current issues in child phonology', in Moreland, D. and Morehead, A. (eds) *Normal and Deficient Child Language*. Baltimore: University Park Press, 1976, pp. 5–27.
12   Kemler Nelson, D. 'When experimental findings conflict with everyday observations: reflections on children's category learning.' *Child Development* **61** (3), 606–10, 1990.
13   Stubbs, M. *Language and Literacy*. London: Routledge and Kegan Paul, 1980.
14   Halliday, M. *Learning How to Mean: Explorations in the Development of Language*. London: Edward Arnold, 1975.
15   Bernstein, B. *Class Codes and Control*. London: Routledge and Kegan Paul, 1975.
16   Heath, S. *Ways with Words: Language, Life and Work in Communities and Classrooms*. Cambridge: Cambridge University Press, 1983.
17   Tough, J. *Listening to Children Talking*. London: Ward Lock, 1973.
18   Carroll, L. *Through the Looking Glass*. London: Oxford University Press, 1982.
19   M'Neill, D. *The Acquisition of Language: The Study of Developmental Psycholinguistics*. New York: Harper and Row, 1970.

CHAPTER 6: REFERENCES

1   Diack, H. *In Spite of the Alphabet: A Study of the Teaching of Reading*. London: Chatto and Windus, 1965.
2   Tansley, P. and Panckhurst, J. *Children with Specific Learning Difficulties: A Critical Review of Research*. London: Nelson, 1981.
3   E.g. Gattegno, C. *Words in Colour*. London: Educational Explorers, 1962.
4   Pitman, J. and St John, J. *Alphabets and Reading*. London: Pitman, 1969.
5   Smith, F. *Understanding Reading: A Psycholinguistic Analysis of Reading and Learning to Read*. New York: Holt, Rinehart and Winston, 1971.
6   Goodman, K. *Language and Literacy*. Boston, MA: Routledge and Kegan Paul, 1982.
7   Bettelheim, B. and Zelan, K. *On Learning to Read*. London: Thames and Hudson, 1982.
8   Groff, P. *Phonics: Why and How*. New Jersey: General Learning Press, 1978.
9   Somerville, D. and Leach, D. 'Direct or indirect instruction? An evaluation of three types of intervention programme for assisting students with specific reading difficulties.' *Educational Research* **30** (1), 46–53, 1988.
10   Ehri, L. and Wilce, L. 'Does learning to spell help beginners to learn to read words?' *Reading Research Quarterly* **22** (1), 47–65, 1987.
11   Bondy, E. 'Seeing it their way: what children's definitions of reading tell us about improving teacher education.' *Journal of Teacher Education* **41** (5), 33–45, 1990.
12   Goodman, K. *op. cit.*
13   Shute, R. 'Treating dyslexia with tinted lenses: a review of the evidence.' *Research in Education* **46**, 39–48, 1991.
14   Bosmajian, H. 'Tricks of the text and acts of reading by censors and adolescents.' *Children's Literature in Education* **18** (2), 89–96, 1987.
15   Baker, C. and Freebody, P. *Children's First School Books: Introductions to the Culture of Literacy*. Oxford: Basil Blackwell, 1989.

CHAPTER 7: REFERENCES

1   Bloom, L. and Capatides, J. 'Expression of affect and the emergence of language.' *Child Development* **58** (6), 1513–22, 1987.
2   Garnica, O. and King, M. *Language, Children and Society*. Oxford: Pergamon, 1979.
3   Cox, M. and Parkin, C. 'Young children's human figure drawing: cross sectional and longitudinal studies.' *Educational Psychology* **6** (4), 353–68, 1986.
4   Silk, A. and Thomas, G. 'Development and differentation in children's figure drawings.' *British Journal of Psychology* **77**, 399–410, 1986.
5   Ferreiro, E. and Teberosky, A. *Literacy before Schooling*. London: Heinemann, 1983.
6   Söter, A. 'Recent research on writing: implications of writing across the curriculum.' *Journal of Curriculum Studies* **19** (5), 425–38, 1987.
7   Cullingford, C. *The Inner World of the School*. London: Cassell, 1991.
8   Cox, M. and Parkin, C. *op. cit.*
    Silk, A. and Thomas, G. *An Introduction to the Psychology of Children's Drawings*. Hemel Hempstead: Harvester Wheatsheaf, 1990.
9   Graves, D. *Writing, Teachers and Children at Work*. Portsmouth, NH: Heinemann, 1984.
    Blatchford, P. 'Academic self-assessment at 7 and 11 years: its accuracy and association with ethnic group and sex.' *British Journal of Educational Psychology* **62** (1), 35–44, 1992.
10 Getzels, J. and Smilansky, J. 'Individual differences in pupil perceptions of school problems.' *British Journal of Educational Psychology* 307–16, 1983.
11 Barnes, D., Britton, J. and Rosen, H. (eds) *Language, the Learner and the School*. Harmondsworth: Penguin, 1969.
12 Austin-Ward, B. 'English, English teaching and English teachers: the perceptions of 16 year olds.' *Educational Research* **28** (1), 32–42, 1986.
13 Perera, K. *Children's Writing and Reading: Analysing Classroom Language*. Oxford: Basil Blackwell, 1984.
14 Graves, D. *op. cit.*

CHAPTER 8: REFERENCES

1   Short, J., Williams, E. and Christie, B. *The Social Psychology of Telecommunications*. London: John Wiley, 1976.
2   Baddeley, A. *Human Memory: Theory and Practice*. London: Lawrence Erlbaum, 1990.
3   Heath, S. *Ways with Words: Language, Life and Work in Communities and Classrooms*. Cambridge: Cambridge University Press, 1983.
4   Farrar, M. 'Why do we ask comprehensive questions? A new conception of comprehensive instruction.' *The Reading Teacher* **37** (6), 452–6, 1984.
5   Bennett, N., Desforges, C., Cockburn, A. and Wilkinson, B. *The Quality of Pupil Learning Experiences*. London: Lawrence Erlbaum, 1984.
6   Davies, B. *Life in the Classroom and Playground: The Accounts of Primary School Children*. London: Routledge, 1982.
7   Wood, H. and Wood, D. 'Questioning the pre-school child.' *Educational Review* **35** (2), 149–62, 1983.
8   Wood, H. and Wood, D. *ibid.*
9   Atherley, K. 'Shared reading: an experiment in peer tutoring in the primary classroom.' *Educational Studies* **15** (2), 145–53, 1989.
10 Burden, M., Emsley, M. and Constable, H. 'Encouraging progress in collaborative group work.' *Education 3–13* **16** (1), 51–6, 1988.
11 Baker, C. and Perrott, C. 'The news sessions in infants and primary school classrooms.' *British Journal of Sociology of Education* **9** (1), 19–38, 1988.
12 Edwards, D. and Mercer, N. *Common Knowledge*. London: Methuen, 1987.
13 Courage, M. 'Children's inquiry strategies in referential communication and in the game of Twenty Questions.' *Child Development* **60** (4), 877–86, 1989.

14 Ong, W. *Orality and Literacy: The Technologising of the Word*. London: Methuen, 1982.
15 McDevitt, T., Spivey, N., Sheehan, E., Lennon, R. and Story, R. 'Children's beliefs about listening: is it enough to be still and quiet?' *Child Development* **61** (3), 713–21, 1990.
16 Bryant, P. and Bradley, L. *Children's Reading Problems: Psychology and Education*. Oxford: Basil Blackwell, 1985.
17 Ong, W. *op. cit.*
18 Houghton, S., Wheldall, K., Jukes, R. and Sharpe, A. 'The effects of limited private reprimands and increased private praise on classroom behaviour in four British secondary school classes.' *British Journal of Educational Psychology* **60** (3), 255–65, 1990.

CHAPTER 9: REFERENCES

1   MacLean, B. and Schuler, M. 'Conceptual development in infancy: the understanding of containment.' *Child Development* **60** (5), 1126–37, 1989.
    Kazmak, S. and Gelman, R. 'Young children's understanding of random phenomena.' *Child Development* **57** (3), 559–66, 1986.
    Thorkildsen, T. 'Pluralism in children's reasoning about social justice.' *Child Development* **60** (4), 965–72, 1989.
    Wellman, H. *The Child's Theory of Mind*. Boston, MA: MIT Press, 1990.
2   Pye, J. *Invisible Children: Who Are the Real Losers at School?* Oxford: Oxford University Press, 1989.
3   Davies, B. *Life in the Classroom and Playground*. London: Routledge, 1982.
4   Watts, E. *Authority*. London: Croom Helm, 1982.
5   Dunn, Y. *The Beginnings of Social Understanding*. Oxford: Basil Blackwell, 1988.
6   Cullingford, C. *The Inner World of the School*. London: Cassell, 1991.
7   Cullingford, C. *Parents, Teachers and Schools*. London: Robert Royce, 1986.
8   Davies, B. *op. cit.*
9   Miller, P. and Alois, P. 'Young children's understanding of the psychological causes of behaviour.' *Child Development* **60** (2), 257–85, 1989.
10 Measor, L. and Sikes, P. *Gender and Schools*. London: Cassell, 1992.
11 Tizard, J., Moss, P. and Perry, J. *All Our Children: Pre-School Services in a Changing Society*. London: Temple Smith, 1976.
12 Fryer, M. and Collings, J. 'Teachers' views about creativity.' *British Journal of Educational Psychology* **61** (2), 207–19, 1991.
13 Flowers, J. 'A behavioural method of increasing self-confidence in elementary school children: treatment and modelling results.' *British Journal of Educational Psychology* **61** (1), 13–18, 1991.
14 Cullingford, C. 'Children's views on gender issues in school.' *British Educational Research Journal* **19** (5), 555–63, 1993.
15 Bronfenbrenner, U. *Two Worlds of Childhood*. London: Allen and Unwin, 1971.
16 Chapman, J., Lamborne, R. and Silva, P. 'Some antecedents of academic self-concept: a longitudinal study.' *British Journal of Educational Psychology* **60** (2), 142–52, 1990.
17 Foot, H. and Barron, A. 'Friendship and task management in children's peer tutoring.' *Educational Studies* **16** (3), 237–50, 1990.
18 Lane, D. 'Violent histories: bullying and criminality', in Tattum, D. and Lane, D. (eds) *Bullying in Schools*. Stoke-on-Trent: Trentham Books, 1989, pp. 95–104.
19 Bettelheim, B. *A Good Enough Parent: The Guide to Bringing Up Your Child*. London: Thames and Hudson, 1987.
20 Besag, V. *Bullies and Victims in Schools: A Guide to Understanding and Management*. Milton Keynes: Open University Press, 1989.
21 Pollard, A. *The Social World of the Primary School*. London: Holt, Rinehart and Winston, 1985.
22 Mark, J. *Feet*. London: Walker, 1985.

23 Lillard, A. 'Pretend play skills and the child's theory of mind.' *Child Development* **64** (2), 348–71, 1993.
Hutt, J., Tyler, S., Hutt, C. and Christopherson, H. *Play: Exploration and Learning: A Natural History of the Pre-School.* London: Routledge, 1989.
24 Nias, J. *Primary Teachers Talking: A Study of Teaching as Work.* London: Routledge, 1989.
25 Pye, J. *op. cit.*
26 Dunn, J. *op. cit.*
Cassidy, J. and Asher, S. 'Loneliness and peer relations in young children.' *Child Development* **63** (2), 350–68, 1992.
27 Vandell, D., Henderson, K. and Wilson, K. 'A longitudinal study of children with day-care experiences of varying quality.' *Child Development* **59** (5), 1215–29, 1988.
28 Lampa, M. and Turiel, F. 'Children's conceptions of adult and peer authority.' *Child Development* **57** (2), 405–12, 1986.

CHAPTER 10: REFERENCES

1 Bennett, N. 'Cooperative learning in classrooms: processes and outcomes.' *Journal of Child Psychology and Psychiatry* **32** (4), 581–95, 1991.
2 Stanford University. *Cross-Age Tutoring.* Stanford, CA: Stanford University, 1984.
3 Foot, H. and Barron, A. 'Friendship and task management in children's peer tutoring.' *Educational Studies* **16** (3), 237–50, 1990.
4 Blatchford, P., Burke, J., Farquhar, C., Plewis, I. and Tizard, B. 'A systematic observation study of children's behaviour in an infant school', in Woodhead, A. and McGrath, A. (eds) *Family, School and Society.* London: Hodder and Stoughton, 1988, pp. 96–111.
5 Croll, P. and Moses, D. 'Teaching methods and time on task in junior classrooms,' *Educational Research* **30** (2), 90–7, 1988.
6 Galton, M. and Williamson, J. *Group Work in the Primary Classroom.* London: Routledge, 1992.
7 Bennett, N. 'Cooperative learning in classrooms.' *Journal of Child Psychology and Psychiatry* **32** (4), 581–94, 1991.
8 Bennett, N., Andreae, J., Hegarty, P. and Wade, B. *Open Plan Schools: Teaching, Curriculum, Design.* Windsor: NFER, 1980.
9 Slavin, R. 'Student teams and achievement divisions.' *Journal of Research and Development in Education* (12), 39–49, 1978.
Slavin, R. *Cooperative Learning.* New York: Longman, 1983.
10 Marshall, S. *An Experiment in Education.* Cambridge: Cambridge University Press, 1976.
11 Pye, J. *Invisible Children: Who Are the Real Losers at School?* Oxford: Oxford University Press, 1989.
12 Blatchford, P., Burke, J., Farquhar, C., Plewis, I. and Tizard, B. 'Teacher expectations in infant schools: associations with attainment and progress, curriculum coverage and classroom interaction.' *British Journal of Educational Psychology* **59** (1), 19–30, 1989.
13 Burden, M., Emsley, M. and Constable, H. 'Encouraging progress in collaborative group work.' *Educational 3-13* **16** (1), 51–6, 1988.
14 Alexander, R., Willcocks, J. and Kinder, K. *Changing Primary Practice.* London: Falmer, 1989.
15 Bennett, N. and Cass, A. 'The effects of group composition on group interaction processes and pupil understanding.' *British Educational Research Journal* **15** (1), 19–32, 1988.

CHAPTER 11: REFERENCES

1 Cullingford, C. *The Nature of Learning.* London: Cassell, 1990.
2 Sylva, K., Roy, C. and Painter, M. *Childwatching at Playgroup and Nursery School.* London: Grant McIntyre, 1980.
   Sylva, K. 'The effects of pre-school education: hard data and soft speculation. Quality education provision for 3–7 year olds: its implications and implementation.' 2nd European Conference on the Quality of Early Childhood Education. Worcester, August 1992.
3 Cullingford, C. *Children and Television.* Aldershot: Gower, 1984.
   Hodge, B. and Tripp, D. *Children and Television: A Semiotic Approach.* Cambridge: Polity Press, 1986.
4 Cullingford, C. *Parents, Teachers and Schools.* London: Robert Royce, 1986.
5 Goodacre, E. *School and Home.* Windsor: NFER, 1970.
6 Cullingford, C. *Parents, Teachers and Schools. op. cit.*
7 *ibid.*
8 Tizard, J., Schofield, W. and Hewison, J. 'Collaboration between teachers and parents in assisting children's reading.' *British Journal of Educational Psychology* 52, 1–15, 1982.
9 Sluckin, A. *Growing Up in the Playground.* London: Routledge, 1981.
10 Cullingford, C. *Children and Television. op. cit.*
11 Tidhar, C. and Peri, S. 'Deceitful behaviour in situation comedy: effects on children's perception of social reality.' *Journal of Educational Television* 16 (2), 61–76, 1990.
12 Das Gupta, P. and Bryant, P. 'Young children's causal inferences.' *Child Development* 60 (5), 1138–46, 1989.
13 Donaldson, M. *Children's Minds.* London: Fontana Croom Helm, 1978.
14 Flavell, J., Flavell, E., Green, F. and Moses, L. 'Young children's understanding of fact beliefs versus value beliefs.' *Child Development* 61 (4), 915–28, 1990.
   Woolley, J. and Wellman, H. 'Young children's understanding of realities, non-realities and appearances.' *Child Development* 61 (4), 946–61, 1990.
15 Buckingham, D. *Children Talking Television: The Making of Television Literacy.* London: Falmer Press, 1993.
   Lull, J. 'The social uses of television.' *Human Communication Research* 6 (3), 197–209, 1980.
16 Choat, E., Griffin, H. and Hobart, D. 'Language, educational television and young children.' *Journal of Educational Television* 12 (3), 175–87, 1986.
17 Tizard, A. and Hughes, M. *Young Children Learning.* London: Fontana, 1984.
18 Sturm, H. *Fernsehdiktate: Die Veränderung von Gedanken und Gefühlen.* Gütersloh: Bertelsmann Stiftung, 1991.
19 Pramling, I. 'Developing children's thinking about their own learning.' *British Journal of Educational Psychology* 58 (3), 266–78, 1988.
20 Cullingford, C. *Children and Society.* London: Cassell, 1992.
21 Perry, W. *Forms of Intellectual and Ethical Development in the College Years: A Scheme.* New York: Holt, Rinehart and Winston, 1970.

CHAPTER 12: REFERENCES

1 Keys, W. and Fernandez, C. *What Do Children Think about School?* A Report for the National Commission on Education. Slough: NFER, 1993.
2 Cullingford, C. *The Inner World of the School.* London: Cassell, 1991.
   Davies, B. *Life in the Classroom and Playground.* London: Routledge, 1982.
   Goodnow, J. and Burns, A. *Home and School: A Child's Eye View.* Hemel Hempstead: Allen and Unwin, 1985.
3 White, R. with Brockington, D. *Tales Out of School: Consumers' Views of British Education.* London: Routledge, 1983.
   Blatchford, P. 'Children's attitudes to work at 11 years.' *Educational Studies* 18 (1), 107–18, 1992.

4 Barrett, G. *Disaffection from School? The Early Years*. London: Falmer Press, 1989.
5 Pye, J. *Invisible Children*. Oxford: Oxford University Press, 1988.
6 Cullingford, C. *op. cit.*
7 Giles, H. and Smith, P. 'Accommodation theory: optimal levels of convergence', in Giles, H. and St Clair, R. *Language and Social Psychology*. Oxford: Basil Blackwell, 1979, pp. 45–65.
8 Galton, M., Simon, B. and Croll, P. *Inside the Primary Classroom*. London: Routledge and Kegan Paul, 1980.
9 Baker, C. and Freebody, P. *Children's First School Books: Introductions to the Culture of Literacy*. Oxford: Basil Blackwell, 1989.
   King, R. 'Multiple realities and their reproduction in infants' classrooms', in Richards, C. *New Directions in Primary Education*. Lewes: Falmer Press, 1982.
10 King, R. *All Things Bright and Beautiful? A Sociological Study of Infants' Classrooms*. Chichester: John Wiley, 1978.
   Perry, W. *Forms of Intellectual and Ethical Development in the College Years*. New York: Holt, Rinehart and Winston, 1970.
11 Edwards, A. and Furlong, V. *The Language of Teaching: Meaning in Classroom Interaction*. London: Heinemann, 1978.
12 Knight, P. 'A study of children's understanding of people in the past.' *Educational Review* **41** (3), 207-20, 1989.
13 Ginsburg, G. and Bronstein, P. 'Family factors related to children's intrinsic/extrinsic motivational orientation and academic performance.' *Child Development* **64** (6), 1461-74, 1993.
14 Dreyfus, A. 'Pupils' selection and application of oversimplified principle.' *British Educational Research Journal* **15** (3), 331-40, 1989.
15 Turner, J. *Made for Life: Coping, Competence and Cognition*. London: Methuen, 1980.
16 Houghton, S., Wheldall, K., Jukes, R. and Sharpe, A. 'The effects of limited private reprimands and increased private praise on classroom behaviour in four British secondary school classes.' *British Journal of Educational Psychology* **60** (3), 253-65, 1990.
17 Sharp, R. and Green, A. *Education and Social Control*. London: Routledge and Kegan Paul, 1975.
18 Bennett, N., Desforges, C., Cockburn, A. and Wilkinson, B. *The Quality of Pupil Learning Experiences*. London: Lawrence Erlbaum, 1984.
19 Elias, N. *The Civilising Process*: Vol. 1, *The History of Manners*; Vol. 2, *State Formation and Civilisation*. Oxford: Basil Blackwell, 1978 and 1982.

CHAPTER 13: REFERENCES

1 Kozeki, B. and Entwistle, N. 'Describing and utilizing motivational styles in education.' *British Journal of Educational Studies* **31** (3), 184-97, 1983.
2 E.g. Hudson, L. *Frames of Mind*. London: Methuen, 1968.
   Compare Eysenck Personality Tests.
3 *ibid.*
4 Rosenthal, R. and Jacobsen, L. *Pygmalion in the Classroom*. New York: Holt, Rinehart and Winston, 1968.
5 Sodian, B., Zaitchik, D. and Carey, S. 'Young children's differentiation of hypothetical beliefs from evidence.' *Child Development* **62** (4), 753-66, 1991.
6 Galton, M., Simon, B. and Croll, P. *Inside the Primary Classroom*. London: Routledge and Kegan Paul, 1980.
7 Burns, R. *Self Concept Development and Education*. London: Holt, Rinehart and Winston, 1982.
8 Eshel, Y. and Kurman, J. 'Academic self concept, accuracy of perceived ability and academic attainment.' *British Journal of Educational Psychology* **61** (2), 187-96, 1991.
9 Blatchford, P. 'Children's attitudes to work at 11 years.' *Educational Studies* **18** (1), 107-18, 1992.

10   Eder, R. 'Uncovering young children's psychological selves: individual and developmental difficulties.' *Child Development* **61** (3), 849–63, 1990.
11   Stipek, D. and MacIver, D. 'Developmental change in children's assessments of intellectual competence.' *Child Development* **60** (3), 521–38, 1989.
12   Chapman, J., Lambourne, R. and Silva, P. 'Some antecedents of academic self-concept: a longitudinal study.' *British Journal of Educational Psychology* **60** (2), 142–52, 1990.
13   Flowers, J. 'A behavioural method of increasing self-confidence in elementary school children: treatment and modelling results.' *British Journal of Educational Psychology* **61** (1), 13–18, 1991.
14   Compare Egan, K. *Education and Psychology.* New York: Teachers College, 1983.
15   Witkin, M., Moore, C., Goodenough, D. and Cox, P. 'Field-dependent and field-independent cognitive styles and their educational implications.' *Review of Educational Research* **47**, 1–64, 1977.
16   Pask, G. and Scott, B. 'Learning strategies and individual competence.' *International Journal of Man–Machine Studies* **4**, 217–53, 1972.
17   Entwistle, N. and Ramsden, P. *Understanding Student Learning.* London: Croom Helm, 1982.
18   Riding, R. and Cheema, I. 'Cognitive styles: an overview and integration.' *Educational Psychology* **11** (3), 193–216, 1991.
19   Randell, G. 'Gender differences in pupil–teacher interaction in workshops and laboratories', in Weiner, G. and Arnot, M. (eds) *Gender under Scrutiny.* 1987.
20   Kolb, D. *Learning Styles Inventory.* Boston, MA: McBer, 1976.
21   Entwistle, N. and Ramsden, P. *op. cit.*
22   Ramsden, P. and Entwistle, N. 'Effects of academic departments on students' approaches to studying.' *British Journal of Educational Psychology* **51**, 368–83, 1981.
23   Fransson, A. 'On qualitative differences in learning: effects of motivation and test anxiety on process and outcome.' *British Journal of Educational Psychology* **47**, 244–57, 1977.
24   Ferrell, G. 'A factor analytic comparison of four learning styles instruments.' *Journal of Educational Psychology* **75** (1), 33–9, 1983.
25   Reay, D. 'Intersections of gender, race and class in the primary school.' *British Journal of Sociology of Education* **12** (2), 163–82, 1991.
     King, R. *The Best of Primary Education?* London: Falmer Press, 1989.
     Worrall, N. and Tsarna, H. 'Teachers' reported practices towards girl and boys in science and language.' *British Journal of Educational Psychology* **57** (3), 300–12, 1987.
26   Ramsden, P. and Entwistle, N. 'Effects of academic departments on students' approaches to studying.' *British Journal of Educational Psychology* **51**, 368–83, 1981.
27   Compare de Bono, E. *Teaching Thinking.* London: Temple Smith, 1976.
28   Houghton, S., Wheldall, K., Jukes, R. and Sharpe, A. 'The effects of limited private reprimands and increased private praise on classroom behaviour in four British secondary school classes.' *British Journal of Educational Psychology* **60** (3), 255–65, 1990.
29   Blatchford, P. *op. cit.*

CHAPTER 14: REFERENCES

1   Bennett, N., Andreae, J., Hegarty, P. and Wade, B. *Open Plan Schools: Teaching, Curriculum, Design.* Windsor: NFER, 1980.
2   Doyle, W. 'Academic work.' *Review of Educational Research* **53** (2), 159–99, 1983.
3   Courage, M. 'Children's enquiry strategies in referential communication and in the game of Twenty Questions.' *Child Development* **60** (4), 877–86, 1989.
     McDevitt, T., Spivey, N., Sheehan, F., Lennon, R. and Story, R. 'Children's beliefs about listening: it is enough to be still and quiet?' *Child Development* **61** (3), 713–21, 1990.
4   Bennett, N. 'Cooperative learning in classrooms: processes and outcomes.' *Journal of Child Psychology and Psychiatry* **32** (4), 581–94, 1991.
5   E.g. Bennett, N. *Teaching Styles and Pupil Progress.* London: Open Books, 1976.

6   Blatchford, P., Burke, J., Farquhar, C., Plewis, I. and Tizard, B. 'Teacher expectations in infant school: associations with attainment and progress, curriculum coverage and classroom interaction.' *British Journal of Educational Psychology* **59** (1), 19–30, 1989.
7   Galton, M., Simon, B. and Croll, P. *Inside the Primary Classroom*. London: Routledge and Kegan Paul, 1980.

CHAPTER 15: REFERENCES

1   Cullingford, C. *The Inner World of the School*. London: Cassell, 1991.
2   Doyle, W. 'The use of non-verbal behaviour: toward an ecological model of classrooms.' *Merrill-Palmer Quarterly* **23**, 174–92, 1977.
3   Caffyn, R. 'Attitudes of British secondary school teachers and pupils to rewards and punishments.' *Educational Research* **31** (3), 210–20, 1989.
4   Cullingford, C. 'Wall displays – children's reactions.' *Education 3-13* **6**, 12–15, 1978.
5   Nash, R. 'The effects of classroom spatial organisation on four and five year old children's learning.' *British Journal of Educational Psychology* **51** (1), 144–55, 1981.
6   Mares, C. and Stephenson, R. *Inside Outside: An Action Plan for Improving the Primary School Environment*. Tidy Britain Group Schools Research Project. Brighton Polytechnic, 1988.
7   Compare the erstwhile East German approach that made school gardens a complete subject.
8   Lawrence, D. 'Counselling of retarded readers by non-professionals.' *Educational Research* **15** (1), 48–51, 1972.
9   Thomas, G. in Cullingford, C. (ed.) *The Primary Teacher*. London: Cassell, 1989, pp. 56–74.
10 Thomas, G. 'The new classroom teams.' *Education 3-13* **21** (2), 22–6, 1993.

CHAPTER 16: REFERENCES

1   Skinner, B. *The Technology of Teaching*. New York: Appleton-Century-Crofts, 1968.
2   Lumsdaine, A. and Glaser, R. *Teaching Machines and Programmed Learning*. Washington: National Education Association of the United States, 1960.
3   Toffler, A. *Future Shock*. London: Bodley Head, 1970.
4   Roehler, L. and Duffy, G. 'What makes one teacher a better explainer than another?' *Journal of Education for Teaching* **12** (3), 273–84, 1986.
5   Chandra, P. 'How do teachers view their teaching and the use of teaching resources?' *British Journal of Educational Technology* **18** (2), 102–11, 1987.
6   Cullingford, C. *Children and Television*. Aldershot: Gower, 1984.
7   Bates, A. 'Towards a better research framework for evaluating the effectiveness of educational media.' *British Journal of Educational Technology* **12** (3), 215–33, 1981.
8   Lesser, G. 'Learning, teaching and television production for children: the experience of "Sesame Street".' *Harvard Educational Review* **42** (2), 232–72, 1972.
9   Belson, W. *The Impact of Television: Methods and Findings in Programme Research*. London: Crosby Lockwood, 1967.
10 Sturm, H. *Fernsehdiktate: Die Veränderung von Gedanken und Gefühlen*. Gütersloh: Bertelsmann Stiftung, 1991.
11 Choat, E. and Griffin, H. 'Young children, television and learning: comparison of the effects of reading and story telling by the teacher and television story viewing.' *Journal of Educational Television* **12** (2), 91–104, 1986.
    Robinson, G. *Emotional Effects of Media: The Work of Hertha Sturm*. Working Papers in Communications. Montreal: McGill University, 1987.
12 Romiszowski, A. *The Selection and Use of Instructional Media*. London: Kogan Page, 1988.

13   Underwood, J. and Underwood, G. *Computers and Learning: Helping Children Acquire Thinking Skills*. Oxford: Basil Blackwell, 1990.

CHAPTER 17: REFERENCES

1   McLuhan, M. *The Gutenberg Galaxy: The Making of Typographic Man*. Toronto: Toronto University Press, 1962.
McLuhan, M. *Understanding Media P: The Extensions of Man*. New York: McGraw-Hill, 1964.
McLuhan, M. and Fiore, Q. *The Medium Is the Massage*. Harmondsworth: Penguin, 1967.
2   King, R. *All Things Bright and Beautiful? A Sociological Study of Infants' Classrooms*. Chichester: John Wiley, 1978.
King, R. 'Multiple realities and their reproduction in infant classrooms,' in Richards, C. (ed.) *New Directions in Primary Education*. Lewes: Falmer Press, 1982, pp. 237–46.
3   Cullingford, C. '"I am a firefly, she is the moon": the nature of learning in young children.' *Primary Life* 2 (2), 23-6, 1993.
4   *ibid.*
5   Baker, C. and Freebody, P. *Children's First School Books: Introductions to the Culture of Literacy*. Oxford: Basil Blackwell, 1989.
6   Cullingford, C. 'Why children like Enid Blyton.' *The Media*: London New Society Social Studies Reader, 1980, pp. 22-3.
7   Meadows, S. and Cashdan, A. *Teaching Styles in Nursery Education*. London: SSRC, 1983.
8   Iser, W. *The Art of Reading: A Theory of Aesthetic Response*. London: Routledge and Kegan Paul, 1976.

CHAPTER 18: REFERENCES

1   Blatchford, P. 'Academic self-assessment at 7 and 11 years: its accuracy and association with ethnic group and sex.' *British Journal of Educational Psychology* 62 (1), 35-44, 1992.
2   Eshel, Y. and Kurman, J. 'Academic self-concept, accuracy of perceived ability and academic attainment.' *British Journal of Educational Psychology* 61 (2), 187-96, 1991.
Stipek, D. and MacIver, D. 'Developmental change in children's assessment of intellectual competence.' *Child Development* 60 (3), 521-38, 1989.
3   Blatchford, P., Burke, J., Farquhar, C., Plewis, I. and Tizard B. 'Teacher expectations in infant school: associations with attainment and progress. Curriculum coverage and classroom interaction.' *British Journal of Educational Psychology* 59 (1), 19-30, 1989.
4   Task Group on Assessment and Testing. *A Report*. Department of Education and Science, 1988.
5   Blatchford, P. *et al., op. cit.*
Flowers, J. 'A behavioural method of increasing self-confidence in elementary school children: treatment and modelling results.' *British Journal of Educational Psychology* 61 (1), 13-18, 1991.
6   Kelley, H. 'Attribution theory in social psychology', in Levine, D. (ed.) *Nebraska Symposium on Motivation*. Lincoln: University of Nebraska Press, 1967.
7   Rosenthal, R. and Jacobson, L. *Pygmalion in the Classroom*. New York: Holt, Rinehart and Winston, 1968.

CHAPTER 19: REFERENCES

1   Cullingford, C. *The Inner World of the School*. London: Cassell, 1991.
Roehler, L. and Duffy, G. 'What makes one teacher a better explainer than another?' *Journal of Education for Teaching* 12 (3), 273-84, 1986.

Goodnow, J. and Burns, A. *Home and School: A Child's Eye View*. Hemel Hempstead: Allen and Unwin, 1985.

2 Turner, J. *Made for Life: Coping, Competence and Cognition*. London: Methuen, 1980.

3 Davies, B. *Life in the Classroom and Playground*. London: Routledge and Kegan Paul, 1982.

4 Pye, J. *Invisible Children*. Oxford: Oxford University Press, 1989.
Sharp, R. and Green, A. *Education and Social Control*. London: Routledge and Kegan Paul, 1975.

5 Worrall, N., Worrall, C. and Meldrum, C. 'Children's reciprocation of teacher evaluation.' *British Journal of Educational Psychology* **58** (1), 78–88, 1988.

6 Charlton, T., Jones, K. and Ogilvie, M. 'Primary, secondary and special school teachers' perceptions of the qualities of good schools.' *Educational Studies* **15** (3), 229–39, 1989.
Nias, J., Southworth, G. and Yeomans, R. *Staff Relationships in the Primary School: A Study of Organizational Cultures*. London: Cassell, 1989.

7 Larsson, S. 'Learning from experience: teachers' conceptions of changes in their professional practice.' *Journal of Curriculum Studies* **19** (1), 35–43, 1987.

8 Charlton, T. *et al., op. cit.*

9 Rogers, P. and Aston, F. 'Teaching method, memory and learning: an enquiry with primary school children.' *Educational Studies* **18** (2), 129–43, 1992.

10 Larsson, S. *op. cit.*

11 Cullingford, C. *The Nature of Learning*. London: Cassell, 1990.

12 Bennett, N., Desforges, C., Cockburn, A. and Wilkinson, B. *The Quality of Pupil Learning Experience*. London: Lawrence Erlbaum, 1984.

13 Kagan, D. and Smith, K. 'Beliefs and behaviours of kindergarten teachers.' *Educational Research* **30** (1), 26–35, 1989.

14 Broadfoot, P., Osborn, M. with Gilly, M. and Paillet, A. 'Teachers' conceptions of their professional responsibility: some international comparisons.' *Comparative Education* **23** (3), 287–302, 1987.

15 Salzberger-Wittenberg, I., Henry, G. and Osborne, E. *The Emotional Experience of Learning and Teaching*. London: Routledge and Kegan Paul, 1983.

16 Osborn, M. and Broadfoot, P. 'A lesson in progress? Primary classrooms observed in England and France.' *Oxford Review of Education* **18** (1), 3–16, 1992.

17 Blatchford, P., Burke, J., Farquhar, C., Plewis, I. and Tizard, B. 'Teacher expectations in infant schools: associations with attainment and progress, curriculum coverage and classroom interaction.' *British Journal of Educational Psychology* **59** (1), 19–30, 1989.

18 Fryer, M. and Collings, J. 'Teachers' views about creativity.' *British Journal of Educational Psychology* **61** (2), 207–19, 1991.

19 Alexander, R. *Policy and Practice in Primary Education*. London: Routledge, 1992.

20 *ibid.*

CHAPTER 20: REFERENCES

1 Alexander, R., Willcocks, J. and Kinder, K. *Changing Primary Practice*. London: Falmer, 1989.

2 Vold, E. and Nomisham, D. 'Teacher appraisal,' in Cullingford, C. *The Primary Teacher*. London: Cassell, 1989, pp. 130–47.

3 Thomas, G. 'The new classroom teams.' *Education 3–13* **21** (2), 22–6, 1993.

4 Hoggart, R. *Speaking to Each Other: About Society*. London: Chatto and Windus, 1970.

5 Hannon, P., Weinberger, J. and Nutbrown, C. 'A study of work with parents to promote early literacy development.' *Research Papers in Education* **6** (2), 77–98, 1991.

6 Laosa, L. 'School, occupation, culture and family: the impact of parental schooling on the parent–child relationship.' *Journal of Educational Psychology* **74** (6), 791–827, 1982.

7 Hannon, P. and James, S. 'Parents' and teachers' perspectives on pre-school literacy development.' *British Educational Research Journal* **16** (3), 259–72, 1990.

8 *ibid.*

9   Cullingford, C. *Parents, Teachers and Schools*. London: Robert Royce, 1986.
10 Bettelheim, B. *A Good Enough Parent*. London: Thames and Hudson, 1987.
11 Broadfoot, P., Osborn, M. with Gilly, M. and Paillet, A. 'Teachers' conceptions of their professional responsibility: some international comparisons.' *Comparative Education* **23** (3), 287–302, 1987.
12 Hewison, J. and Tizard, J. *Journal of Educational Psychology* **50**, 209–15, 1980.
    Tizard, J., Schofield, W. and Hewison, J. 'Collaboration between teachers and parents in assisting children's reading.' *British Journal of Educational Psychology* **52**, 1–15, 1982.
13 Maynard, T. and Furlong, J. 'Learning to teach and models of mentoring', in McIntyre, D., Hagger, H. and Wilkin, M. (eds) *Mentoring: Perspectives on School-Based Teacher Education*. London: Kogan Page, 1993, pp. 69–85.
14 Stern, H. *Parent Education: An International Survey*. Hull: Hull University Press, 1960.
15 Hannon, P. and James, S. *op. cit.*
16 Bettelheim, B. *op. cit.*

CHAPTER 21: REFERENCES

1   John, P. and Osborn, A. 'The influence of school ethos on pupils' citizenship attitudes.' *Educational Review* **44** (2), 153–66, 1992.
2   Rutter, M., Maughan, B., Mortimore, P. and Ouston, J. *Fifteen Thousand Hours: Secondary Schools and Their Effect on Children*. London: Open Books, 1979.
    Mortimore, P., Sammons, P., Stoll, L., Lewis, D. and Ecob, R. *School Matters: The Junior Years*. Wells: Open Books, 1988.
3   Burris, A. and Chittenden, E. *Analysis of an Approach to Open Education*. Princeton, NJ: Educational Testing Service, 1970.
4   Domingos, A. 'Influence on the social context of the school of the teachers' pedagogic practice.' *British Journal of Sociology of Education* **10** (3), 351–66, 1989.
5   Cooper, P. 'Learning from pupils' perspectives.' *British Journal of Special Education* **20** (4), 129–33, 1993.
6   Joyce, B. and McKibbin, M. 'Teacher growth status and school environment.' *Educational Leadership* **40** (2), 36–41, 1982.
7   Plowden, B. (Chair). *Children and Their Primary Schools: A Report of the Central Advisory Council for Education*. London: HMSO, 1967.
    Blenkin, G. and Kelly, A. *The Primary Curriculum*. London: Harper and Row, 1981.
8   Joyce, B. and McKibbin, M. *op. cit.*
9   Gray, H. *The Management of Educational Institutions: Theory, Research and Consultancy*. Lewes: Falmer Press, 1982.
10 Reynolds, D. 'The search for effective schools', in Smetherham, D. (ed.) *School Organisation*. London: Falmer Press, 1982.
11 Mortimore, P. *et al. op. cit.*
12 Fox, D. 'Personal theories of teaching.' *Studies in Higher Education* **8** (2), 151–63, 1983.

Index